Meeting Point 2de

Josette STARCK
Lycée Richelieu, Rueil-Malmaison
Formateur IUFM Versailles

Pascale CAMPS-VAQUER
Collège Les Vallées, La Garenne-Colombes
Formateur IUFM Versailles

Dominique SANTONI
Collège-Lycée Buffon, Paris

Isabelle ZIMMER
Lycée Léonard de Vinci, Saint-Michel-sur-Orge

Marie BARRILLON
Lycée Richelieu, Rueil-Malmaison

Paul LARREYA
Professeur de linguistique anglaise

Avec la participation de **Ruth PHAN**,
Lycée Charles de Gaulle, Poissy

Hatier

Les auteurs tiennent à remercier Véronique Jaubert, professeur au lycée Jacques Prévert à Longjumeau, et Anne Vallet, professeur au lycée Charles de Gaulle à Poissy, pour leur précieuse collaboration.

Conception maquette et mise en page :
Marc & Yvette - Graphismes (2010)
Illustrations : Pénélope Paicheler - Juliette Baily (2010)
Cartographie : Corédoc
Iconographie : Hatier Illustrations
Édition : Catherine de Bernis

ISBN : 978-2-218-**94428**-4

Discovering the world through English

Travelling broadens the mind.

Meeting Point 2de est un lieu de rencontres. Les unités du manuel ont été conçues pour vous donner envie de découvrir le monde anglophone et de nouveaux horizons. Apprendre une langue étrangère, c'est voyager dans le temps et dans l'espace, vous initier à d'autres modes de vie, de nouveaux auteurs, ainsi qu'à la culture et à l'histoire des arts de pays très divers.

Try, and you will achieve!

Meeting Point 2de vous permettra aussi d'être acteur de votre apprentissage. Des mises en situation authentiques, concrètes et vivantes vous sont proposées au cours et à la fin de chaque unité (double page YOUR TASK). Ces tâches finales vous aideront à mobiliser vos connaissances, à réinvestir les acquis des cours précédents, à être créatif et à prendre la parole.

Speak, and don't let others speak for you!

De plus, les encadrés Help!, les doubles pages de réflexion sur la langue et les exercices vous permettront d'enrichir votre lexique et de fixer les points de grammaire étudiés.

Au fil des unités, vous vous sentirez en confiance face à des documents nouveaux et / ou des interlocuteurs différents. Conformément au Cadre Européen Commun de Référence pour les Langues, vous passerez ainsi d'une compréhension de documents simples et de la production d'énoncés simples (Niveau A2) à des documents plus riches et une expression plus organisée (Niveau B1).

Des évaluations pour mesurer vos progrès tout au long de l'année

À votre entrée en classe de seconde, les ÉVALUATIONS DIAGNOSTIQUES vous aideront à connaître votre niveau d'anglais par rapport aux critères du Cadre Européen Commun de Référence pour les Langues et à prendre conscience des progrès à accomplir.

Chaque grande partie s'achève par ailleurs sur une ÉVALUATION SOMMATIVE. Pour préparer ces évaluations finales, des entraînements avec corrigés vous sont fournis.

Get help when you're not sure.

Des ressources complémentaires pour un entraînement personnel

- Les fiches de compréhension écrite et orale du **Workbook** vous aideront à mettre au point des stratégies d'écoute et de lecture, à découvrir et analyser des documents de façon autonome.
- Sur le **site compagnon**, vous trouverez des **documents audio** que vous pourrez télécharger pour vous entraîner à la compréhension de l'oral. Ces enregistrements sont accompagnés de fiches à travailler individuellement. MP3
- Toutes les rubriques ***Improve your pronunciation*** ont également été enregistrées pour faciliter votre travail personnel.
- Les **pages lexique** proposent des exercices pour chaque unité du manuel. Elles seront un excellent moyen de tester et d'enrichir votre vocabulaire.
- Le **précis grammatical** à la fin du manuel vous permettra de revoir et d'approfondir certains points de grammaire dont vous avez besoin pour communiquer.
- Les **pages de méthodologie** serviront à consolider vos compétences en compréhension écrite et orale ainsi qu'en production écrite et orale, ou à acquérir des connaissances en analyse iconographique et cinématographique.

Turn your brain on!

Teachers open the door, but you must enter by yourself.

Les auteurs

DÉROULEMENT

OUVERTURE

Annonce de la tâche finale, détaillée dans la double page de fin

Introduction de la thématique et du champ lexical de l'unité

AIDES LEXICALES

Pour développer la prise de parole

Vocabulaire à mémoriser (enregistré sur le CD classe)

Help!

Description

Noms
- hair roller: *bigoudi*
- shopping cart (US) = trolley (UK)
- stack of products / items: *pile de produits*
- wide breasts / hips: *forte poitrine / hanches larges*
- housewife

Adjectifs
- overweight = obese /əʊ'bi:s/
- tight: *serré*
- ugly /'ʌgli/: *laid*

Verbes et expresssions
- be full to the brim: *être plein à ras bord*
- overeat

Reaction and artist's goals

- harsh criticism /'krɪtɪsɪzəm/: *critique acerbe*
- consumer society: *société de consommation*
- drawback /'drɔ:bæk/: *défaut*
- revolting /rɪ'vəʊltɪŋ/
- gross /grəʊs/ (familiar): *(ici) dégoûtant*
- realistic
- brainwash into + V-ing
- exaggerate
- denounce / expose
- be aware of: *être conscient de*

Voyelle accentuée

Phonétique

Traduction

Amorces de phrases pour guider la production

- To me...
- What you are saying is shocking...
- I'm surprised / amazed...
- In my opinion, he / she... should / shouldn't + BV...

LES DOCUMENTS (DE 4 À 6 PAGES)

Renvoi au DVD-Rom

La compétence langagière en jeu lors de cette activité

La ou les compétences langagières travaillées sur l'ensemble de la page ou de la double page

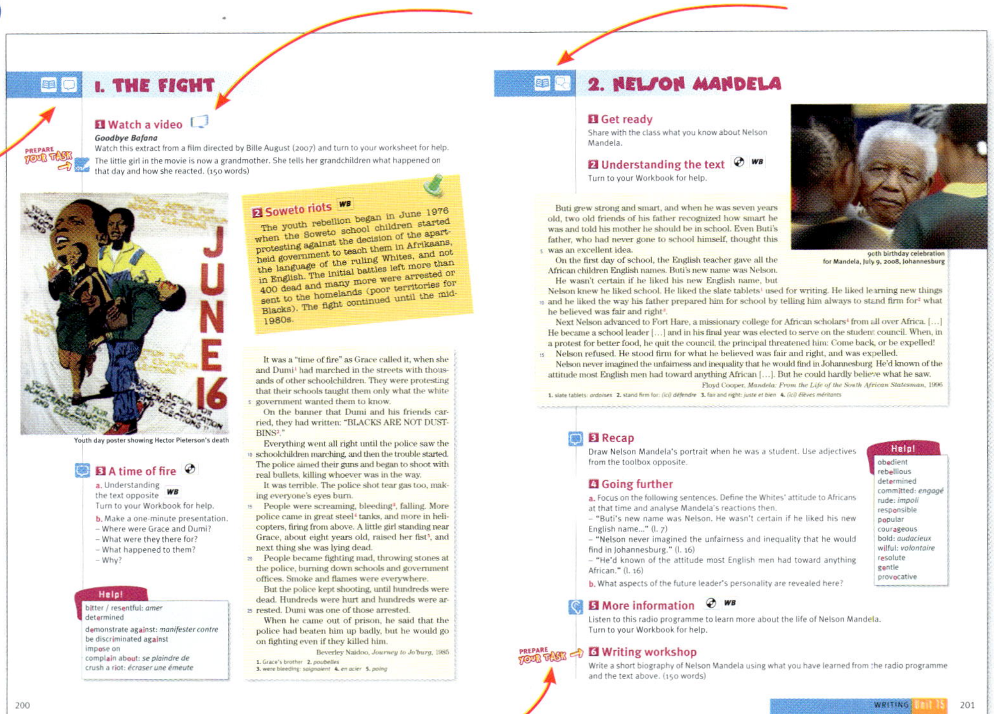

Tâche intermédiaire préparant à la tâche finale

D'UNE UNITÉ

LANGUAGE AT WORK

Objectifs linguistiques liés à la thématique de l'unité

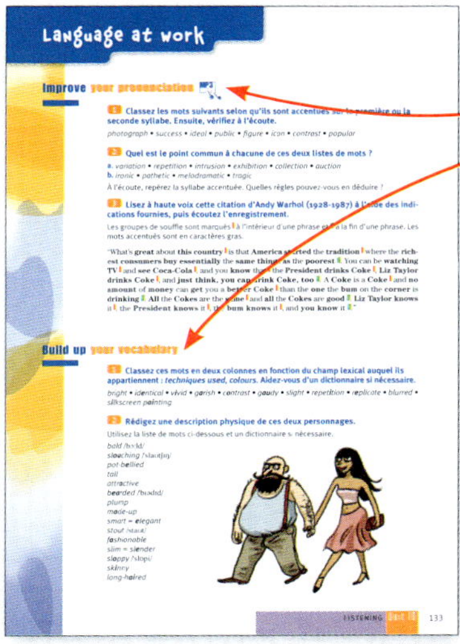

Exercices de phonologie s'appuyant sur des enregistrements disponibles sur le CD élève (travail individuel)

Lexique : enrichissement et renforcement

Réflexion sur la langue : observation et déduction

Mise en pratique en contexte

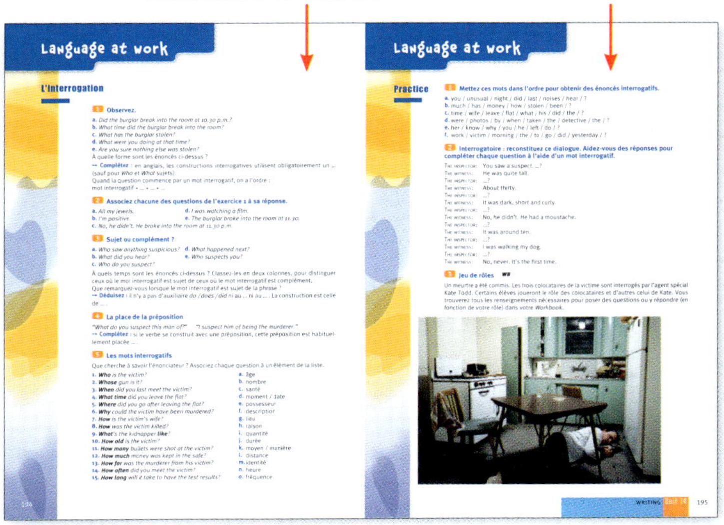

Reprise de l'énoncé de la tâche

YOUR TASK

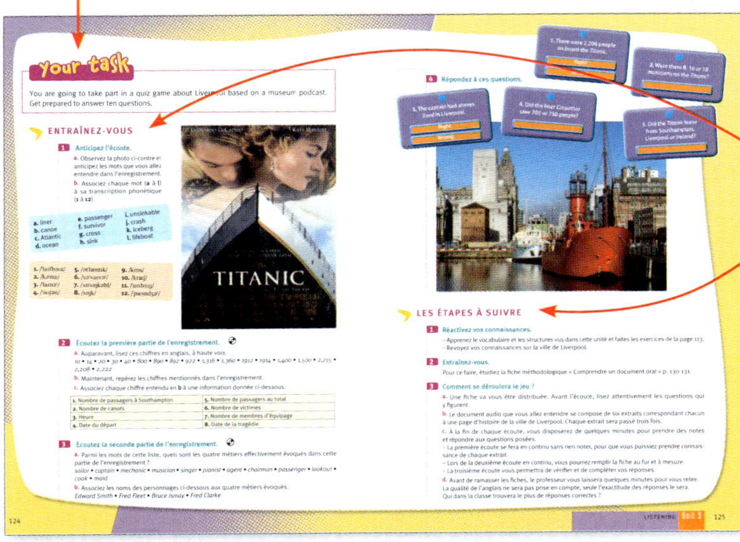

Documents servant à la mise en œuvre de la tâche

Mise en œuvre concrète et guidée de la tâche finale

PICTOS UTILISÉS DANS CE MANUEL

Lire

Écrire

Écouter

Parler en continu

Parler en interaction

WB Renvoi au cahier d'activités

Renvoi au CD classe

Renvoi au DVD-Rom

MP3 À télécharger sur le site compagnon : **www.editions-hatier.fr/meetingpoint**. Les fichiers comprennent tous les exercices *Improve your pronunciation* et *Your task* ainsi que 12 documents nouveaux.

ÉVALUATION

ÉVALUATIONS DIAGNOSTIQUES

Découvrir ce qu'est l'évaluation diagnostique à l'entrée en seconde

Qu'est-ce-qu'une évaluation diagnostique ?
Dans quel but ?

Grille des compétences évaluées par le CECRL

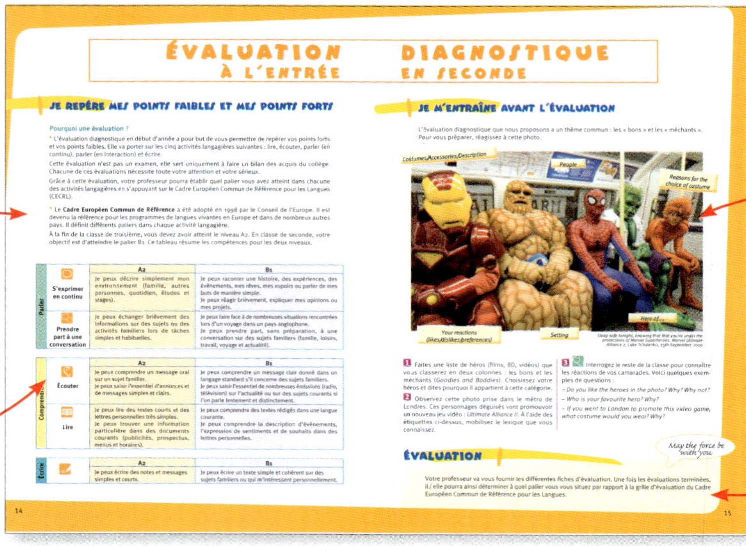

Entrer dans le thème des évaluations

Déroulement des évaluations diagnostiques

FICHES D'ÉVALUATION DIAGNOSTIQUE

Évaluer les compétences langagières à l'entrée en seconde

Fiches distribuées par le professeur

Compréhension de l'écrit

Un extrait de roman, *Dracula*, Bram Stocker

- Fiche d'évaluation accompagnée d'un barème
- Critères de répartition en groupes de compétences

Compréhension de l'oral

Interview (fichier MP3) : William Anderson

- Fiche d'évaluation accompagnée d'un barème
- Critères de répartition en groupes de compétences

Expression écrite

De l'expression guidée à l'expression libre

- Exercices gradués
  - Mobilisation du lexique
  - Repérage des éléments constitutifs d'une phrase
  - Complexification des énoncés à l'aide de mots de liaison
  - Repérage d'erreurs
  - Écrire un récit à partir d'un support visuel
- Barème et critères de répartition en groupes de compétences

Prise de parole en continu

Monologue

- Présenter un héros à l'aide d'une fiche (5 sujets différents)
- Barème et critères de répartition en groupes de compétences

Prise de parole en interaction

Dialogue

- Échanger avec quelqu'un à partir de 5 situations différentes
- Barème et critères de répartition en groupes de compétences

MODE D'EMPLOI

ÉVALUATIONS SOMMATIVES

Évaluer les compétences langagières à la fin de chaque partie

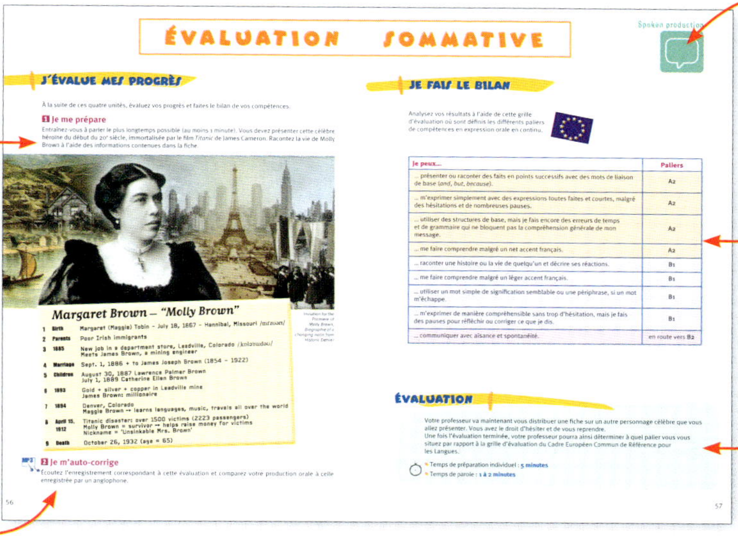

La compétence testée dans cette évaluation

Entraînement et auto-évaluation à la fin de chaque partie et dans chaque compétence

Grille d'évaluation du CECRL pour faire le point sur ses acquis et prendre conscience des progrès à accomplir

Déroulement des évaluations sommatives

Corrigé fourni pour repérer ses erreurs

FICHES D'ÉVALUATION SOMMATIVE

Compréhension de l'écrit

Deux extraits de roman de niveaux différents

- Fiche d'évaluation accompagnée d'un barème
- Critères de répartition en groupes de compétences

Compréhension de l'oral

Interview (fichier MP3) : Marie Macklin

- Fiche d'évaluation accompagnée d'un barème
- Critères de répartition en groupes de compétences

Expression écrite

Expression libre

- 3 types de production écrite
- Barème et critères de répartition en groupes de compétences

Prise de parole en continu

Monologue

- Présenter un personnage célèbre à l'aide d'une fiche (2 sujets différents)
- Barème et critères de répartition en groupes de compétences

Prise de parole en interaction

Dialogue

- Échanger avec quelqu'un à partir d'un document visuel (2 documents)
- Barème et critères de répartition en groupes de compétences

Fiches distribuées par le professeur

S O M M

Spoken production

Unit 1 SONG OF MYSELF • sentiment d'appartenance

Unit 2 HALL OF FAME • sentiment d'appartenance

Unit 3 MAKE A WISH • vision d'avenir • sentiment d'appartenance

Unit 4 HEROES • sentiment d'appartenance • vision d'avenir

Reading

Unit 5 CITY OF GLASS • sentiment d'appartenance • vision d'avenir

Unit 6 WILD WILD WEST • sentiment d'appartenance • vision d'avenir

Unit 7 ROBOT DREAMS • vision d'avenir • mémoire

Listening

Unit 8 TRUE BRITS • sentiment d'appartenance • mémoire

YOUR TASK

Choose a British icon and justify your choice.

Unit 9 DESTINATION LIVERPOOL • sentiment d'appartenance • mémoire

YOUR TASK

Take part in a quiz game based on a museum podcast.

Unit 10 LIFE IS ART • sentiment d'appartenance • mémoire

YOUR TASK

Decide which of these two audio guides is the better one.

Speaking interaction

Unit 11 A WORLD OF GEEKS • vision d'avenir • sentiment d'appartenance

Unit 12 MOTHER EARTH • vision d'avenir • sentiment d'appartenance

Unit 13 ALL THE WORLD'S A STAGE • sentiment d'appartenance • vision d'avenir • mémoire

Writing

Reading corner

Art project: New York City in art

Documents vidéo disponibles sur le DVD-Rom

ÉVALUATION À L'ENTRÉE

JE REPÈRE MES POINTS FAIBLES ET MES POINTS FORTS

Pourquoi une évaluation ?

• L'évaluation diagnostique en début d'année a pour but de vous permettre de repérer vos points forts et vos points faibles. Elle va porter sur les cinq activités langagières suivantes : lire, écouter, parler (en continu), parler (en interaction) et écrire.

Cette évaluation n'est pas un examen, elle sert uniquement à faire un bilan des acquis du collège. Chacune de ces évaluations nécessite toute votre attention et votre sérieux.

Grâce à cette évaluation, votre professeur pourra établir quel palier vous avez atteint dans chacune des activités langagières en s'appuyant sur le Cadre Européen Commun de Référence pour les Langues (CECRL).

• Le **Cadre Européen Commun de Référence** a été adopté en 1998 par le Conseil de l'Europe. Il est devenu la référence pour les programmes de langues vivantes en Europe et dans de nombreux autres pays. Il définit différents paliers dans chaque activité langagière.

À la fin de la classe de troisième, vous devez avoir atteint le niveau A2. En classe de seconde, votre objectif est d'atteindre le palier B1. Ce tableau résume les compétences pour les deux niveaux.

		A2	B1
Parler	**S'exprimer en continu**	Je peux décrire simplement mon environnement (famille, autres personnes, quotidien, études et stages).	Je peux raconter une histoire, des expériences, des événements, mes rêves, mes espoirs ou parler de mes buts de manière simple. Je peux réagir brièvement, expliquer mes opinions ou mes projets.
	Prendre part à une conversation	Je peux échanger brièvement des informations sur des sujets ou des activités familiers lors de tâches simples et habituelles.	Je peux faire face à de nombreuses situations rencontrées lors d'un voyage dans un pays anglophone. Je peux prendre part, sans préparation, à une conversation sur des sujets familiers (famille, loisirs, travail, voyage et actualité).

		A2	B1
Comprendre	**Écouter**	Je peux comprendre un message oral sur un sujet familier. Je peux saisir l'essentiel d'annonces et de messages simples et clairs.	Je peux comprendre un message clair donné dans un langage standard s'il concerne des sujets familiers. Je peux saisir l'essentiel de nombreuses émissions (radio, télévision) sur l'actualité ou sur des sujets courants si l'on parle lentement et distinctement.
	Lire	Je peux lire des textes courts et des lettres personnelles très simples. Je peux trouver une information particulière dans des documents courants (publicités, prospectus, menus et horaires).	Je peux comprendre des textes rédigés dans une langue courante. Je peux comprendre la description d'événements, l'expression de sentiments et de souhaits dans des lettres personnelles.

		A2	B1
Écrire		Je peux écrire des notes et messages simples et courts.	Je peux écrire un texte simple et cohérent sur des sujets familiers ou qui m'intéressent personnellement.

DIAGNOSTIQUE EN SECONDE

JE M'ENTRAÎNE AVANT L'ÉVALUATION

L'évaluation diagnostique que nous proposons a un thème commun : les « bons » et les « méchants ». Pour vous préparer, réagissez à cette photo.

Luke Tchalenko, *Sleep safe tonight, knowing that you're under the protection of Marvel Superheroes. Marvel Ultimate Alliance 2*, 25th September 2009

1 Faites une liste de héros (films, BD, vidéos) que vous classerez en deux colonnes : les bons et les méchants (*Goodies and Baddies*). Choisissez votre héros et dites pourquoi il appartient à cette catégorie.

2 Observez cette photo prise dans le métro de Londres. Ces personnages déguisés vont promouvoir un nouveau jeu vidéo : *Ultimate Alliance II*. À l'aide des étiquettes ci-dessus, mobilisez le lexique que vous connaissez.

3 Interrogez le reste de la classe pour connaître les réactions de vos camarades. Voici quelques exemples de questions :

– *Do you like the heroes in the photo? Why? Why not?*

– *Who is your favourite hero? Why?*

– *If you went to London to promote this video game, what costume would you wear? Why?*

ÉVALUATION

May the force be with you!

Votre professeur va vous fournir les différentes fiches d'évaluation. Une fois les évaluations terminées, il / elle pourra ainsi déterminer à quel palier vous vous situez par rapport à la grille d'évaluation du Cadre Européen Commun de Référence pour les Langues.

Senator Barack Obama speaks to a crowd on the steps of City Hall in Oakland, California, on March 17, 2007.

Spoken production

Unit 1 SONG OF MYSELF

- Discover the personality of teenagers from the USA, Jamaica or Canada.
- Find out your personality through music.
- Introduce yourself and speak about your likes and dislikes.

YOUR TASK

You are entering a casting for the TV programme of your choice. Introduce yourself, explain who you are, your likes and dislikes, and why you want to take part in the programme.

→ P. 23

Unit 2 HALL OF FAME

- Describe people's looks and feelings.
- Draw the portrait of a famous person or hero you admire very much.

YOUR TASK

Your class has decided to create a Hall of Fame (i.e. a group of people you find remarkable). You have to choose a famous person, a star, or a book / film hero. Justify your choice and say why you admire him or her very much.

→ P. 29

Unit 3 MAKE A WISH

- What do people dream of?
- Can we fulfil all our dreams?

YOUR TASK

You are taking part in a drama contest. You have to choose a poem or an excerpt from a famous speech. Learn it by heart. Then justify your choice in a few sentences and recite it in front of your class.

→ P. 40

Unit 4 HEROES

- Learn about various heroes: record-breakers, explorers, peace-makers, Human Rights fighters and environmentalists.

YOUR TASK

You are in a newly-built school. A name for this school has to be found. Each member of the community has to suggest a hero's name, and justify his or her choice.

→ P. 52

Unit 1

SONG OF MYSELF

YOUR TASK AT THE END OF THIS UNIT

You are entering a casting for the TV programme of your choice. Introduce yourself, explain who you are, your likes and dislikes, and why you want to take part in the programme. → P. 23

TUNE IN!

1 Get ready

Look at the two passports, then listen to four interviews.

a. Pick out as many clues as you can to recognize who is speaking.

b. Sum up what you have learnt about Shani and Sara.

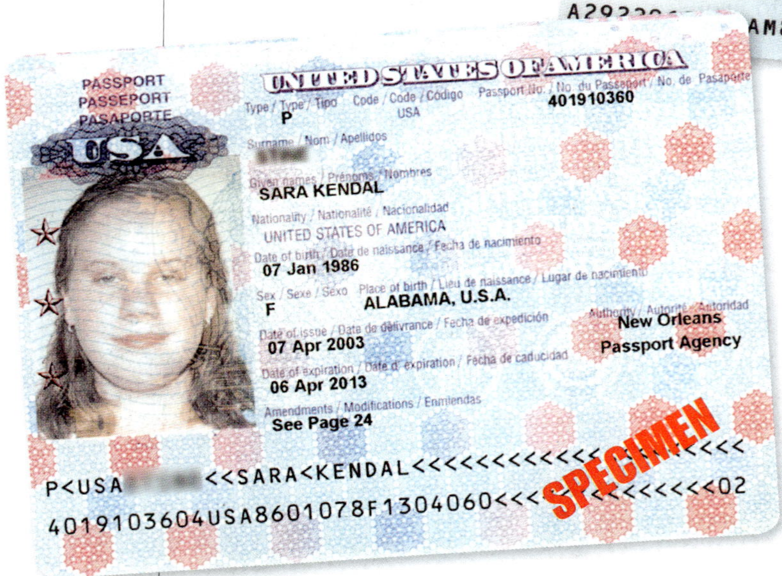

Help!

Canadian /kə'neɪdiən/
British
Jamaican
American /ə'merɪkən/
South African /saʊθ'æfrɪkən/
Australian /ɒs'treɪliən/
Irish /'aɪərɪʃ/
Welsh /welʃ/
Scottish /'skɒtɪʃ/
be a citizen /'sɪtɪzn/: *être citoyen*

PREPARE YOUR TASK →

2 Tell me more

Now, ask your partner questions to get to know him / her better (name, age, nationality, date and place of birth, family...). Then, present him / her to the class.

PREPARE YOUR TASK →

3 What about you? WB

Fill in your ID page in your Workbook. Make a one-minute speech with the help of this page.

I. PERSONALITY QUIZ

1 What's your music personality?

Do the questionnaire to find out what kind of music best suits your personality. Note down your results on a separate piece of paper.

1. What do you most appreciate about music?

a. The melody.
b. How your favourite musicians look.
c. The skill of the musicians involved.
d. The lyrics.

2. When you are at a party, do you:

a. spend the same amount of time equally dancing and chatting to friends?
b. dance with your group of friends whenever the music you like comes on?
c. ask for a song which only you and a few others want to hear?
d. stand with your friends saying how bad the music is and talk about leaving?

3. Do you most often find yourself:

a. humming[1] tunes you can't remember the title of or who sang them?
b. dancing in your bedroom alone?
c. rehearsing[2] with the band you started with a few friends at school?
d. researching information about your favourite music on the Internet?

4. When you meet a boy / girl that you find attractive, their musical taste is:

a. not so important. You might be able to exchange CDs and broaden[3] your tastes.
b. quite important, but their looks and fitness are much more significant.
c. unimportant, as long as they don't stop you from doing your own thing.
d. vital. If they don't like the same kind of music as you, they can't go out with you.

5. What is the role of music in your life?

a. To give you pleasure in everyday life.
b. To dance.
c. It is a serious business and you don't care what others think about your tastes.
d. It represents your culture and identity, who you are.

1. *chantonner* 2. *répéter* 3. *élargir*

ANALYSIS

➤ **Mainly a:** You have a pop personality. You are balanced[1] and down-to-earth[2]. You like music, but it isn't your whole life – other things are just as important. You don't like people who are too extreme. Your friends love you for your honesty and lack[3] of affectation.

➤ **Mainly b:** You have a dance personality. You are a tidy[4], organized person. You are concerned with appearance and try to look your best. You choose friends who do the same things as you. It takes time getting to know the real you, but people appreciate your good judgement.

➤ **Mainly c:** You have a rock personality. You like things that have a big impact. You don't care about appearance and are very direct in the way you speak to people. You are unafraid of taking risks and work hard to achieve your goals.

➤ **Mainly d:** You have a rap personality. You are extremely precise in the way you dress and who you make friends with. You are a perfectionist and have an incredible drive[5] to succeed. You sometimes seem a bit mysterious at first, but you are a loyal friend and people can always rely on[6] you.

Mary Glasgow Magazines, *Timesaver Personality Quizzes*, 2003

1. *équilibré* 2. *terre à terre* 3. *manque* 4. *ordonnée* 5. *désir* 6. rely on: *compter sur*

PREPARE YOUR TASK

2 React

What do you think of this quiz? Do the quiz results correspond to your personality?

2. "I AM" POEMS

1 Me, myself and I

Read the following poems and find the differences between them.

Trilingual and funny

I am trilingual and funny
I like travelling to new places
I love soccer
I hate country music
I want to be successful
I am trilingual and funny

I can learn languages easily
I cannot play baseball
I must finish my studies
I must not procrastinate[1] so much
I need to listen to music everyday
I am trilingual and funny

I'd like to visit Australia
I'd like to be a famous actor
I'd like to have a sportscar
I'd like to learn about philosophy
I'd like to see a volcano erupt
I am trilingual and funny

Sebastien Schmoranz, 2008

1. *remettre au lendemain*

Down-to-earth and cool

I am down-to-earth[1] and cool
I'd like to be more like my Dad who is
athletic and tall
I must tidy my room which is an utter pigsty[2]
I mustn't be impolite

I am down-to-earth and cool
I dream of visiting New Zealand
I try to wake up early. It doesn't happen.
I worry about my grandmother who is 85 and
lives alone
I remember my dreams

I am down-to-earth and cool
I can be angry when mocked
I can be friendly when flirting
I feel sad when I am homesick
I feel moved when I listen to jazz
I believe in holidays spent at the beach
I love playing Scrabble and watching tennis

Shani Robinson, 2009

1. I am down-to-earth: *j'ai les pieds sur terre* 2. /pɪgstaɪ/ *porcherie*

PREPARE YOUR TASK

2 Train your ears WB

Listen to the recording of the poems and work on rhythm and intonation in your Workbook.

3 Over to you WB

a. Which of these poems do you prefer? Say why.

PREPARE YOUR TASK

b. Read aloud the poem you like best.

c. Write your own "I am" poem with the help of your Workbook.

3. I AM THE MAN OF YOUR FUTURE

1 Get ready

a. What is the situation in the picture?

b. Before listening to the recording, match each word with its phonetic transcription. Then, read all the words aloud.

1. cafeteria 2. promote 3. potential
4. reliable 5. equally 6. unnoticed

a. /prə'məʊt/ b. /pəʊ'tenʃəl/ c. /ʌn'nəʊtɪst/
d. /ˌkæfɪ'tɪəriə/ e. /rɪ'laɪəbl/ f. /'i:kwəli/

Hyde Park, Speaker's Corner

2 A man for the job WB

Listen to the speech and turn to your Workbook for help.

PREPARE YOUR TASK →

3 Recap WB

Give a one-minute oral account of the recording. Use your notes in your Workbook.

- The recording deals with...
- First, he explains...
- Then, he asks... because he wants to...
- Finally he mentions...
- He wants to convince them to...
- He insists on... because...
- He gives the reasons why he wants to...

4. REAL TV

A. The Amazing Race

B. Fear Factor

C. American Idol

1 Read and match

Read the descriptions of TV programme candidates can participate in, and match them with the corresponding title.

1 A show where contestants have to perform outrageously disgusting or terrifying activities like eating worms or jumping out of airplanes to win a cash prize.

2 A group of aspiring pop stars compete against each other to win a recording contract. They are criticized by a panel of judges.

3 Teams of two or three contestants go on a world-wide scavenger hunt[1] to win a cash prize. Their travels are filmed for entertainment purposes and viewers can watch as teams make key decisions that will affect the outcome of the competition.

1. scavenger hunt: treasure hunt

2 Watch a video

Poor Little Rich Girls

Watch this extract from a reality show. Turn to your worksheet for help.

Language at work

Le présent simple

1 Observez.

a. *I hate big cities, but Mark loves them.*
b. *We spend a lot of time on the Internet.*
c. *He often travels abroad and meets many different people.*
d. *They have many hobbies.*

Chacun de ces énoncés contient un verbe au présent. Qu'est-ce qui différencie la forme de ces verbes ? Décrivez le fonctionnement de ces formes :
– sujet (3e personne du singulier) + ... + ...
– sujet (autres personnes) + ...

2 Comparez.

a. *I come from Ireland. Where do you come from?*
b. *I don't understand this sentence. What does it mean?*
c. *She is not very fit. Does she do any sport?*

Classez les formes soulignées : forme affirmative, forme négative, forme interrogative. Que remarquez-vous ?

3 Analysez.

a. *She goes to the theatre twice a year.*
b. *We go camping every summer.*
c. *She always cycles to school.*
d. *They never arrive late.*

Dans les énoncés **a**, **b**, **c** et **d**, quels sont les mots qui donnent une indication de temps ? Quel temps est utilisé pour le verbe ? Qu'exprime-t-il ?

4 Comparez et déduisez.

a. *She looks very pretty.* **b.** *He enjoys playing soccer.* **c.** *He lives in Scotland.*

Dans les énoncés **a**, **b** et **c**, il n'y a pas d'indication explicite de temps. Pourquoi ?

5 Récapitulez.

a. On utilise le présent simple pour faire le portrait de quelqu'un, pour parler de ses ... (**1. a**), de son ... (**4. a**), de tout ce qui le ... (**4. c**).

b. On emploie aussi le présent simple pour parler d'une ... (**3. a, b, c** et **d**).

Practice

Lisez la légende de ce *cartoon*. Puis continuez le récit d'une journée type du maître et de la maîtresse des deux animaux.

"Everything is automatic. The coffee turns on at 7:00. The coffee smell goes upstairs at 7:10. They come down at 7:20. They go to work at 7:25 and we go up and get in their bed."

your task

You are entering a casting for the TV programme of your choice. Introduce yourself, explain who you are, your likes and dislikes, and why you want to take part in the programme.

LES ÉTAPES À SUIVRE

1. Choisissez l'émission à laquelle vous souhaitez participer.
2. Prenez en note les points essentiels de votre présentation. Utilisez uniquement les mots clés, ne faites pas de phrases entières.
3. Vous devez inclure les points suivants dans votre discours :
– *key information about yourself (name, surname, age)*
– *skills you can rely on*
– *qualities that can be used for the programme you are entering*
– *hobbies*
– *musical tastes*
– *books you like*
– *goals you can achieve*

RAPPEL En anglais, on utilise **le verbe *BE*** pour exprimer l'âge.

CONSEILS POUR VOTRE PRESTATION

1. Veillez à réutiliser les outils linguistiques travaillés dans cette unité.
2. ⚠ Pour parler de vous, utilisez des adjectifs précis, comme ceux appris dans cette unité :
– *~~good at~~ → excellent at, clever at, brilliant at*
– *~~cool~~ → calm, patient, relaxed*
– *~~nice~~ → kind, friendly*
3. ⚠ Faites des phrases courtes.
4. Accentuez les mots porteurs de sens.
I stand before you to promote myself as a potential candidate for the show.
5. Veillez à la syllabe accentuée des mots de plus de deux syllabes.
*c**a**ndidate, id**ea**l, t**a**lented, person**a**lity...*
6. Veillez à l'alternance entre formes pleines et réduites ainsi qu'aux liaisons consonnes - voyelles.
I'm friendly and‿always‿in‿a good mood.
7. Parlez distinctement et lentement.
8. Parlez suffisamment fort pour être entendu(e) même au fond de la salle.
9. Utilisez des *gap fillers* si vous hésitez (manuel p. 54).

– Let me see / think...
– I mean...
– ..., you know, ...
– ..., just a moment, ...
– ..., you see, ...
– ..., well, ...
– Um... / Er...

Unit 2

HALL OF FAME

YOUR TASK AT THE END OF THIS UNIT

Your class has decided to create a Hall of Fame (i.e. a group of people you find remarkable). You will have to choose a famous person, a star or a book / film hero. Justify your choice and say why you admire him or her very much.

→ P. 29

TUNE IN!

1 Your favourites WB

a. Observe the posters. Then listen to young people talking about their favourite films.
b. Guess what film each of them is talking about. To find the title of the movie, pick out as many clues as you can.
c. Which of these posters do you like better? Why? What sort of film does it advertise?

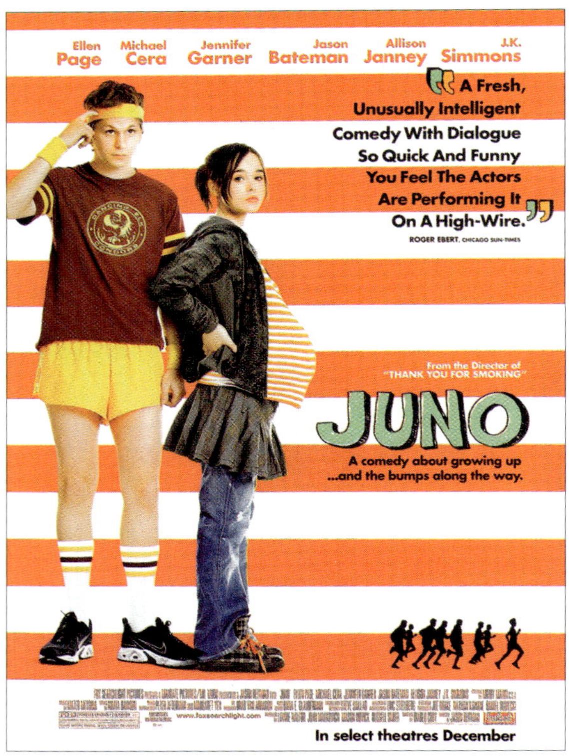

Help!
- romantic comedy
- adventure / social / action film
- horror /hɒrəʳ/ movie
- detective story
- character /kærɪktəʳ/
- hero /hɪərəʊ/

PREPARE YOUR TASK →

2 Your choice

Choose a film poster you like, or simply a photo of your favourite star, and say why you like it very much.

I. THE ACTORS' STUDIO

1 Bruce and George

Compare the two actors with their caricatures.

2 Guess who?

a. Find out whose caricature it is, and justify your answer orally.

PREPARE YOUR TASK → **b.** Which caricature makes you laugh? Why?

Help!

Physical description	Reactions
hair: straight /streɪt/ ≠ curly /ˈkɜːli/, frizzy, wavy /ˈweɪvi/ red, dark ≠ fair, blond, chestnut-brown **face**: pointed /ˈpɔɪntɪd/ ≠ round /raʊnd/, oval /ˈəʊvəl/ cleanshaven /kliːnˈʃeɪvn/ full lips: *lèvres charnues*	caricature /ˈkærɪkətʃʊəʳ/ ridiculous distorted /dɪsˈtɔːtɪd/ good-looking, cute handsome (only for men) pretty /ˈprɪti/ (only for women) ugly /ˈʌgli/: *laid* look + adj.: *avoir l'air*

2. HAPPY BIRTHDAY

Part 1

Saturday April 2nd
Manchester Railway Station.

Got here by fish lorry[1]. Pretended to be asleep in order to avoid[2] driver's conversation.

10.31 a.m. I wonder[3] what my Mum and Dad have bought me for my birthday. I hope they are not too worried[4]. Perhaps I ought to ring them and convince them that I am well and happy.

12.15 p.m. We have been ordered out of the railway station café by a bad-tempered waitress. It's the stupid dog's fault. It kept going behind the counter and begging for bits of bacon. Yet I bought it a bacon roll all to itself this morning.

3 p.m. Nobody has said "Happy Birthday" to me.

3.05 p.m. I'm not well (I've got a cold) and I'm not happy. In fact, I'm extremely unhappy.

5.30 p.m. Bought myself a birthday card. Inside I wrote:

To our darling first-born child
on his sixteenth birthday.
With all the love it is possible
to give,
From your admiring and loving
parents.

PS. Come home son. Without you
the house is devoid of[5] life and
laughter.

1. *camion* 2. *éviter* 3. *me demande*
4. anxious 5. devoid of: with no

Part 2

6.15 p.m. There was nothing about me on the six o'clock news.

7.30 p.m. Can't face another night in the open.

9 p.m. Park bench.[1]

I have asked three policemen the time, but none of them have spotted[2] me as a runaway. It's obvious that my description hasn't been circulated.

9.30 p.m. Just rang the police station, using a disguised voice. I said:

"Adrian Mole, a sixteen-year-old runaway, is in the vicinity of the Blood Transfusion Headquarters. His description is as follows: small for his age, slight build, mousey[3] hair, disfigured skin. He is wearing a green school blazer. Orange waterproof trousers. A blue shirt. Balaclava helmet[4]. Brown Doc Martens. With him is a mongrel[5] dog, of the following description: medium height, hairy face, squint in left eye. Wearing a tartan collar and matching lead[6]."

The desk sergeant said: "April Fool's Day was yesterday, sonny." [...] There is never one around when you need one.

Sue Townsend, *The Growing Pains of Adrian Mole*, 1984

1. *banc* **2.** *remarqué* **3.** /maʊsi/ chestnut brown **4.** balaclava helmet: *passe-montagne* **5.** *bâtard* **6.** *laisse*

1 Get ready

Skim through the whole text and answer the following questions:

a. Who is the narrator (name and age)?
b. Find a date. What makes it special?
c. Find the name of a big city in Great Britain and locate it on the map in the front flap of your book.
d. Who are the other characters mentioned?
e. Find four different places where the main character was.

2 Understanding the text WB

Turn to your Workbook for help.

PREPARE YOUR TASK

3 Story telling

Tell Adrian's story. Include these points:

– Who?
– Where?
– What happened?
– What is the problem?
– What are the character's feelings?

Help!

Feelings	Parent /child relationships
happy, cheerful /tʃɪəfʊl/ ≠ sad, miserable /mɪzərəbl/	look after sb = take care /kɛəʳ/ of sb ≠ neglect
embarrassed, ill-at-ease	care for
lonely /ləʊnli/ = isolated /aɪsəʊleɪtɪd/	celebrate a birthday
shy /ʃaɪ/: *timide*	offer /ɒfəʳ/ presents
nice, kind /kaɪnd/ ≠ nasty, mean /mi:n/	take no notice /nəʊtɪs/ of
worried /wʌrɪd/, anxious, desperate /despərət/	react /ri'ækt/
	be reported missing to the police /pə'li:s/

PREPARE YOUR TASK

4 Follow-up work WB

Observe Norman Rockwell's painting in your Workbook. Compare it with the characters in the text.

Language at work

Le comparatif des adjectifs

1 Observez.

a. *Bruce Willis looks* ***younger*** *on the caricature* ***than*** *on the photo.*
b. *Britney Spears looks* ***more attractive*** *in reality.*
c. *Mr Bean's caricature is* ***as funny as*** *the other ones.*
d. *I think* Juno *is* ***not as thrilling as*** The Lord of the Rings.
e. *Amy Winehouse is a* ***better*** *singer* ***than*** *Britney Spears.*
f. *George Clooney looks* ***smarter*** *on the photo.*
g. *Mr Bean is* ***funnier than*** *all the others.*
h. *Look at his nose! It's* ***bigger than*** *in reality.*

2 Classez les éléments de comparaison dans un tableau de ce type, sur papier libre.

Comparatif de supériorité	Comparatif d'infériorité	Comparatif d'égalité

3 Déduisez-en les règles de formation des comparatifs.

4 Observez les comparatifs suivants.

better • nicer • funnier • bigger
– Retrouvez les adjectifs à la base de ces comparatifs.
– Identifiez les exceptions et les modifications orthographiques.

Practice

1 Utilisez les éléments donnés entre parenthèses pour comparer ces différents personnages de films ou de dessins animés.

a. James Bond / Indiana Jones: (attractive) and (good-looking)
b. South Park / The Simpsons: (lazy) and (funny)
c. Cinderella / Ugly Betty: (romantic) and (pretty)
d. Ironman / Spiderman: (energetic) and (strong)
e. Terminator / Mr Bean: (determined) and (crazy)

2 Comparez.

Your task

Your class has decided to create a Hall of Fame (i.e. a group of people you find remarkable). You have to choose a famous person, a star or a book / film hero. Justify your choice and say why you admire him or her very much.

LES ÉTAPES À SUIVRE

1. Choisissez votre personnage dans un livre, une BD ou un film. Trouvez une illustration, un poster, une photo ou apportez un livre ou un magazine dans lequel il figure.

2. Présentez le film ou le livre dont est issu votre personnage. Dites pourquoi ce film ou ce livre est votre préféré et expliquez pourquoi ce personnage vous plaît.

3. Vous devez inclure les points suivants :
– *A description of the character (face, general features, style, clothes...).*
– *His / her personality (qualities and defects).*
– *His / her hobbies, tastes and passions.*
– *What he / she is famous for.*
– *What he / she does in the film / book.*
– *Compare him / her with other characters in the same story or in similar fiction.*

***Spiderman III*, Sam Raimi, 2004**

CONSEILS POUR VOTRE PRESTATION

Vocabulaire

Utilisez des adjectifs précis, comme ceux appris ou revus dans cette unité. Cela vous aidera à nuancer votre description.
– ~~*lovely*~~ → *attractive, cute, handsome, good-looking, charming, pretty, well-dressed...*
– ~~*intelligent*~~ → *clever, smart, cunning, quick, sharp, humorous...*
– ~~*strong*~~ → *muscular, broad-shouldered, energetic, athletic, powerful, active...*

Grammaire

Utilisez :
– le présent simple – le comparatif – *can* + base verbale – *be good at + V-ing*

Prononciation

– Accentuez les mots porteurs de sens (ce sont les mots-clés de votre présentation). L'anglais est en effet une langue mélodique où l'on accentue les mots qui apportent des informations.
– À l'aide d'un dictionnaire, vérifiez quelle syllabe est accentuée dans les mots de plus de deux syllabes. Ainsi, pour *character,* vous trouverez /ˈkærɪktəʳ/. Le signe ˈ correspond à un accent tonique et indique que la syllabe suivante est accentuée.
– Parlez distinctement et lentement. Marquez des pauses pour respirer. Parlez suffisamment fort.
– Si vous hésitez, utilisez des *gap fillers* (voir p. 54).

Unit 3

MAKE A WISH

YOUR TASK AT THE END OF THIS UNIT

You are taking part in a drama contest. You will have to choose a poem or an excerpt from a famous speech. You will learn it by heart, justify your choice in a few sentences and recite it in front of your class. → p. 40

TUNE IN!

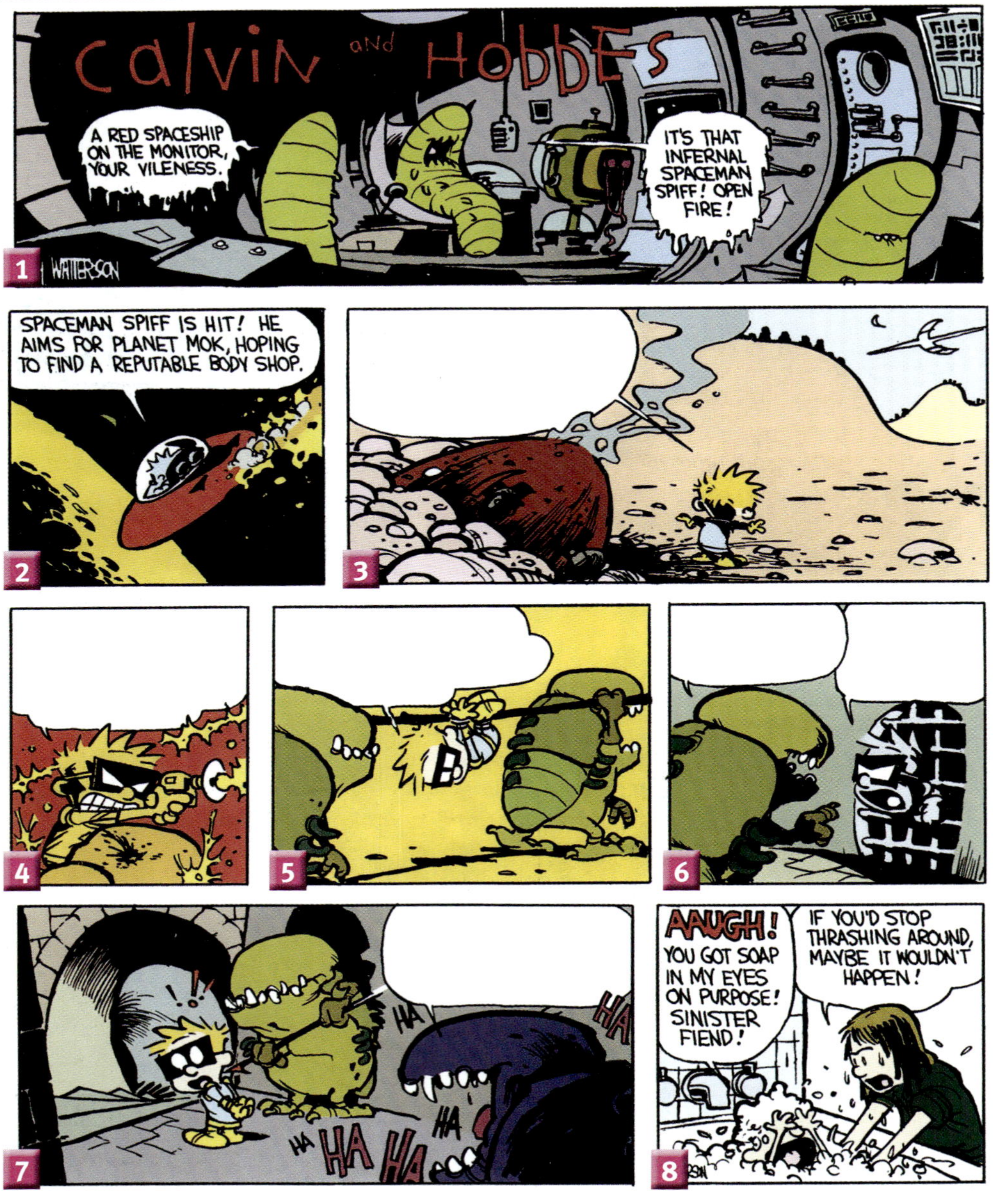

Frame 1. monitor: *écran de contrôle* **Frame 8.** fiend /fi:nd/: *monstre* • if you'd stop thrashing around: *si tu voulais bien cesser de te débattre*

Bill Watterson, *Lazy Sunday Book*, 1990

1 Understanding the comic strip

a. Read the comic strip carefully.

b. Observe frames 1 and 8. Where does the scene take place? Who are the main characters? Describe the situation in each frame.

c. What is happening to Calvin? Sum up the main events briefly.

2 Re-order the text

a. Match each sentence with the corresponding balloon. Use the pictures and the key words in the text to help you.

A. Still won't talk, eh, Spiff? We'll see about *that*!

B. Surrounded, our hero is taken prisoner, and carried to a subterranean dungeon!

C. The daring Spaceman Spiff lays waste with his Death Ray Zorcher, but he is hopelessly outnumbered!

D. You'll never get anything from me, Space Squid!

E. You had your chance, Earthling! Take him to the interrogation room and *wash his hair*!

F. We join our hero after a crash landing on the hostile planet Mok. Ominous figures appear on the horizon.

b. Confront your results and justify the order orally.

3 Dreams versus reality

a. Compare Calvin's situation in reality and in his dream. Use the toolbox below to make as many sentences as you can.

Help!

Dream	hero /ˈhɪərəʊ/ space astronaut adventure enemy jail = prison prisoner	thrilling = exciting brave courageous /kəˈreɪdʒəs/ bold /bəʊld/: *intrépide* fearless vicious	travel fly: *voler (dans les airs)* fight send He wishes he were /wɜːʳ/... He wishes he could + BV
Reality	(have) a bath		hate + V-ing torture take sb for: *prendre qqn pour* daydream escape obey sb

PREPARE YOUR TASK

b. Do you often daydream? When? Why? Present your ideas to the class.

I. A BETTER WORLD?

1 Get ready

Look at the illustration and read the title. What can you guess about the themes of the song?

Imagine

Imagine there's no heaven[1]
It's easy if you try
No hell[2] below us
Above us only sky
Imagine all the people
Living for today...

Imagine there's no countries
It isn't hard to do
Nothing to kill or die for
And no religion too
Imagine all the people
Living life in peace...

You may say I'm a dreamer
But I'm not the only one
I hope someday you'll join us
And the world will be as one

Imagine no possessions[3]
I wonder if you can
No need for greed[4] or hunger
A brotherhood of man
Imagine all the people
Sharing all the world...

You may say I'm a dreamer
But I'm not the only one
I hope someday you'll join us
And the world will live as one

John Lennon, *Imagine*, 1971

1. /ˈhevn/ *paradis*
2. /hel/ *enfer*
3. /pəˈzeʃənz/
4. *l'appât du gain, du pouvoir...*

2 Understanding the text

a. What is the singer's message in stanza 1? (Several possible answers)
– He wants us to forget about good and evil *(le bien et le mal)*.
– He wants people to be judged on their actions once they are dead.
– He says people should fear *(craindre)* God's judgement.
– He wants people to be free from all judgements.

b. Who does "You" refer to?

c. In each stanza, pick out all the words referring to:
– the singer's dream,
– the consequences this dream would have if it came true.
Then, classify them in two columns (Dreams and Consequences).

d. What does John Lennon denounce in this song? Why?

Help!

Stanza 2	Chorus	Stanza 4
border: *frontière* conflict = dispute soldier army cause of war territory jingoism = strong belief that your country is better than others extremism /ɪksˈtriːmɪzəm/ optimism /ˈɒptɪmɪzəm/ pessimism /ˈpesɪmɪzəm/ denounce criticize	a utopia peace activist unity hopeful ≠ hopeless idealistic committed: *engagé* act for peace believe come true = become true urge sb to do sth: *inciter fortement qqn à faire qqch*	jealousy rivalry solidarity the rich ≠ the poor powerful strong ≠ weak /wiːk/ steal sth from sb help one another respect one another

PREPARE YOUR TASK

3 Recap WB

Prepare a one or two-minute oral account of the song. Use your notes and the following link words to present the song to the class: first • secondly • then • finally.

4 "I have a dream"

Read this short excerpt from Martin Luther King's most famous speech. What is his vision of the world? Are Luther King's and Lennon's goals similar or different?

"I have a dream that my four little children will one day live in a nation where they will not be judged by the color of their skin but by the content of their character.
I have a dream today!
I have a dream that one day, […] right there in Alabama little black boys and black girls will be able to join hands with little white boys and white girls as sisters and brothers.
I have a dream today!"

Martin Luther King, Lincoln Memorial, Washington D.C., August 28, 1963

PREPARE YOUR TASK

5 Song writing

Write a stanza of your own, beginning with the phrase "I imagine" or "I have a dream" and read it aloud to the class.

2. BUMS IN THE ATTIC

Andrew Wyeth, *Christina's World*, 1948

I want a house on a hill[1] like the ones with the gardens where Papa works. We go on Sundays, Papa's day off. I used to go. I don't anymore. You don't like to go out with us, Papa says. Getting too old? Getting too stuck-up, says Nenny. I don't tell them I am ashamed–all of us staring out the *window* like the hungry. I am tired of looking at what we can't have. When we win the lottery... Mama begins, and then I stop listening.

People who live on hills sleep so close to[2] the stars they forget those of us who live too much on earth. They don't look down at all except to be content to live on hills. They have nothing to do with last week's garbage[3] or fear of rats. Night comes. Nothing wakes them but[4] the wind.

One day I'll own my own house, but I won't forget who I am or where I came from. Passing bums[5] will ask, Can I come in? I'll offer them the attic[6], ask them to stay, because I know how it is to be without a house.

Some days after dinner, guests and I will sit in front of a fire. Floorboards will squeak upstairs. The attic grumble[7].

Rats? they'll ask.

Bums, I'll say, and I'll be happy.

Sandra Cisneros, *The House on Mango Street*, 1991

1. *colline* **2.** close to: near **3.** rubbish **4.** except **5.** *clochards* **6.** *grenier* **7.** *grincera*

1 Get ready

Read the first sentence:
"I want a house on a hill like the ones with the gardens where Papa works."
What can you guess about the narrator (age, social status, dream)?

2 Understanding the text WB

Read the text and turn to your Workbook for help.

Check the narrator's age and his / her social status. Find out about the narrator's feelings and dream.

Report your findings to the class. The rest of the class will listen and complete with the missing information. What can you deduce about the narrator's personality?

3 Speak in chains WB

a. Give an oral account of this passage with the help of your notes in your Workbook. Student A starts giving a sentence. Student B continues with another one.

b. With the information you have on the narrator, decide whether or not the painting is a good illustration of the narrator's dream and explain your view.

3. DREAMS

Hold fast to dreams
For if dreams die
Life is a broken-winged bird
That cannot fly.

Hold fast to dreams
For when dreams go
Life is a barren field
Frozen with snow.

Langston Hughes, *The Collected Poems of Langston Hughes*, 1994

1 Understanding the poem WB

a. Read the poem with the help of your Workbook.

PREPARE YOUR TASK → b. Say briefly what the message of the poem is.

2 How to pronounce WB

Work on the pronunciation with the help of your Workbook, then read the poem aloud.

3 More about Langston Hughes

Find information about Langston Hughes: dates, ethnic group, social background, career, name of the movement he belonged to, and what influenced him. Then report to the class.

– **Group 1** will read "From Busboy to Poet" on the following website:
www.americaslibrary.gov/cgi-bin/page.cgi/aa/writers/hughes

– **Group 2** will read "A Renaissance Man":
www.americaslibrary.gov/cgi-bin/page.cgi/aa/writers/hughes/renaiss_1

4. CHILDHOOD DREAMS WB

a. Listen to George Lucas talking about his dreams when he was in High School. Then report to the class.

PREPARE YOUR TASK → b. Role play
You are a radio journalist. Introduce George Lucas to your listeners in a two-minute report. Use your notes, and the words and expressions given in your Workbook.

5. THE NEW GENERATION GAP

1 Get ready

a. Look at the text and the photograph. What sort of document is this text? Name its different elements.

b. "The daughters of immigrants often make career choices their moms don't understand. The dreams of parents and children often clash..." (l. 1-3) What may the text deal with?

THE DAUGHTERS OF IMMIGRANTS OFTEN MAKE CAREER CHOICES THEIR MOMS DON'T UNDERSTAND.

The dreams of parents and children often clash, but the conflict can be especially painful in first-generation immigrant families where the parents have made enormous sacrifices. [...]

The contrast between parents' dreams and children's realities can be particularly acute [...]. Their mothers often come from countries where opportunities for women were severely limited, which makes the daughters' choices even more inexplicable. [...]

Sparlha Swa, 27, [...] believes that following her bliss[1] is the best way to honor her mother's sacrifice. Juliet Hart brought her three children to the United States from Jamaica for the opportunities. Sparlha and her brothers were straight-A students[2], and she went on to major in[3] anthropology at Stanford[4]. Sparlha held a series of jobs but soon found she could make money heeding[5] her passion for music. She's now a singer-songwriter, and has performed around the world. One of her most personal songs is called "Mama," and includes the lines: *"Who worked 16 hours just the other day breaking her back, her pride, her bones? So that we wouldn't ever have to do the same, never have to groan and moan[6], when we were[7] on our own."* Sparlha says her mother is now her biggest fan. "My mom's life has been inspirational because she has served the family instead of serving her own dreams. Because she didn't get to live her dreams, I have to."

Newsweek, January 21, 2008

1. total happiness **2.** straight A-students: *élèves brillants* **3.** major in: *se spécialiser en* **4.** one of the most prestigious American universities **5.** *en tenant compte de* **6.** *gémir* **7.** when we were: *(ici) quand nous serions*

2 Understanding the text

a. Find out the name of the girl and her age in the article.

b. Pick out all the words in the text related to the main character's:
– mother (name, country of origin, job and working conditions),
– education,
– dream,
– relationship with her mother.

c. List all the words referring to music.

d. What words are connected with conflict?

e. What word is repeated four times in the text?

PREPARE YOUR TASK →

3 Invent a dialogue

A journalist is interviewing Sparlha Swa in a talk show. The singer relates her experience. Act the dialogue out.

Language at work

Improve your pronunciation MP3

1 Lisez ces mots à haute voix.

/sək'ses/ • /sək'si:d/ • /'dɪfɪkəlt/ • /'dɪfɪkəlti/ • /'pɜ:pəs/

2 Accent de mot

a. À l'aide d'un dictionnaire, vérifiez l'accentuation de ces mots.
obstacle • advantage • opportunity • achieve • prevent • fulfil • optimistic • determined

b. Classez les mots ci-dessus selon qu'ils s'accentuent sur la première, la deuxième ou la troisième syllabe.

Première syllabe	Deuxième syllabe	Troisième syllabe

3 Lisez silencieusement ces citations.

– "Imagination is more important than knowledge." Albert Einstein
– "You must do the thing you think you cannot do." Eleanor Roosevelt
– "Continuous effort – not strength or intelligence – is the key to unlocking our potential." Winston Churchill

Quels mots sont non accentués ? Parmi ceux qui restent, lesquels allez-vous mettre particulièrement en relief ? Pourquoi ?

4 Lisez les trois phrases ci-dessus à haute voix.

Build up your vocabulary

1 Donnez le contraire de ces mots ; aidez-vous d'un dictionnaire si nécessaire.

success • successful • advantage • difficult • safe

2 À l'aide d'un dictionnaire, trouvez un synonyme pour chacun des mots suivants.

a goal • a way of • a try • determination • give up • hopeful

3 Reformulez cette phrase.

He fulfilled his dream. → *His dream ....*

4 À l'aide d'un dictionnaire, complétez ces phrases avec la préposition ou la particule verbale qui convient.

a. *She succeeds ... all she does.*
b. *We haven't made ... our minds about going abroad yet.*
c. *I have taken ... playing the guitar lately.*
d. *They met ... a lot of difficulties during their trip.*

5 À l'aide d'un dictionnaire, trouvez la traduction des phrases suivantes.

a. Il a surmonté de nombreuses difficultés.
b. *We shall overcome one day.*

Language at work

Le prétérit simple : valeur imaginaire
Les phrases conditionnelles : *If...*

1 Observez.

a. *If she* ***wins*** *the lottery, she* ***will buy*** *her own house.*
b. *If she* ***won*** *the lottery, she* ***would buy*** *her own house.*
c. *If she* ***had*** *a house of her own, she* ***would be*** *happier.*

De quels éléments est composée chaque forme verbale soulignée ?

Qu'exprime la proposition en *if* dans chaque phrase ? Associez chaque phrase à son sous-entendu dans cette proposition :

1. l'hypothèse ne se réalisera probablement pas dans l'avenir.
2. l'hypothèse se réalisera peut-être dans l'avenir.
3. l'hypothèse n'est pas réalisée en ce moment.

Sur une feuille séparée, récapitulez le fonctionnement de ces formes en remplissant un tableau de ce type.

If + ...	... + ...
If + ...	... + ...

2 Traduisez les énoncés a, b, et c ci-dessus.

3 Observez les formes soulignées ci-dessous.

If she were rich enough, she would have a big garden.
If I were you, I would try again.
If people were intelligent enough, they would not fight.

a. Que remarquez-vous ?
b. La forme soulignée ci-dessous appartient-elle à la langue courante ou soutenue ?
"If I was hungry, you would feed me." Katie Melua

4 Observez.

They wish they ***had*** *money to do what they want.*
She wishes she ***lived*** *in a more comfortable house.*
The mother wishes her daughter ***were*** *not a singer.*
The mother wishes her daughter ***were*** *a professor.*
The child wishes his parents ***allowed*** *him to do what he wants.*

Quel verbe exprime le regret de la situation présente ?
Quelle forme verbale est utilisée dans la subordonnée (verbe en gras) ?

I wish peut se traduire par « je regrette ». Traduisez les phrases en entier. Quels changements remarquez-vous lorsque l'on traduit ces phrases en français ?

5 Remplacez *they wish...* par *if only...* dans les phrases suivantes et traduisez en français les énoncés obtenus.

– *She wishes she could fulfil her dreams.* → *If only...*
– *I wish I owned my own house.* → *If only...*

6 Autres emplois : observez la forme en caractères gras, puis traduisez en français l'énoncé ci-dessous.

It's time you ***stopped*** *dreaming.*

Language at work

Practice

1 *If...*

Associez chaque début de phrase (à gauche) à la fin qui lui convient (à droite).

1. If they accepted my project, I would make a fortune.	**A.** I may fly to Dublin.
2. If I had enough money, I would fly to Dublin.	**B.** I'm not sure he will.
3. If I have enough money, I will fly to Dublin.	**C.** Unfortunately it still exists.
4. If he managed to reach his goals, he would be very happy.	**D.** But I can't afford the ticket.
5. If racism was eradicated, people would live in harmony.	**E.** But I don't think they ever will.

2 **Complétez ces phrases.**

Example: If I were a genius, I would only have A's in school without doing my homework!
– *If I were as small as a fly, ...*
– *If I won the lottery, ...*
– *If I didn't have to work later, ...*
– *If my teachers were replaced by computers, ...*
– *If only more women were managers, ...*
– *If school wasn't compulsory, ...*
– *If guns disappeared, ...*

3 **Complétez.**

– *If ..., I wouldn't have to work.*
– *If ..., people would be on holiday all the time.*

4 **Catastrophes en série.**

Example: It will be terrible if I forget my best friend's birthday.
À vous de trouver quatre autres catastrophes.

5 **Laissez libre cours à votre imagination.**

a. Lisez cette bande dessinée.

Bill Watterson, *It's a Magical World*, 1997

b. Vous aussi, vous avez sûrement des milliers d'idées. À votre tour de les exprimer.

I wish...
Possible topics: pupils... / the cafeteria...
teachers... / my timetable...

your task

You are taking part in a drama contest. You have to choose a poem or an excerpt from a famous speech. Learn it by heart. Then justify your choice in a few sentences and recite it in front of your class.

WHAT IF

Last night, while I lay[1] thinking here,
Some Whatifs crawled inside[2] my ear
And pranced[3] and partied all night long
And sang their same old Whatif song:
Whatif I'm dumb[4] in school?
Whatif they've closed the swimming pool?
Whatif I get beat up?
Whatif there's poison in my cup?
Whatif I start to cry?
Whatif I get sick and die?
Whatif I flunk that test[5]?
Whatif green hair grows on my chest[6]?
Whatif nobody likes me?
Whatif a bolt of lightning[7] strikes me?
Whatif I don't grow tall?
Whatif my head starts getting smaller?
Whatif the fish won't bite?
Whatif the wind tears up my kite[8]?
Whatif they start a war?
Whatif my parents get divorced?
Whatif the bus is late?
Whatif my teeth don't grow in straight[9]?
Whatif I tear my pants?
Whatif I never learn to dance?
Everything seems swell[10], and then
The nighttime Whatifs strike again!

Shel Silverstein, *A Light in the Attic*, 1981

1. lie, lay, lain **2.** crawled/krɔːld/ inside: *sont entrés en rampant*
3. /prɑːnst/ *se sont pavanés* **4.** /dʌm/ *bête, stupide*
5. I flunk that test: *je suis collé à l'examen* **6.** *poitrine*
7. bolt of lightning: *éclair* **8.** /kaɪt/ *cerf-volant* **9.** *droit*
10. *formidable*

LISTEN TO THE MUSTN'TS

Listen to the MUSTN'TS[1], child,
Listen to the DON'TS
Listen to the SHOULDN'TS[2]
The IMPOSSIBLES[3], the WON'TS
Listen to the NEVER HAVES.
Then listen close[4] to me –
Anything can happen, child,
ANYTHING can be.

Shel Silverstein, *Where the Sidewalk Ends*, 1974

1. /ˈmʌsnts/ **2.** /ˈʃʊdnts/ **3.** /ɪmˈpɒsəblz/ **4.** /kləʊs/

BETTER FUTURE

I chose to run for president at this moment in history because I believe deeply that we cannot solve the challenges of our time unless we solve them together – unless we perfect[1] our union by understanding that we may have different[2] stories, but we hold common hopes; that we may not look the same and we may not have come from the same place, but we all want to move in the same direction – towards a better future for our children and our grandchildren.

Barack Obama, Constitution Center,
Philadelphia, Pennsylvania, March 18, 2008

1. /pəˈfekt/ **2.** /ˈdɪfrənt/

LES ÉTAPES À SUIVRE

1 Choisissez votre texte.

a. Lisez silencieusement les deux poèmes et l'extrait du discours de Barack Obama.

b. Assurez-vous de bien les comprendre. Utilisez le dictionnaire pour vérifier le sens des mots que vous ne connaissez pas.

c. Choisissez avec soin l'un des deux poèmes (le plus long bénéficie d'un bonus) ou le discours : n'oubliez pas de justifier votre choix. Utilisez vos notes sur cette unité pour reformuler ce que vous avez compris.

MP3

2 Travaillez la prononciation. *WB*

a. Prononcez tous les mots donnés avec leur transcription phonétique (ci-contre).

b. Servez-vous des rimes pour trouver comment se prononcent les mots en fin de vers.

c. Posez-vous les questions suivantes :
– Quels mots sont accentués ?
– Quelles sont les formes réduites ?
– Quels mots allez-vous particulièrement mettre en relief ?
– Où se feront les liaisons ?
– À quels endroits allez-vous respirer ?

d. Lisez le texte choisi à haute voix et vérifiez votre prononciation en écoutant l'enregistrement sur le site compagnon (U3 - Your task (1), (2), (3)).

MP3

3 Apprenez votre texte par cœur.

a. Écoutez l'enregistrement de votre document, puis récitez-le en même temps que le modèle de l'enregistrement.

b. N'attendez pas le dernier moment pour le mémoriser : **entraînez-vous** tous les jours et **à haute voix**.

c. Mettez-vous **en situation** : restez debout et regardez autour de vous. Déplacez-vous dans l'espace.

d. Karaoké
Pour vous habituer à produire de l'anglais en continu, chantez les chansons suivantes sur le thème du rêve :
– Katie Melua : *If I Were a Sailboat*
– Ben Harper : *With My Own Two Hands*
– Elvis Presley : *If I Can Dream*

Keith Haring, *Untitled*, 1982

CONSEILS POUR VOTRE PRESTATION

1 Expliquez votre choix.

– Donnez votre **opinion** : *to me/as far as I'm concerned /in my opinion...* (cf. p. 54)
– Réutilisez les **structures** vues dans l'unité pour partager vos sentiments : *I wish... /If only...*
– Réemployez le **vocabulaire** étudié. N'utilisez pas ~~I like it because, it's nice...~~, mais : *It makes me feel /it makes me think of /it symbolizes /it stands for /it highlights...*

2 Parlez lentement, tout en regardant votre auditoire.

Le professeur n'est pas votre seul interlocuteur. Vous n'en serez que plus convaincant !

HEROES

YOUR TASK AT THE END OF THIS UNIT

You are in a newly-built school. A name for this school has to be found. Each member of the community has to suggest a hero's name, and justify his or her choice.
→ P. 52

TUNE IN!

1 React to this book cover

a. Does the man in the picture make you think of heroes from books or films you know?

b. What makes this man look like a hero?
– What angle / shot is used here? (see p. 280). What impact does it have on you?
– Justify your answer by listing his basic qualities.

Help!

Physical description

pilot /ˈpaɪlət/
gear /gɪəʳ/: *équipement*
leather /ˈleðəʳ/ jacket
helmet /ˈhelmɪt/
goggles /ˈgɒglz/: *lunettes protectrices*
gloves /glʌvz/
sporty /ˈspɔːti/
upright: *très droit*

Angle / shot

shot: *plan*
look / seem to be
He reminds /rɪˈmaɪndz/ me of...

Impact on the viewer

courageous / brave
triumphant /traɪˈʌmfənt/
fearless / daring
enterprising
proud /praʊd/
self-satisfied /selfˈsætɪsfaɪd/
determined /dɪˈtɜːmɪnd/
impressive
achieve one's goal: *atteindre son but*
risk one's life
overcome difficulties
give up: *abandonner*

PREPARE YOUR TASK →

2 Role play

You work for a publishing company and you have found this photo for a new book called "How to Be a Hero". You have to justify your choice; give five arguments.

1. ROLE MODELS

1 Do you know them?

a. Have a look at the names in each card. Which of these heroes do you know?

b. Read each biographical card and learn more about these heroes.

c. Classify each hero in the corresponding category in the middle of the page and justify your answers using key words from the cards.

A Cathy Freeman
(born in 1973) is an Australian field track athlete and fearless promoter of the Aboriginal culture. She became the star of the 2000 Sydney Olympic Games.

D ALEXANDER FLEMING
(1881-1955) was a Scottish bacteriologist who discovered penicillin and is considered the father of modern medicine.

F EMMELINE PANKHURST
/ˈpæŋkhɜːst/ (1858-1938) was an English woman who stood up for the women's cause. After many fights, she accomplished her dream of giving women the right to vote in 1938.

B Robert Gould Shaw
(1837-1863) was a brave young colonel in the American Civil War who led the first all-black regiment in their fearless charge of Fort Wagner.

1. record-breaker
2. peace-maker
3. explorer
4. scientist
5. athlete
6. war hero
7. Human Rights fighter
8. earthkeeper

G Neil Armstrong
(born in 1930) was the first man to walk on the moon during the Apollo 11 mission in 1969.

C JOHN MUIR
/mjʊəʳ/ (1838-1914) devoted most of his life to the protection of nature, and is seen as the founder of the American National Parks.

E Amelia Earhart
(1897-1937) was the first woman to fly across the Atlantic Ocean. She broke many records such as speed and altitude. She opened aviation to women.

H Martin Luther /luːθəʳ/ King
(1929-1968) was awarded the Nobel Peace Prize for his passive resistance to racism and segregation in the USA. He also fought against poverty and the war in Vietnam.

2 Pairwork WB

Make your partner guess the two heroes you have selected with the help of their biography card.

PREPARE YOUR TASK →

3 Writing a back cover WB

Now your publishing company wants to publish a book about one of the eight heroes above. Choose one of them and write the back cover corresponding to him / her. Include the following elements:

– a definition of a hero.
– the main biographical elements of your hero's life.
– your hero's role and field of achievement.

Help!

Biography	Qualities
be born /bɔːn/ ≠ die /daɪ/	adventurous /ədˈventʃərəs/
live in the nineteenth / twentieth century	clever = intelligent
become /bɪˈkʌm/	devoted /dɪˈvəʊtɪd/ = dedicated /ˈdedɪkeɪtɪd/
discover	energetic
be awarded /əˈwɔːdɪd/	generous
fight /faɪt/ for ≠ against	persevering
spend his / her life + V-ing	reckless /ˈreklɪs/: *téméraire*
be famous for + V-ing	selfless /ˈselflɪs/: *altruiste*

2. ON BEING A CHAMPION

Mattie Stepanek was a young American poet who died in June 2004 of a rare hereditary disease called myopathy. By the age of 13 he had written thousands of poems.

A champion is a winner,
A hero...
Someone who never gives up[1]
Even when the going gets rough[2].
A champion is a member of
A winning team...
Someone who overcomes[3] challenges
Even when it requires[4] creative solutions.
A champion is an optimist,
A hopeful spirit...
Someone who plays the game,
Even when the game is called life.
There can be a champion in each of us,
If we live as a winner,
If we live as a member of a team,
If we live with a hopeful spirit,
For life.

Mattie Stepanek, *Journey through Heartsongs*, 2001

1. *abandonne* **2.** when the going gets rough /rʌf/: *quand il devient difficile d'avancer* **3.** *surmonte* **4.** *nécessite*

1 Get ready

Close your books and listen to the poem. Can you remember the first word(s) and the last one(s)? What other words did you recognize and memorize? Write them down on a separate piece of paper.

2 Understanding the poem WB

a. What groups of words are repeated?

b. Find the sentence that best sums up the poem.

c. What are the most important values for Mattie? Choose from the list.
love • friendship • solidarity • energy • joy • hope • success • courage • competitive spirit • honesty • loyalty • money • peace • determination • will-power

PREPARE YOUR TASK →

3 Recap

Prepare a one-minute oral account.

a. Who can be a hero? What qualities are needed?
b. Do you agree with the definition of a hero given in the poem?
c. Why do you think Mattie Stepanek has become a hero?
d. Do you like this poem? Why? Why not?
e. What are the most important values for you in life?

- A hero is someone who is... and who has...
- He / She embodies *(incarne)*...
- He / She can... ; yet he / she must...
- He or she never... , on the contrary, he / she always...

4 Speak up WB

Read the poem aloud. Turn to your Workbook for help.

3. LITTLE BIG MAN

A Subway Superhero

A New York City man saves a stranger from an oncoming train and receives high honors.

Wesley Autrey can't fly, but he is still being called a real-life Superman! Last week, the courageous 50-year-old rescued Cameron Hollopeter, 20, from being hit by a train. The train was entering a subway station in New York City. The young man had fallen from the station's platform[1] and onto the train tracks[2] a few feet below.

1. *quai* **2.** *voies*

Heroic Rescue

Autrey, a construction worker and Navy veteran, was with his two young daughters when he saw Hollopeter fall. Autrey made a quick decision and jumped onto the tracks. He then rolled himself and Hollopeter into a gap, or opening, between the rails. Autrey used his own body to shield[3] the young man. Five of the train's cars passed over the two before stopping completely. The two men were both unharmed[4]. Hollopeter's stepmother [...] called Autrey an "angel". Autrey visited the New York Film Academy student in hospital on Wednesday.

3. *faire écran à, protéger* **4.** *indemnes*

Rewards for Bravery

For his bravery, Autrey was given a hero's welcome at City Hall. New York City Mayor Michael Bloomberg presented Autrey with the Bronze Medallion. It is the highest award[5] for achievements[6] by its citizens. Mayor Bloomberg called Autrey "a great man – a man who makes us all proud to be New Yorkers".

After the ceremony at City Hall, a limousine took Autrey to a meeting with multi-millionaire businessman Donald Trump. Trump awarded Autrey with $10,000. The heroic father also received $5,000 from the New York Film Academy, a trip to Disney World, and one year of free subway rides[7].

Even after all this attention, Autrey still doesn't see himself as a Superman. "I did it out of a split-second[8] reaction", Autrey said on CBS *The Early Show*. "And if I had to do it again, I probably would."

5. /əˈwɔːd/ *récompense* **6.** *réalisations, exploits* **7.** free subway rides: *trajets gratuits dans le métro*
8. *fraction de seconde*

Time for Kids, January 8, 2007

1 Understanding the text WB

a. Skim through the first paragraph.
- Find a city name, the rescuer's and the victim's names.
- What do "50" and "20" correspond to?
- Pick out two words related to transport.

b. Concentrate on the second paragraph.
- Who is Autrey? (age, job, past experience, family)
- Who is Hollopeter? (age, occupation)
- List Autrey's actions in chronological order.

c. Focus on the last paragraphs.
- Who are Michael Bloomberg and Donald Trump?
- List the rewards Autrey got.
- What are Autrey's nicknames? According to you, are they justified?

PREPARE YOUR TASK →

2 Role play

You are a radio journalist. Introduce Wesley Autrey to your listeners in a two-minute news flash.

a. Sum up the main facts and the reasons why the Mayor of New York gave him an award.
b. Give your reactions to what Autrey did.
c. What sort of hero is Wesley Autrey?
d. Compare him with the role models on page 43.

- Wesley was...
- Suddenly he saw... and decided...
- Fortunately...
- Later...
- For his bravery... and...
- But Autrey thinks... , because he considers...

4. GORILLAS IN THE MIST

Gorillas are mammals.
– diet: omnivore
– average lifespan: 35 years
– size (standing): 1.2 to 1.8m
– weight: 135 to 220kg
– protection status = endangered

1 Get ready

a. How much do you know about gorillas? Look at the chart on the right for one minute then close your book. What can you remember?

b. Look at the photo. What can you guess about Dian Fossey (job, relationships with the gorillas)?

2 More about Dian Fossey

Read these paragraphs on Dian Fossey's life. Can you re-order them chronologically?

A The Canadian orang-utan expert, Dr. B. Galdikas, has written of her colleague, Dian Fossey: "[…] In her devotion to these animals, Dian will be remembered for generations as one of the heroes of the twentieth century. Without her work, it is doubtful that mountain gorillas would have survived to the twenty-first."

B In 1980 she went to England to attend Cambridge University, where she obtained a PhD[1] in zoology.

C In 1985, she was found murdered in her cabin. No one has ever found her killer, although it is suspected that the person was a gorilla poacher[2]. […]

D Her work took her to Zaire and then to Rwanda, where she opened the Karisoke Research Center. After years of patient observation, the gorillas came to know and trust her, and she found that she could sit in the midst[3] of a group and even play with their young. She came to know the animals as individuals, and even gave them names.

E Thanks to her work, the world's awareness of the endangered status of the mountain gorilla has increased, and the animals are now protected by the government of Rwanda and various international conservation organizations, including the Dian Fossey Gorilla Fund.

F She wrote an account of her experiences in Rwanda. In 1983, it was published as *Gorillas in the Mist*[4]. The next year she returned to the Karisoke Research Center to continue her fieldwork.

G Dian Fossey […] decided to study the endangered mountain gorilla in Africa. […]

H When her favorite gorilla, Digit, was killed (in 1977) by poachers for his hands, Fossey began a campaign against poaching. Her outspokenness, unfortunately, made her a target for violence.

www.myhero.com, 2009

1. *doctorat* 2. *braconnier* 3. in the middle 4. *brume*

3 Watch a video

Mountain Gorillas

Thanks to Dian Fossey, has the situation evolved in Rwanda?
Turn to your worksheet for help.

PREPARE YOUR TASK →

4 Role play

You have just watched this report and read the text. You try to convince your friends to join the Dian Fossey Gorilla Fund and adopt a gorilla. Include the following points:
– Who was Dian Fossey? What is she famous for? Where did she work?
– Who opposed her work? Why?
– Why is she considered one of the heroes of the twentieth century?

5. OVER OCEANS AND MOUNTAIN TOPS

Sir Edmund Hillary, Everest conqueror, dies

On the 29 May, 1953, Hillary made history by becoming the first person to reach the peak of Everest alongside Sherpa Tenzing Norgay. The victory, which was achieved on the eve[1] of Queen Elizabeth II's coronation[2], was seen as a huge accomplishment against nature as many attempts[3] had previously[4] failed. Shortly after the climb a heated debate broke out amongst the public over who had actually[5] reached the peak first – Sir Edmund or Tenzing.

Both insisted that they had got there at exactly the same time but Tenzing revealed years later in his book that Sir Edmund had been a few steps ahead.

The New Zealander went on to devote much of his life to aiding the mountain people of Nepal and set up the Himalayan Trust through which he built schools, hospitals and bridges in the region. He never liked to be known as a hero, preferring to be called "Ed" and considering himself just an ordinary beekeeper[6].

Despite winning international renown[7] as one of the 20th century's greatest adventurers, Sir Edmund remained humble to the end.

The mountaineer, known to friends and family simply as Ed, said he wished to be remembered mostly for his humanitarian work.

[...] New Zealand's Prime Minister, Helen Clark, paid tribute to Sir Edmund early today as "a quintessential Kiwi[8]". "Sir Ed described himself as an average New Zealander with modest abilities," she said. "In reality, he was a colossus. He was a heroic figure who not only 'knocked off' Everest but lived a life of determination, humility, and generosity. He is the best-known New Zealander ever to have lived."

[...] His philosophy of life was simple: "Adventuring can be for the ordinary person with ordinary qualities, such as I regard myself," he said in a 1975 interview.

The Telegraph, January 13, 2008

1. *la veille* **2.** *couronnement* **3.** *tentatives* **4.** *auparavant* **5.** *effectivement* **6.** *apiculteur* **7.** *renommée* **8.** Kiwi is the nickname used internationally for New Zealanders.

1 Understanding the text WB

Read the article and find information about Sir Edmund Hillary.

– What was his native country?
– When did he become famous? What for?
– Pick out all the words related to Edmund Hillary's humanitarian work.
– Find examples of Sir Edmund's humility.

2 Who's your hero? WB

Now listen to Susie, a mountaineer. She will tell you why Sir Edmund is a role model for her.

PREPARE YOUR TASK

3 A famous Kiwi WB

Use your notes and explain why Sir Edmund is portrayed on this banknote. Useful words :
admire • inspire • lead • accomplish • overcome • succeed in + V-ing • the first... • the best... • the most...

– He was chosen... because...
– He was an explorer who...

6. WAR AND PEACE

1 War times WB

Look at the front cover of the book, then read the back cover. Find as much information as you can about Ishmael Beah. Turn to your Workbook for help.

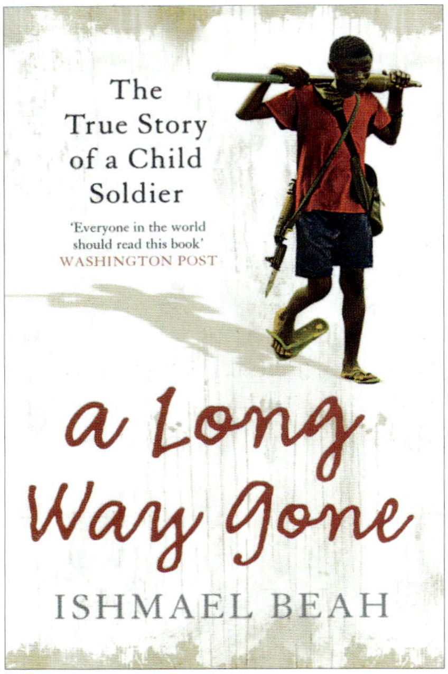

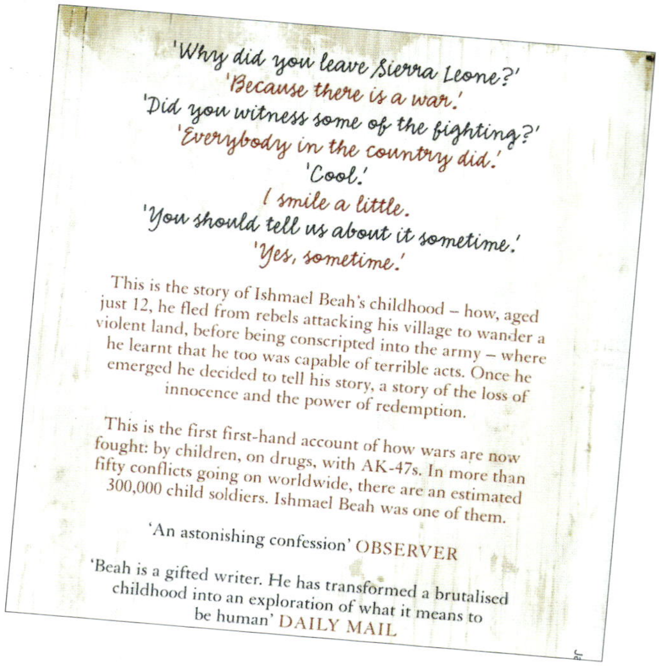
'Why did you leave Sierra Leone?'
'Because there is a war.'
'Did you witness some of the fighting?'
'Everybody in the country did.'
'Cool.'
I smile a little.
'You should tell us about it sometime.'
'Yes, sometime.'

This is the story of Ishmael Beah's childhood – how, aged just 12, he fled from rebels attacking his village to wander a violent land, before being conscripted into the army – where he learnt that he too was capable of terrible acts. Once he emerged he decided to tell his story, a story of the loss of innocence and the power of redemption.

This is the first first-hand account of how wars are now fought: by children, on drugs, with AK-47s. In more than fifty conflicts going on worldwide, there are an estimated 300,000 child soldiers. Ishmael Beah was one of them.

'An astonishing confession' OBSERVER

'Beah is a gifted writer. He has transformed a brutalised childhood into an exploration of what it means to be human' DAILY MAIL

2 Rebel with a cause

a. Read this extract from Ishmael's book and list the reasons why he became a soldier.

I am from Sierra Leone[1], and the problem that is affecting us children is the war that forces us to run away from our homes, lose our families, and aimlessly roam[2] the forests. As a result, we get involved in the conflict as soldiers, carriers of loads, and in many other difficult tasks. All this is because of starvation[3], the loss of our families, and the need to feel safe and be part of something when all else has broken down. I joined the army really because of the loss of my family and starvation. I wanted to avenge the deaths of my family. I also had to get some food to survive, and the only way to do that was to be part of the army. It was not easy being a soldier, but we just had to do it. I have been rehabilitated[4] now, so don't be afraid of me. I am not a soldier anymore; I am a child.

The issue[5] of children in war is not only an African issue, it's a global issue and my trauma is a small price to pay to expose[6] what continues to happen to children all over the world.

Ishmael Beah, *A Long Way Gone*, 2007

1. /sɪ'eralɪ'əʊn/ or /sɪ'eralɪ'əʊne/ a country in West Africa **2.** *errer (dans)* **3.** *famine* **4.** *réinséré* **5.** problem **6.** denounce

b. Explain why he is now a member of Human Rights Watch and has spoken before the United Nations on several occasions.

Help!

ill-treated defenceless weak /wi:k/: *faible* committed: *engagé* positive outraged / indignant widespread phenomenon: *phénomène répandu*	speak out: *s'exprimer publiquement en faveur de qqn* stand by sb: *être solidaire de qqn* ban: *interdire* improve: *améliorer*

PREPARE YOUR TASK →

3 Role play

A journalist interviews Ishmael Beah. Prepare questions and answers and act the dialogue out in front of the class.

Language at work

Improve your pronunciation MP3

Après l'écoute, lisez ces phrases à haute voix en prêtant particulièrement attention à la prononciation de *were / weren't, there are / there were, was* et *are / aren't.*

1. The Beatles were /wə/ four young men from Liverpool.
2. They were /wə/ the number one rock group for years.
3. They weren't /wɜːnt/ the only rock group at the time.
4. Fans were /wə/ crazy about them.
5. They were /wə/ amazing on stage.
6. There are /ə/ many songs by the Beatles about love.
7. There were /wə/ thousands of fans wherever they went.
8. In 1970 the band was /wəz/ dissolved.
9. John Lennon was /wəz/ murdered in New York City.
10. Many songs written by Lennon and McCartney are /ə/ cult songs now.
11. Paul McCartney's recent songs aren't /ɑːnt/ as good.
12. I'm sure the Beatles are /ə/ the best.

Build up your vocabulary

1 Reconnaître la nature d'un mot

a. Sur papier libre, classez les mots suivants selon leur catégorie grammaticale.
dead /ded/ • *death* /deθ/ • *die* /daɪ/ • *life* /laɪf/ • *live* /lɪv/ • *lived* • *born* • *birth* /bɜːθ/ • *work* /wɜːk/ • *worked* • *belief* • *believe* • *succeed* /sək'siːd/ • *success* • *successful*

⚠ ATTENTION : un de ces mots sera classé dans deux colonnes à la fois.

Nom	Adjectif	Participe passé	Verbe

b. Complétez ce texte avec les mots de la liste ci-dessus. Faites les modifications grammaticales nécessaires.

My hero is Abraham Lincoln; he was ... 1 in 1809. He ... 2 all his ... 3 first on his father's farm, then as a lawyer, and eventually he became the 16th American President. He ... 4 all men were equal and consequently made slavery illegal in 1863. His biggest ... 5 was winning the Civil War. He was shot in Washington where he ... 6 . His ... 7 in 1865 was a real shock for the nation.

2 Fabriquer des adjectifs à partir de noms communs

a. Observez :
- *success* → *successful*
- *help* → *helpful*

Que constatez-vous ?

D'autres schémas existent :
- *courage* → *courageous*
- *knowledge* → *knowledgeable*
- *luck* → *lucky*
- *friend* → *friendly*

b. Fabriquez des adjectifs à partir de ces noms, puis vérifiez vos réponses à l'aide d'un dictionnaire et donnez leur traduction.
honour • *peace* • *respect* • *adventure* • *hope* • *faith* • *thought* • *pain* • *fame* • *joy* • *skill*

Language at work

Le superlatif

1 Repérez les superlatifs dans les énoncés suivants.

– *Usain Bolt is the fastest sprinter of all times.*
– *Einstein was one of the most intelligent scientists ever.*
– *I am Marilyn Monroe's biggest fan. To me, she was the prettiest film star of all. But her lonely and desperate suicide was the worst death one can imagine.*
– *Oprah Winfrey is the richest African-American woman. But she is also the most successful and the best TV presenter in the US. She is the most generous star I can think of.*

2 Identifiez les adjectifs à partir desquels ces superlatifs sont formés. Classez-les en trois colonnes : adjectifs courts, longs, ayant un superlatif irrégulier.

Récapitulez : pour exprimer le **superlatif de supériorité** (= « le plus... »), on emploie :
– ... + **terminaison** ... pour les adjectifs d'... syllabe et ceux de ... syllabes se terminant par ...
– ... + ... pour les autres adjectifs.

3 Quelles modifications orthographiques remarquez-vous dans ces superlatifs ?

the luckiest • *the prettiest* • *the happiest* • *the biggest*
Déduisez : – ... devient ... s'il est précédé d'une consonne
– une consonne finale qui suit une voyelle est ... .

4 Observez les compléments des superlatifs dans les phrases de l'exercice 1. Par quelles prépositions sont-ils introduits ?

Être ou avoir

1 Lisez ce texte écrit par une admiratrice de Charlie Chaplin.

I love Charlie Chaplin who was the best comic actor of the silent movies. Nothing prepared him to be such a star: He was only five foot three tall, and shabby-looking *(d'aspect minable)*. And yet he became the most famous actor of his time. Chaplin's mother was a poor unsuccessful English actress, but there were many jobs in a theatre for a young intelligent child. In 1910, he was not afraid to go to New York. There he was lucky to get a job and became the brilliant actor we know. Chaplin's genius was limitless. Consider *The Gold Rush* (1925), *Modern Times* (1936), *The Great Dictator* (1940), which are masterpieces I watch over and over again. When Chaplin died he was 78 years old.

a. Traduisez en français les expressions soulignées. Que constatez-vous ?
b. À quels temps sont les verbes dans le texte ? Pourquoi ?

2 À quoi correspond 's dans les phrases suivantes ?

– *Ishmael's a peace-maker.*
– *Ishmael's book is entitled* A Long Way Gone.
– *He's just read a book on the Himalayas.*

Écoutez l'enregistrement et classez chaque énoncé dans la colonne correspondante.

Ex: Ishmael's a peace-maker.	Ex: Ishmael's book...	Ex: He's just read...

Practice

1 Mettez les adjectifs entre parenthèses au superlatif.

a. Abraham Lincoln was (tall) president ever in the White House: He was six foot four (= nearly 2 metres) tall. He was also (honest), that's why his nickname was "Honest Abe".

b. Thomas Edison was (young) American inventor: He started when he was 16. He became (good) inventor of modern times when he invented the light bulb, his (important) discovery.

c. Ellen MacArthur broke the world record for the (fast) solo travel around the globe on 7th February 2005. She is (brave) sailor I've learnt about. She is also (young) person to be awarded the title of Dame Commander of the Order of the British Empire.

2 Traduisez ces phrases.

a. Il y a beaucoup de records détenus par des Américains.
b. Quand il a eu 20 ans, il a écrit son premier roman.
c. Mon héros a les cheveux bruns.
d. Shackleton n'avait jamais froid et n'avait jamais peur !
e. Tu as raison, il a eu de la chance de ne pas mourir.

3 Recopiez cette biographie et complétez-la avec les formes verbales qui conviennent.

Margaret Brown (become) famous as one of the lucky survivors of the *Titanic* tragedy and (be) then nicknamed "The Unsinkable Molly". She (be born) in Missouri in 1867. Later she (move) to Colorado where she (meet) her husband James who (work) for the silver mines. He (strike) it immensely rich and the family (go) to live in Denver. Molly (travel) around the world. She (be) on her way home on the transatlantic liner *Titanic* when the ship (hit) an iceberg and (sink). During the disaster she (help) victims and everybody (acclaim) her heroism. Back home she (give) money to poor immigrants who (be) on board. She (be) an incredible woman who (speak) her mind and (join) many causes such as the rights of women or the education of all children.

4 Rédigez une biographie de Terry Fox avec les éléments suivants.

Canadian humanitarian, athlete and cancer activist, one of Canada's greatest heroes
– **July 28, 1958:** birth in Winnipeg, Manitoba
– **Childhood** near Vancouver
– **1977:** bone cancer and right leg amputation above the knee
– **In hospital:** decides to run across Canada and raise money for cancer research
– **Name of his journey:** the Marathon of Hope
– **Goal:** get attention, collect money, raise $1 from each Canadian citizen
– **Preparation:** 18 months, 5,000 kilometers (3,107 miles)
– **Starting point:** St John's, Newfoundland
– **Departure:** April 12, 1980
– **Distance every day:** 42 kilometers (26 miles) through Quebec and Ontario
– **September 1, 1980:** end of the run after 143 days and 5,373 kilometers (3,339 miles)
– **June 28, 1981:** death
– **2005:** issue of the Terry Fox dollar; first Canadian on coins
– **Today:** organization of the Terry Fox Run around the world every year; goal: raise money for cancer research

Ottawa, Canada

Your task

You are in a newly-built school. A name for this school has to be found. Each member of the community has to suggest a hero's name, and justify his or her choice.

AVANT DE VOUS LANCER

1 Lisez les déclarations suivantes.

"My hero is Princess Diana. She was Princess of Wales, married to Prince Charles. She was such a lovely lady! She was both beautiful and the most generous person I've heard and read about. For example, she cared about the poor, the homeless, the handicapped, the orphaned. She was also involved in the fight against landmines. Sadly she died in a car accident in Paris."

Susie from Reading, Berkshire, England

"My hero is David Beckham because he is a fantastic English soccer player. He is 34 years old, athletic and he's so good-looking. He inspires me because he is the world's best soccer player. Beckham played for my favorite team, Manchester United, and for Real Madrid. To conclude, I wish I could be as good as him. I think he's awesome!"

Scott from Denver, Colorado, USA

"I wish our school was named after Rosa Parks. Rosa Parks was certainly the most courageous woman in Alabama in the 60s. She refused to give up her seat to a white passenger. She was an amazing person because she stood up for what she believed in. She started a one-year boycott against racism and segregation in buses. Thousands of people followed her. For me, she is a symbol of dignity, courage and hope. She serves as an example and is a true inspiration to me and many others. That's why she received many awards over the years. She died a few years ago."

Alison from Virginia Beach, Virginia, USA

a. Relevez dans ces trois textes les expressions utilisées pour :
exprimer son admiration • structurer le discours (connecteurs logiques) • donner son opinion

b. Classez les expressions suivantes à l'aide des trois rubriques ci-dessus : *in my opinion* • *consequently* • *he /she's incredible* • *later on* • *he is a great guy (colloquial)* • *he /she's a tremendous hero* • *that's how* • *to my mind* • *what a genius!* • *thanks to him /her* • *eventually*

c. Écoutez l'enregistrement puis lisez toutes ces expressions à haute voix.

2 Entraînez-vous à prendre des notes.

⚠ Votre tâche consiste à présenter votre héros ou votre héroïne à l'oral. Vous ne devez pas rédiger de phrases, mais vous entraîner à prendre la parole à partir de notes uniquement.

A. "My hero is Bethany Hamilton."

"My hero is a young surfer called Bethany Hamilton. She intended to become professional and was very talented. She was surfing with friends on Halloween morning in sunny Hawaï when a 14-foot tiger shark bit and took off her left arm. Her courage was tremendous: Not only did she swim to safety and save her life, but she went back surfing a month later with only one arm. She turned a negative into a positive and she was my age, only 14, when it happened. She inspired me to go on with my dream. I am her biggest fan!"

a. Écoutez le texte et repérez les mots accentués.

b. Lisez ce texte à haute voix, de façon expressive, et en accentuant les mots porteurs de sens.

B. "Let me tell you about Sebastian Clover."

Sebastian Clover sailed Atlantic solo 15 (2003)
Hero: youngest person to cross ocean alone
Left Tenerife, reached Antigua 24 days later
Most fantastic moments = when saw dolphins + whales swimming near boat
Worst day = bad weather & mast nearly broken → spent 20 hours repairing
Dream = sleep real bed + eat a lot of chocolate
Admire him → love sailing + know difficult and dangerous
Think both courageous + strong = awesome experience!

a. Un élève américain a pris ces notes pour faire son exposé. Que remarquez-vous ? Quels mots les signes utilisés remplacent-ils ? Rétablissez à l'oral les éléments manquants.
b. Maintenant, écoutez l'élève parler de son héros et comparez avec votre production.
c. Réécoutez l'enregistrement en faisant particulièrement attention aux mots accentués.

LES ÉTAPES À SUIVRE

1 Choisissez le héros ou l'héroïne dont le nom pourrait être donné à votre lycée. Renseignez-vous sur sa vie dans une encyclopédie, un dictionnaire ou en allant sur le site Internet *myhero.com*.

2 Revoyez les documents étudiés dans l'unité et apprenez le lexique utile avec sa prononciation.

3 **Pour préparer vos notes**, pensez :
– aux principaux éléments biographiques (nom, nationalité, âge, date de naissance et éventuellement de mort, titre, métier, passe-temps...)
– aux raisons pour lesquelles cette personne est un héros à vos yeux (dans un des domaines vus dans *Role Models* page 39 par exemple), aux récompenses éventuellement reçues
– aux qualités qui lui ont permis de se surpasser ou d'atteindre son but.
Justifiez votre choix en expliquant ce qui la rend admirable à vos yeux (en faisant le lien avec vos centres d'intérêt, vos loisirs, votre expérience ou votre vie).

4 **Choisissez la forme grammaticale** qui convient (le prétérit pour des événements vus comme coupés du présent, le présent simple pour les goûts et les habitudes, le *present perfect* pour les expériences et les faits inachevés).

5 **Employez des superlatifs** pour montrer le caractère exceptionnel de cette personne.

CONSEILS POUR VOTRE PRESTATION

⚠ **Vous n'aurez que vos notes sous les yeux !**

Lors de votre exposé devant la classe (de 1 minute 30 à 2 minutes) :
– parlez distinctement et lentement
– réalisez correctement les formes réduites qui seront prises en compte dans l'évaluation
– marquez des pauses pour respirer
– si vous hésitez, utilisez des *gap fillers* (voir p. 54).

PRENDRE LA PAROLE EN CONTINU

A Améliorez votre prononciation

1 Écoutez cette interview, puis lisez ces extraits du script.

a. My greatest hobby is soccer. I absolutely love this sport and have been involved in it for a long time.
b. In Canada and in France, I referee soccer games. I enjoy watching games on TV. Lyon and Monaco are my favourite French teams.
c. Surprisingly, even though I'm Canadian, I don't really like hockey very much. I don't enjoy American football very much either.
d. I like to travel and have visited many parts of Europe and North America. It's fun to see new places and experience different cultures and languages. I like going to the movies and when I go, I usually watch comedies or action movies.

2 Repérez.

a. Quels mots sont accentués dans l'extrait **a** ? Quels mots sont inaccentués dans l'extrait **b** ?
→ Quelle règle en déduisez-vous ? Tous les mots d'une phrase ne sont pas accentués. On ... les mots porteurs de sens, c'est-à-dire les mots lexicaux (noms, verbes, adjectifs, adverbes, etc.). Certains mots d'une syllabe, appelés mots grammaticaux, sont ... .
b. Quels mots sont particulièrement mis en relief dans l'extrait **c** ?
c. Écoutez l'extrait **d** en prêtant attention aux pauses qui correspondent aux groupes de sens.

3 Lisez à haute voix la fin de l'interview.

– Accentuez les mots porteurs de sens et respectez les groupes de souffle.
– Attention : parlez lentement, haut et fort.

When I'm not watching soccer on TV, I like to watch crime shows like *CSI: Las Vegas*. My other guilty pleasure is video games. I've always loved playing console games with friends or playing computer games on my own.

B Enrichissez votre prise de parole

Vous demandez la permission de commencer.
– *Shall I start?*

Vous voulez donner votre opinion.
– *To my mind...*
– *In my view...*
– *In my opinion...*
– *According to us / them...*
⚠ On ne dit pas : ~~according to me.~~

Vous voulez conclure.
– *In conclusion...*
– *To conclude...*

Vous voulez changer de sujet.
– *By the way...*
– *Before I forget...*
– *I nearly forgot...*

Vous hésitez (*gap fillers*).
– *... , er / um...*
– *Let me see / think...*
– *... , you know, ...*
– *... , now what's the word for ...?*
– *Actually... / In fact...*
– *What else?*

Vous voulez dire les choses différemment.
– *In other words...*
– *..., I mean, ...*

Vous voulez vérifier qu'on vous a compris(e).
– *Do you know / see what I mean?*
– *... , if you see what I mean.*

C Réagissez à la prise de parole de quelqu'un

1 Exprimez votre admiration.

Formel
– *It was a very good performance.*
– *Your performance was superb.*

Usuel
– *Congratulations!*
– *Well done!*
– *Super! Splendid! Fantastic! Brilliant!*
– *Awesome! (US)*
– *Good job! / Neat job! (US)*
– *You were just great* /greɪt/.
– *That's great! This is really nice!*

2 Analysez la prestation.

Points positifs
– *It was very good.*
– *It was quite good.*
– *It was rather good.*
– *Not bad!*
– *It was OK.*
– *You were (very / quite) fluent* /ˈfluːənt/.
– *You stressed the right words.*
– *It was well-organized.*
– *You used a lot of vocabulary.*
– *It was lively* /ˈlaɪvli/.: C'était vivant.

Points à améliorer
– *You didn't look at us.*
– *You looked at your notes most of the time.*
– *You didn't speak loud enough* /ɪˈnʌf/.
– *Your voice was monotonous.*
– *You hesitated a little / a lot.*
– *You skipped a line / a sentence.*
– *You didn't know your text very well.*
– *It was too short / slow.*
– *You left out important points.*
– *You mispronounced...*
– *You made a few mistakes, for example...*
– *You said* /sed/*..., but you should have* /əv/ *said...*

D Évaluez votre propre prestation

Critères d'auto-évaluation de la prise de parole en continu	Oui	Non
1. Prise en compte de l'auditoire		
a. J'ai regardé l'auditoire en m'adressant à lui.	1	0
b. J'ai parlé sans lire mes notes.	1	0
c. J'ai parlé distinctement et assez fort pour qu'on m'entende.	1	0
2. Qualité du discours		
a. J'ai essayé de garder la parole, en limitant les pauses et les faux démarrages.	1	0
b. J'ai fait un exposé précis, complet et clair.	2	0
c. J'ai enchaîné plusieurs phrases à la suite, avec des liens logiques.	1	0
d. J'ai donné mon point de vue.	1	0
e. J'ai utilisé des *gap fillers* lorsque j'hésitais.	1	0
3. Langue orale employée		
a. J'ai fait attention à accentuer les mots porteurs de sens.	2	0
b. J'ai respecté les groupes de souffle.	1	0
c. J'ai respecté le rythme (formes pleines et réduites).	1	0
d. J'ai pris garde à prononcer correctement les phonèmes des mots nouveaux.	1	0
4. Lexique et grammaire		
a. J'ai utilisé un lexique approprié et précis.	2	0
b. J'ai eu recours à des périphrases pour compenser le lexique inconnu.	2	0
c. J'ai limité mes erreurs et elles ne gênent pas la compréhension.	1	0
d. J'ai été capable de m'auto-corriger.	1	0

TOTAL = ... / 20 POINTS

ÉVALUATION

J'ÉVALUE MES PROGRÈS

À la suite de ces quatre unités, évaluez vos progrès et faites le bilan de vos compétences.

1 Je me prépare

Entraînez-vous à parler le plus longtemps possible (au moins 1 minute). Vous devez présenter cette célèbre héroïne du début du 20e siècle, immortalisée par le film *Titanic* de James Cameron. Racontez la vie de Molly Brown à l'aide des informations contenues dans la fiche.

Invitation for the Première of *Molly Brown, Biography of a changing nation* from *Historic Denver*

Margaret Brown – "Molly Brown"

1	**Birth**	Margaret (Maggie) Tobin - July 18, 1867 - Hannibal, Missouri /mɪˈzʊəri/
2	**Parents**	Poor Irish immigrants
3	**1885**	New job in a department store, Leadville, Colorado /ˌkɒləˈrɑːdəʊ/ Meets James Brown, a mining engineer
4	**Marriage**	September 1, 1886 to James Joseph Brown (1854–1922)
5	**Children**	August 30, 1887 Lawrence Palmer Brown July 1, 1889 Catherine Ellen Brown
6	**1893**	Gold + silver + copper in Leadville mine James Brown: millionaire
7	**1894**	Denver, Colorado Maggie Brown → learns languages, music, travels all over the world
8	**April 15, 1912**	Titanic disaster: over 1500 victims (2223 passengers) Molly Brown: survivor → helps raise money for victims Nickname: 'Unsinkable Mrs. Brown'
9	**Death**	October 26, 1932 (age = 65)

MP3 2 Je m'auto-corrige

Écoutez l'enregistrement correspondant à cette évaluation et comparez votre production orale à celle enregistrée par un anglophone.

SOMMATIVE

JE FAIS LE BILAN

Analysez vos résultats à l'aide de cette grille d'évaluation où sont définis les différents paliers de compétences en expression orale en continu.

Je peux…	Paliers
… présenter ou raconter des faits en points successifs avec des mots de liaison de base (*and*, *but*, *because*).	**A2**
… m'exprimer simplement avec des expressions toutes faites et courtes, malgré des hésitations et de nombreuses pauses.	**A2**
… utiliser des structures de base, mais je fais encore des erreurs de temps et de grammaire qui ne bloquent pas la compréhension générale de mon message.	**A2**
… me faire comprendre malgré un net accent français.	**A2**
… raconter une histoire ou la vie de quelqu'un et décrire ses réactions.	**B1**
… me faire comprendre malgré un léger accent français.	**B1**
… utiliser un mot simple de signification semblable ou une périphrase, si un mot m'échappe.	**B1**
… m'exprimer de manière compréhensible sans trop d'hésitation, mais je fais des pauses pour réfléchir ou corriger ce que je dis.	**B1**
… communiquer avec aisance et spontanéité.	en route vers **B2**

ÉVALUATION

Votre professeur va maintenant vous distribuer une fiche sur un autre personnage célèbre que vous allez présenter. Vous avez le droit d'hésiter et de vous reprendre.
Une fois l'évaluation terminée, votre professeur pourra ainsi déterminer à quel palier vous vous situez par rapport à la grille d'évaluation du Cadre Européen Commun de Référence pour les Langues.

- Temps de préparation individuel : **5 minutes**
- Temps de parole : **1 à 2 minutes**

Bewitched, Nora Ephron, 2005 (starring Nicole Kidman and Will Ferrell)

Unit 5 CITY OF GLASS

- Explore New York City, visit its monuments and different districts.
- Read about the experience of immigrants when they landed at Ellis Island and one of the most famous monuments in the Big Apple: the Statue of Liberty.

YOUR TASK

You are taking part in a reading contest. Read a leaflet about the Statue of Liberty and fill in the grid your teacher will give you. The one who finishes first will be the winner.

→ P. 70

Unit 6 WILD WILD WEST

- What does “the West” mean to you?
- Discover who Lewis and Clark were and why their true life adventure changed the course of a nation’s history for ever.
- What impact did the Conquest of the West have on Native Americans?

YOUR TASK

Quiz your friends: Prepare a written quiz to find out how much they really know about the Conquest of the West. Use the elements you have learnt in this chapter.

→ P. 82

Unit 7 ROBOT DREAMS

- Are robots man’s best friends?
- What will our future look like?

YOUR TASK

You have been selected to test a robot for a week. You are given the choice of three robots. Which one is your favourite?

→ P. 94

Unit 5

CITY OF GLASS

YOUR TASK AT THE END OF THIS UNIT

You will take part in a reading contest. You will have to read a leaflet about the Statue of Liberty and fill in a grid. The one who finishes first will be the winner.

→ P. 70

TUNE IN!

A

B

C

D

E

1 Which is which? WB

a. Read each description opposite and match it with the corresponding monument or place above. Justify your choice with keywords from the texts.

PREPARE YOUR TASK → **b.** Focus on the five descriptions. Learn how to guess the meaning of words you don't know and find more details about each monument or place with the help of your Workbook.

c. With the help of the descriptions, locate the different monuments or places on the map of Manhattan in your Workbook.

1 **The Chrysler Building** is surely the jewel in the crown of New York City's skyline. The 77-story Art Deco skyscraper was the tallest in the world at the time it was completed in 1930. It quickly became the symbol of big city glamour, excitement, and style. It is recognizable thanks to its spire[1] with the crescent-shaped steps made of steel[2]. The top of the tower reminds us of car radiators which is perfect for the headquarters of an automaker. You can enter the building from three sides: Lexington Avenue, 42nd and 43rd Streets.

1. *flèche* **2.** *acier*

2 **The Flatiron**'s most interesting feature is its triangular shape. It reminds us of a flat iron[1] or of the front of a cruise ship. The building is famous for its architectural aspect. Some consider the Flatiron building to be New York City's first skyscraper. It certainly was one of the first buildings in the city to employ a steel frame[2] to hold up its 285-foot tall façade. It is said that the building created unusual eddies[3] in the wind which would cause women's skirts to fly around as they walked on 23rd Street. This attracted groups of young men who gathered[4] to view the barelegged spectacle.

1. *fer à repasser* **2.** *structure* **3.** *tourbillons* **4.** *se regroupaient*

3 **The United Nations Headquarters**, built in 1952, was the first major International Style building to be constructed in New York City: Its simple, geometric form, the absence of historical references, and its glass walls are typical of the International Style. 192 states are members of the UNO whose goal is to guarantee peace, the respect of Human Rights and the improvement[1] of living conditions all over the world. It is located on the East River bank[2] in the midtown neighborhood. When you walk down First Avenue, you can't miss the tower with its many flags.

1. *amélioration* **2.** *rive*

4 **The Guggenheim Museum** is a modern art museum. It can be found at the corners of 89th Street and Fifth Avenue (overlooking[1] Central Park). Frank Lloyd Wright designed it in 1959. From the street, the building looks approximately like a white ribbon curled[2] around a cylinder[3], wider at the top than the bottom. The round appearance of the building is in contrast with the more typical box-like Manhattan buildings that surround it.

1. *avec vue sur* **2.** ribbon curled: *ruban enroulé* **3.** /ˈsɪlɪndəʳ/

5 **Times Square** is a major intersection in Manhattan at the junction of Broadway and Seventh Avenue and stretching[1] from West 42nd to West 47th Streets. The theaters of Broadway and the huge number of animated neon and flashy billboards[2] have long made it one of New York's famous images.

1. *s'étendant* **2.** *panneaux publicitaires*

2 The Empire State Building

WB

a. Look at the photo and react. (Who? Where? What?)

b. In your opinion, what will the recording be about?

c. Find what words these phonetic transcriptions correspond to:
/gəˈrɪlə/ • /ˈstræpɪŋ/ *costaud* • /ges/ • /ˈspaɪəʳ/ *flèche* • /dɪˈzaɪnd/ • /dɒk/ • /ˈɜːbən/ • /ˈklaɪməʳ/

d. Now listen to the document to learn more about another famous New York skyscraper.

King Kong, Peter Jackson, 2005

1. ELLIS ISLAND

1 Get ready

a. Read these dates aloud: 1895 • 1905 • 1952 • 1924

b. Read these figures aloud: 50 • 60 • 70 • 80 • 90 • 120 • 1,200 • 12,000 • 1,200,000

c. Find the words derived from the roots in the chart opposite.

d. What is the opposite of:
far from • outside?

e. The following words are written phonetically. Read them aloud and write them.
/ɪ'ventʃʊəli/ • /haʊ'evəʳ/

Root	Word derived	Translation
see	noun: ...	*vue*
embody	noun: ...	*incarnation*
think	noun: ...	*pensée*
deport	noun: ...	*expulsion*
expect	adverb: ...	*de façon inattendue*

A recently arrived family of European immigrants at Ellis Island, around 1920

2 Listen and learn WB

Now listen to this document about the history and the role of Ellis Island, the immigrant processing center in New York harbor. Turn to your Workbook for help.

Useful words: /du:md tə/ *condamné à, destiné à* • /'bekən/ *faire signe* • /'hʌdld/ *blotti, regroupé* • /rɪ'meɪn/

3 Watch a video

The Journey

Watch this documentary directed by Maria Iliou (2007).

Learn more about Greek immigrants coming through Ellis Island and settling in New York City. Turn to your worksheet for help.

PREPARE YOUR TASK

4 The Ellis Island experience

WB

Read the following extracts (A to F) about the immigrants' arrival at Ellis Island. The paragraphs have been mixed up. Re-organize them in chronological order.

A

Those who failed[1] to get past both doctors had to undergo a more thorough medical exam. The others moved on to the registration clerk[2], who questioned them with the aid of an interpreter: What is your name? Your nationality? Your occupation? Can you read and write? Have you ever been in prison? How much money do you have with you? Where are you going?

Some immigrants were so flustered[3] that they could not answer. They were allowed to sit and rest and try again.

About one immigrant out of every five or six[4] was detained for additional examinations or questioning.

1. *échouaient* 2. *employé chargé de l'inscription sur les registres* 3. upset 4. *un immigrant sur cinq ou six*

B

The voyage was an ordeal[1], but it was worth it[2]. They were on their way to America.

The great majority of immigrants landed in New York City, at America's busiest port. They never forgot their first glimpse of the Statue of Liberty.

1. *épreuve* 2. *cela en valait la peine*

C

Filing into an enormous inspection hall, the immigrants formed long lines separated by iron railings[1] [...].

Now the examinations began. First the immigrants were examined by two doctors of the United States Health Service. One doctor looked for physical and mental abnormalities. When a case aroused suspicion, the immigrant received a chalk[2] mark on the right shoulder for further inspection: L for lameness[3], H for heart, X for mental defects, and so on.

1. *grilles de fer* 2. /tʃɔːk/ *craie* 3. *claudication (claudiquer = boiter)*

D

Immigrants usually crossed the Atlantic as steerage[1] passengers.

Because steerage conditions were crowded and uncomfortable, passengers spent as much time as possible up on deck[2].

1. *de troisième classe* 2. *pont*

E

The second doctor watched for contagious and infectious diseases[1]. He looked especially for infections of the scalp and at the eyelids[2] for symptoms of trachoma, a blinding[3] disease. Since trachoma caused more than half of all medical detentions, this doctor was greatly feared. He stood directly in the immigrant's path[4]. With a swift movement, he would grab[5] the immigrant's eyelid, pull it up[6], and peer beneath[7] it. If all was well, the immigrant was passed on.

1. illness, sickness 2. *paupières* 3. *qui rend aveugle* 4. *chemin* 5. *attrapait* 6. *retroussait* 7. would peer beneath it: *regardait en dessous*

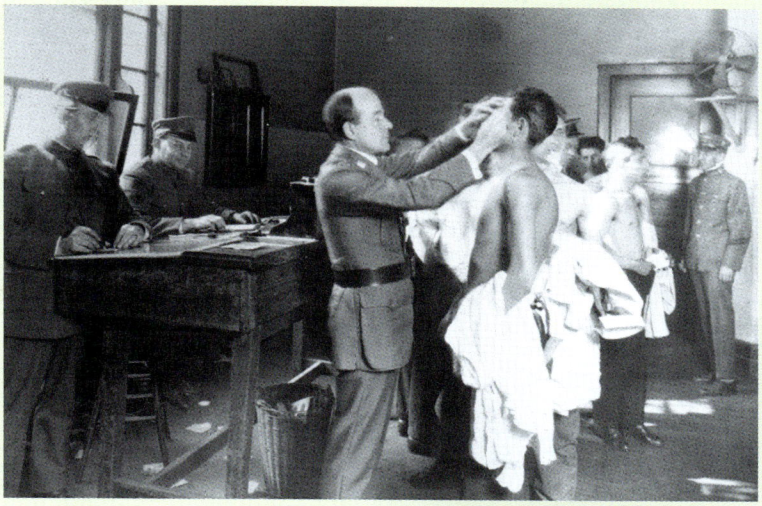

A doctor examining an immigrant at Ellis Island, 1943

F

When their ship docked[1] at a Hudson River pier[2], the immigrants had numbered identity tags pinned to their clothing. Then they were herded[3] onto special ferryboats that carried them to Ellis Island. Officials hurried them along, shouting "Quick! Run! Hurry!" in half a dozen languages.

1. *se mettait à quai* 2. /pɪəʳ/ *jetée* 3. *rassemblés comme un troupeau*

Russell Freedman, *Immigrant Kids*, 1995

2. SCENES OF NEW YORK CITY

PREPARE YOUR TASK →

1 Understanding the text WB

Each group reads one text. Turn to your Workbook for help.

A

"Momma said, just look! Isn't it beautiful! The first snow of the season." Most of the tall trees had lost their leaves, the wind had blown away their leaves that only a few days before had been such bright, beautiful colours, and you could see clearly now the roads curving and dipping[1] through the park, you could see the streams of traffic—yellow taxis, cars, delivery vans, horse-drawn buggies[2], cyclists, you could see the skaters at Wollman Ring, and you could see the outdoor cages of the Children's Zoo which was closed now; you could see the ponds[3] glittering[4] like mirrors laid flat; the park[5] was still green, and seemed to go on forever, you could see to the very end of 110th Street.

Joyce Carol Oates, *Faithless*, 2001

1. *descendant en lacets* 2. /bʌgiz/ *calèches* 3. *plans d'eau* 4. *brillant* 5. Central Park in Manhattan

B

We were of the city, but somehow[1] not in it. Whenever I went off on my favorite walk to Highland Park in the "American" district to the north, on the border of Queens, and climbed[2] the hill[3] to the old reservoir from which I could look straight across to the skyscrapers of Manhattan, I saw New York as a foreign city. There, brilliant and unreal, the city had its life, as Brownsville was ours. [...] We were the end of the line. We were the children of the immigrants who had camped at the city's back door, in New York's rawest[4], remotest[5], cheapest ghetto.

Alfred Kazin, *A Walker in the City*, 1957

1. *d'une certaine manière* 2. /klaɪmd/ *escaladais* 3. *colline* 4. /rɔːɪst/ *(ici) le plus dur* 5. remote: *isolé*

C

When people say the subway frightens them, they are not being silly or irrational. It is no good saying how cheap or how fast it is. The subway is frightening. It is also very easy to get lost on the subway, and the person who is lost in New York City has a serious problem. New Yorkers make it their business to avoid[1] getting lost.

It is the stranger[2] who gets lost. It is the stranger who follows people hurrying into the stairwell[3]: subway entrances are just dark holes[4] in the sidewalk—the stations are below[5] ground. There is nearly always a bus-stop near the subway entrance. People waiting at a bus-stop have a special pitying gaze[6] for people entering the subway.

Paul Theroux, *Sunrise with Seamonsters*, 1981

1. /əˈvɔɪd/ *éviter* 2. *(ici) étranger* 3. *cage d'escalier* 4. *trous* 5. under
6. pitying gaze: *regard de pitié*

2 Recap

Make a one-minute presentation: Sum up the main points in each text and give each of them a title.

Text A

– Who is the narrator? Where does the action take place? What time of year is it? What are the narrator's feelings?
– Does this passage give a positive or a negative image of the city?

Text B

– Who is the narrator?
– What do we learn about his / her social background? What are his / her feelings?

Text C

– What image of the New York subway is given in this passage? Is it a positive or a negative one?

3 Observe and speak

a. Look at the pictures. Match each picture with its corresponding text opposite and justify.
b. What are your impressions? What visions of the city do the pictures give?

1

Subway, George Tooker, 1950

2

3

New York, East Side, 32nd Street, Raymond Depardon, 1981

Help!

Picture 1	Picture 2	Picture 3
subway corridor: *couloir du métro*	ice rink	wooden board: *planche de bois*
stranger: *inconnu*	ice skate	envious
maze /meɪz/: *labyrinthe*	ice skater	tiny /ˈtaɪnɪ/
turnstile: *tourniquet*	crowd	feel excluded = feel left out
ghost /gəʊst/: *fantôme*	gather	tower /ˈtaʊəʳ/: *dominer, surplomber*
miserable	enjoy doing sth	crush /krʌʃ/: *écraser*
depressing	have a good time	peek through a hole: *regarder furtivement par un trou*
gloomy: *sombre*	right in the middle of	segregate / separate
soulless: *sans âme*		integrate into
anonymous		
feel trapped = feel imprisoned		
hide from: *se cacher*		

3. THE MAKING OF AN IMMIGRANT

Storytelling

Use the drawings below to write the story of this immigrant.

– Focus on the following elements in the vignettes: the surroundings (place and atmosphere), and the characters (appearance and actions).

– Imagine the immigrant's everyday life, his hopes and fears.

1

2

3

4

The Arrival, Shaun Tan, 2007

5

6

Language at work

Improve your pronunciation MP3

1 Prononciation de la lettre *-o-*

Prononcez les mots suivants à haute voix. La voyelle accentuée est en gras. Vérifiez ensuite à l'écoute ; vous allez entendre successivement un locuteur britannique, puis américain.
*overwh**e**lmed* • *col**o**ssal* • *w**i**ndow* • *em**o**tion* • *v**o**lume* • ***o**ccupy* • *top* • *torch* • *nose* • *c**o**pper* • *symb**o**lic* • *l**o**bby* • *role*

2 Accent britannique ou américain ?

Les mots de l'exercice **1** vont être utilisés dans des phrases lues soit par un Britannique, soit par un Américain. Sur papier libre, classez les phrases entendues en deux colonnes suivant l'accent.

Build up your vocabulary

1 La dérivation des mots

a. À l'aide d'un dictionnaire, complétez le tableau suivant sur papier libre.

Nom	Verbe	Adjectif	Adverbe
height	*heighten*	*high*	
	lengthen	*long*	
width			
		tall	
		strong	
		deep	*deeply*
		thick	

b. Observez la formation des mots obtenus. Quels suffixes sont ici ajoutés au « mot noyau » pour former un nom ? Quel suffixe est ajouté pour former un adverbe et un verbe ?

2 Les adjectifs composés

a. Observez les adjectifs suivants. Comment sont-ils formés ?
crescent-shaped • *horse-drawn* • *barelegged* • *nationwide*

b. À quoi sert le premier mot par rapport au deuxième ?
→ Le premier mot ... le deuxième.

c. À l'aide des réponses données en **a** et **b**, traduisez ces mots et ces expressions :
– en forme d'étoile • fait en acier • un problème mondial
– *weather-beaten* • *sea-washed* • *wide-eyed* • *homesick*

3 L'ordre des adjectifs

a. Dans chacun de ces groupes nominaux, quel adjectif exprime le point de vue subjectif de l'énonciateur ?
1. *a crazy dark-haired French sculptor*
2. *an original seventy-five story skyscraper*
3. *a scary one-thousand seventy-six step staircase*
4. *a gloomy one-thousand seventy-six step spiral staircase*
5. *an impressive century-old steel building*

→ Complétez la phrase suivante : quand on utilise plusieurs adjectifs devant un nom, on place ... celui ou ceux qui exprime(ent) le point de vue subjectif de l'énonciateur.

b. Observez les mots *story* et *step* dans les énoncés 2, 3 et 4. Que remarquez-vous ?

Language at work

La forme passive

1 Observez.

a. *New York City **is divided** into five boroughs.*
b. *The World Trade Center **was destroyed** in the 9 /11, 2001 attacks.*
c. *The World Trade Center **will be rebuilt**.*
d. *Harlem **has been rehabilitated** over the last few years.*
e. *The skyscrapers that **have been constructed** in New York **are** mostly **concentrated** in Midtown and Lower Manhattan.*

Classez ces énoncés passifs selon qu'ils sont construits avec le présent, le *present perfect,* le modal *will* ou le prétérit.
→ Les formes verbales en gras sont composées des éléments grammaticaux suivants : ... + ... du ... .
→ Quel élément est conjugué ?

2 Comparez les points de vue.

a. *Donald Trump financed the building of the Trump World Tower.*
b. *The Trump World Tower is the tallest of all the towers that were built by Donald Trump.*

Dans quelle phrase s'intéresse-t-on en premier lieu :
– à celui qui a fait construire ?
– à l'objet construit ?

Qui est l'agent (celui qui fait l'action) ?
Par quel élément est-il introduit dans la phrase passive ?

3 L'agent est-il mentionné ou non ?

a. *The Trump World Tower **was designed** by Polish architect Marta Rudzka.*
b. *The building **was** much **admired**.*
– Dans chacune de ces phrases, l'agent est-il mentionné ou non ?
– Traduisez en français les deux énoncés et complétez :
l'équivalent anglais d'une forme française en « ... » est souvent une forme ... .

4 Observez.

a. *New York City **can be called** the most cultural city in the world.*
→ En quoi la forme verbale ci-dessus est-elle différente de celle des énoncés précédents ?
b. *When you visited the Museum of Modern Art, you **must have been** flabbergasted.*
→ Dans la forme verbale ci-dessus, quels éléments expriment le passé ?

Récapitulez.

Emploi des modaux dans une construction passive :
– pour faire référence à un fait présent, la forme verbale se compose de :
auxiliaire modal + ... + ...

– pour faire référence à un fait passé que l'on juge possible, la forme verbale se compose de :
auxiliaire modal + ... + ... + ...

Language at work

Practice

1 Découvrez les origines de la ville de New York.

Transformez les énoncés suivants en énoncés passifs. Utilisez l'élément souligné comme sujet.

a. In 1524 Giovanni da Verrazano discovered the place where New York is located.
b. In the 16th century the Algonquins occupied the area where New York is now situated.
c. The West Indian Company established a trading post (named New Amsterdam) on the island of Manhattan in 1624.
d. The settlement's first governor bought the island for a small sum of money in 1626.
e. The English renamed New Amsterdam New York after they seized the city in 1664.
f. George Washington took the city after the end of the hostilities with the English in 1783.

2 Traduisez les phrases suivantes.

a. On a créé Central Park d'après les plans de Frederick Law Olmsted et de Calvert Vaux.
b. On a bâti le Chrysler Building en 1930, il était alors le plus haut gratte-ciel du monde.
c. On peut acheter de fausses couronnes de la Statue de la Liberté sur le ferry.
d. On connaît le Flatiron dans le monde entier à cause de sa forme bizarre.
e. On rénove *(rehabilitate)* de nombreux quartiers de New York depuis plusieurs années, comme DUMBO.
f. On tourne *(shoot)* beaucoup de films à New York parce que c'est une ville romantique.

3 Décrivez la photo ci-dessous en deux ou trois phrases.

Que se passe-t-il ? Que s'est-il passé ? Que va-t-il se passer ensuite ? Utilisez la forme passive et le vocabulaire du *Help* si besoin est.

The Day after Tomorrow, Roland Emmerich, 2004

Help!

- inhabitants
- the Empire State Building
- violent storm
- tidal /taɪdl/ wave: *raz de marée*
- tornado /tɔːˈneɪdəʊ/ = twister (US)
- heavy rain
- hit
- flood /flʌd/: *inonder*
- drown /draʊn/: *se noyer*
- evacuate
- injure: *blesser*
- knock /nɒk/ down
- collapse: *s'effondrer*
- submerge
- rescue
- survive

Your task

You are taking part in a reading contest. Read this leaflet about the Statue of Liberty and fill in the grid your teacher will give you. The one who finishes first will be the winner.

Statue of Liberty and Ellis Island

Even before it took its place at America's gateway, the Statue of Liberty overwhelmed those who saw it. Parisians, watching the statue's construction in their city in the 1880s, proclaimed it "the eighth marvel of the world." Set atop its pedestal in 1886, it was the tallest structure in New York City – and the tallest statue in the world. A German immigrant whose ship passed by in the 1920 recalled that "my mother rushed us to the window, to see this magic statue standing there. Now we were going to go to heaven."

To visitors today, the statue's sheer size can obscure its meaning. As you explore Liberty Island and the statue, consider the philosophy of its sculptor, Auguste Bartholdi: "Colossal statuary does not consist simply in making an enormous statue, it ought to produce an emotion in the breast of the spectator, not because of its volume, but because its size is in keeping with the idea that it interprets, and with the place which it ought to occupy."

Some statistics

Height from ground to top of torch: 305 ft., 1 in. (92.99m)

Height of statue: 15 ft., 1 in. (46.05m)

Length of nose: 4 ft., 6 in. (1.48m)

Thickness of copper "skin": 3/32 of an inch (2.37mm), about the thickness of two pennies.

1811 Star-shaped Fort Wood is built on Bedloe's (now Liberty) Island.

1865 Laboulaye, Bartholdi, and associates first discuss idea of a monument to liberty.

1871 Bartholdi tours US, chooses site in New York Harbor.

1874 Fundraising for statue begins in France.

1876 Liberty's arm and torch are displayed at the Centennial Exposition in Philadelphia.

1877 Congress authorizes site for statue but no money; private fundraising begins in US for pedestal construction.

1879 Gustave Eiffel designs statue's internal framework.

1881-84 Statue is assembled in Paris. Work begins on foundation on Bedloe's Island. Emma Lazarus writes poem "The New York Colossus".

1884 Richard Morris Hunt completes pedestal design.

1885 Statue is dismantled and shipped to New York. Joseph Pulitzer begins nationwide fundraising for pedestal.

1886 Statue is reassembled on Bedloe's Island. Dedication takes place October 28.

1924 Statue of Liberty is declared a national monument.

1933 National Park Service takes over administration of statue from War Department.

1956 Bedloe's Island is renamed Liberty Island.

1982 Statue of Liberty-Ellis Island Foundation is established to raise money for restoration.

1986 Restoration is completed in time for statue's centennial celebration on July 4.

LES ÉTAPES À SUIVRE

1 Développez des stratégies de lecture.

Lisez les deux premières phrases du dépliant, reproduites ci-dessous :

> Even before it took its place at America's gateway, the Statue of Liberty overwhelmed those who saw it. Parisians, watching the statue's construction in their city in the 1880s, proclaimed it "the eighth marvel of the world."

1. Essayez de déduire le sens des mots en :
– jaune en les décomposant (dérivation, composition) ;
– mauve à l'aide du contexte ;
– gris à l'aide du français (vous pouvez reconnaître ces mots transparents facilement).

2. À l'aide d'un dictionnaire, cherchez le sens du mot en rouge.

2 Procédez de même avec le reste du document.

1. Cherchez dans le dictionnaire le sens des abréviations *ft.* et *in.* et de ces mots :
sheer • *ought to* • *in keeping with* • *lobby*

2. À l'aide des procédés de composition et de dérivation, trouvez la traduction des mots suivants :
atop • *tallest* • *height* • *length* • *thickness*

3. Déduisez le sens de ces mots en vous appuyant sur le contexte :
rushed • *heaven* • *size* • *breast*

4. Repérez les mots clés ainsi que les marqueurs de temps importants.

3 Repérez les informations importantes.

– Matériau utilisé.
– Date de construction.
– Personnages célèbres : Auguste Bartholdi, Gustave Eiffel, Emma Lazarus, Joseph Pulitzer.
– À quelles dates ont eu lieu les événements suivants ?
Laboulaye and Bartholdi started thinking about a monument to liberty.
A site for the statue was authorized by the American Congress.
The statue was erected in Paris.
The Statue of Liberty was declared a national monument.

4 Documentez-vous sur le poème d'Emma Lazarus.

Unit 6

WILD WILD WEST

YOUR TASK AT THE END OF THIS UNIT

Quiz your friends: You will prepare a written quiz to find out how much they really know about the Conquest of the West. You will use the elements you have learnt in this chapter. → P. 82

TUNE IN!

Observe and speak

a. Look at these license plates, then close your books.
b. Which of these state names can you remember? What visual elements struck you?
c. Locate the different states on the map in the back flap of your book.
d. What image of each state is given?

Help!

sand
cactus (plural: cacti /ˈkæktaɪ/)
desert /ˈdezət/
arch
the forest / the woods
whale
eagle
the Rockies
mountain /ˈmaʊntɪn/ range

I. HOW IT ALL BEGAN

1 Get ready

What do you associate the words "Wild West" with? What words, images and films come to mind?

The Stagecoach, Norman Rockwell, 1966

PREPARE YOUR TASK →

2 Understanding the text WB

Turn to your Workbook for help.

For many people, the word "Frontier"[1] brings to mind images of the Wild West. Maybe the word makes you think of cowboys and Indians, or a stagecoach pulled by a team of horses, kicking up a cloud of dust in a vast dry landscape. Or maybe the word paints a scene of a frontier town with horses tied to a hitching post in front of a saloon with swinging doors. Some who hear the word "frontier" see a miner with a long beard and a hat panning for gold in a creek, while others imagine a long train of covered wagons, loaded with pioneers and all their belongings.

The frontier is the edge[2] of what is known—the farthest point of a civilization or settlement, and throughout much of America's history that meant the frontier was to the west. Not long after Europeans settled along the East coast, some settlers began to move west, inland, in search of land, natural resources like water, and animals to hunt. As more Europeans came to the New World to start a new life, and as the population of the colonies began to grow, the desire to explore the West increased. Colonists wanted to claim[3] a piece of the wilderness before someone else did [...]. They wanted good fertile land that could be farmed and hunted [...].

In the early 1800s [...] floods[4] of emigrants streamed into[5] the frontier. Most people were lured[6] to the West by the promise of land, the hope of finding gold, or the idea of a place where they could practice their religion without persecution. And many people developed these expectations when they saw posters known as broadsides, advertisements in newspapers, or letters from family and friends who had already made the journey.

Rachel Dickinson, *Great Pioneer Projects You Can Build Yourself*, 2007

1. /ˈfrʌntɪəʳ/ **2.** *lisière, bord* **3.** *revendiquer* **4.** /flʌdz/ *vagues* **5.** *traversèrent en masse* **6.** attracted

3 Recap

a. Which word in the text corresponds to this definition: *"that part of a settled, civilized country which lies next to an unexplored or undeveloped region"?*

b. Sum up the main points of the text with the help of these words: attract to • magnet: *aimant* • wave: *vague* • settle • land • farm • gold • freedom of thought • look for

2. AN EPIC JOURNEY WEST

A. Jefferson's mission

Jefferson[1] called in his private secretary, Meriwether Lewis. He knew that Lewis had served [...] on the frontier. He asked Lewis to consider leading a group of explorers through the rivers of the Louisiana Territory[2]. Lewis wrote to his friend, William Clark, to ask him to join the group. Both men said yes.

Jefferson wrote instructions to Lewis. He wanted Lewis and Clark to find a Northwest passage, a water route across North America, to bring back maps and written notes about: "the soil and face of the country..., the animals of the country, generally, and especially those not known in the US..., the mineral production of every kind ..., [the] climate as characterized by... proportion of rainy, cloudy and clear days..., the dates at which particular plants put forth or lose their flowers..., times of appearance of particular birds, reptiles, or insects."

Sally S. Isaacs, *America in the Time of Lewis and Clark*, 1998

1. Thomas Jefferson (1743-1826), third US President **2.** /luːˌiːzɪˈænə/ The United States of America bought the Louisiana territory from the French in 1803.

PREPARE YOUR TASK →

Understanding the text

Find the key points of the text:

a. Who sent the expedition west?
b. What for?

B. The members of the expedition

PREPARE YOUR TASK →

1 Who were they? WB

Listen and answer the following questions.

a. How many people were part of the expedition? Who is mentioned in particular?

b. What did Lewis and Clark have in common?

2 Focus on Sacagawea WB

Read the text opposite and find out who Sacagawea was.

PREPARE YOUR TASK →

3 A who's who game WB

Select a member of the expedition and use the information you have learnt to explain his or her role in the expedition. The rest of the class will guess who it is.

Part 1

Sacagawea[1] was born to the Shoshone Indians in the Rocky Mountains (in what is now Idaho) in about 1788. At the age of twelve she was kidnapped by Indians from the plains who took her to what is now North Dakota. She was then sold to the French Canadian fur trapper, Toussaint Charbonneau.

In 1804 Lewis and Clark hired[2] Charbonneau and asked him to bring his wife. Sacagawea was then 16 years old and 6 months pregnant[3]. She was the only woman member of the expedition. It is likely that the expedition was viewed as friendly and peaceful by Native American tribes because Sacagawea had her infant son with her. Clark later noted in his journal: "No woman ever accompanies a war party of Indians in this quarter."

1. /ˌsækədʒəˈwiːə/ **2.** *engagèrent* **3.** *enceinte*

Part 2

Sacagawea spoke both native American languages, Shoshone and Minitari, and the captains realized that she could be a valuable interpreter if the party encountered[1] the Shoshones. Her ability to speak and negociate with the native tribes allowed the expedition to have fresh horses along the way.

On top of her work as a translator she foraged for[2] roots, nuts and berries[3] when food was scarce[4].

She also taught Lewis and Clark the medicinal value of the native plants. In the journal kept by the expedition, she is described as a smart and helpful woman. In one key incident recorded in Clark's journal, she saved records and instruments from being lost overboard during a storm[5].

Although she was largely responsible for the success of the expedition, she wasn't paid for her contributions.

1. *s'ils rencontraient* **2.** *(ici) cherchait* **3.** *baies* **4.** *rare* **5.** *tempête, orage*

C. The expedition

Watch a video

Lewis and Clark

Watch this extract from a documentary on the expedition.
Turn to your worksheet for help.

PREPARE YOUR TASK →

Recap

Recap all the information about the expedition given in the texts and the documentary. You may change some information or include false details, so your listeners must pay attention.

3. Chief Joseph Speaks

1 The white men

The first white men of your people who came to our country were named Lewis and Clark. [...] All the Nez Perce[1] made friends with Lewis and Clark and agreed to let them pass through their country and never to make war on white men. This promise the Nez Perce have never broken. For a short time we lived quietly. But this could not last. White men had found gold in the mountains around the land of the Winding Water. [...]
I labored[2] hard to avoid trouble and bloodshed[3]. We gave up some of our country to the white men, thinking that then we could have peace. We were mistaken[4]. The white men would not let us alone[5]. We could have avenged our wrongs[6] many times, but we did not. Whenever the government has asked for help against other Indians we have never refused. When the white men were few and we were strong we could have killed them off, but Nez Perce wishes to live at peace. [...]

1. /nezˈpɜːˈs/ **2.** tried **3.** *effusions de sang* **4.** *nous nous trompions* **5.** *ne voulaient pas nous laisser tranquilles*
6. *redresser nos torts*

Engraving, 1868

2 At my surrender in the Bear Paw Mountains, 1877

I am tired of fighting. Our chiefs are killed. [...] It is cold and we have no blankets[1]. The little children are freezing to death. My people – some of them have run away to the hills and have no blankets and no food. No one knows where they are – perhaps they are freezing to death. [...] Hear me my chiefs, my heart is sick and sad. From where the sun now stands I will fight no more against the white man. [...]

1. *couvertures*

3 On a visit to Washington D.C., 1879

If the white man wants to live in peace with the Indian he can live in peace. There need be no trouble. Treat all men alike[1]. Give them the same laws. Give them all an even[2] chance to live and grow. All men were made by the same Great Spirit Chief. They are all brothers. The earth is the mother of all people, and all people should have equal rights upon it. [...]
I only ask the government to be treated as all other men are treated. If I cannot go to my own home, let me have a home in a country where my people will not die so fast. [...]
When I think of our condition, my heart is heavy. I see men of my own race treated as outlaws[3] and driven from country to country, or shot down like animals.
I know that my race must change. We cannot hold our own with[4] the white men as we are. We only ask an even chance to live as other men live. We ask to be recognized as men.

1. *de la même façon* **2.** *égale* **3.** /ˈaʊtlɔːz/ *hors-la-loi* **4.** hold our own with: *(ici) résister à*

Chester Anders Fee, *Chief Joseph: The Biography of a Great Indian*, 1936

1 Memory game

a. Read each part silently, then close your book and say which words you remember.

b. – Can you remember the titles of the three parts?
– Did you notice the name of a city?
– Are any dates mentioned?

2 Understanding the text WB

Turn to your Workbook for help.

a. Recap: Part 1
– Who were the first explorers?
– What was the Indians' attitude towards them?
– What marked a turning point in the relationship?
– What did the Indians try to do? Why?

b. Recap: Part 2
– What has just happened to the Indians?
– What were Chief Joseph's feelings then?
– What did he decide?
– Draw a parallel between the photograph and the second part of the text.

A portrait of Chief Joseph by Edward S. Curtis, 1903

c. Recap: Part 3
– What was the situation of the Indians then?
– What does Chief Joseph ask for? What is his main claim?

PREPARE YOUR TASK →

3 Writing workshop

Write a short article for a web encyclopedia. Explain who Chief Joseph was, what happened to him and his tribe and what impact it had on their lives (80 to 100 words). Vote for the best article.

Help!

Part 1	Part 2	Part 3
greed: *avidité, cupidité* gold prospector reliable friendly peaceful faithful: *fidèle* trustworthy /trʌstˌwɜːðɪ/: *digne de confiance* trust sb: *faire confiance à qqn* invade sb's territory deceive: *tromper* retaliate: *riposter, se venger* keep one's promise	defeat fight = struggle sympathy compassion desperate /despərət/ hopeless destitute: *sans ressources* needy give up: *abandonner* yield: *céder* starve to death: *mourir de faim* suffer from hunger	second-class citizen: *citoyen de seconde zone* Human Rights dignity /dɪgnɪti/ be regarded as resent + V-ing: *ne pas admettre de* respect claim: *exiger* be on an equal footing: *être sur un pied d'égalité* live in harmony with nature

4 Reading aloud WB

Read part 2 aloud. Learn how to read this passage with the help of your Workbook.

4. THE WEST GAZETTE

You are a journalist who has spent many years in the West with a Native American tribe. You decide to write an article on what happened to them (about 100 words). You illustrate your article with the following pictures.

Use the preterite and the past perfect (see p. 80 and 260-261).

1

Oscar Berningshaus, 1920

2

Engraving, 1849

3

Engraving inspired by Frederic Remington, 19th century

4

Engraving, 1868

Language at work

Improve your pronunciation MP3

1 Prononciation de *-ed*

Avant l'écoute, prononcez les formes verbales suivantes et classez-les en trois colonnes selon la prononciation de leur suffixe ***-ed***. Vérifiez ensuite à l'écoute.
wanted • pushed • asked • stretched • ended • helped • loaded • followed • decided • walked • cooked • started • travelled • expected

/d/	/t/	/ɪd/

2 *Was* et *were*

a. Dans la phrase suivante, *was* se prononce-t-il /wɒz/ ou /wəz/ ?
The territory through which the explorers travelled was unknown, and the climate was harsh.
b. Écoutez la phrase suivante, puis répétez-la à haute voix.
There were mountains and deserts to cross.

3 Lisez à haute voix.

7,700 miles • 1788 • 1800 • 1804 • in the early 1800s

4 Schéma accentuel

En vous aidant du dictionnaire si nécessaire, représentez sur papier libre le schéma accentuel de ces mots. Vérifiez ensuite à l'écoute.
Exemple : *expedition* → ☐ ☐ ☑ ☐

a. *persecution* **b.** *religion* **c.** *possessions* **d.** *Indian* **e.** *Canadian* **f.** *mission*

Quelle est l'incidence des terminaisons *-ion* et *-ian* sur la place de l'accent principal ?

Build up your vocabulary

1 Associez chacun des mots de la liste a. à un mot de sens voisin pris dans la liste b. Utilisez un dictionnaire si nécessaire.

a. *resist • avenge oneself • defy • fight against • give up • flee • horrible*
b. *escape • yield • challenge • dreadful • retaliate • fight back • struggle against*

2 Les lettres de ces mots ont été mélangées. Retrouvez chacun d'eux.

uffabol • eribt • epete • csalh • wrthapa • treslauhg • attebl • edeatf

3 Remplissez les blancs du texte avec les mots de la liste ci-dessous. Faites les changements grammaticaux nécessaires.

animal • challenge • describe • hero • journey • knowledge • map • pioneer • plant • see • share • succeed • trade • travel • through

Lewis and Clark returned to St. Louis as ... [1]. They were the first United States citizens to ... [2] and ... [3] the West, and they had made ... [4] that would guide future ... [5], described hundreds of ... [6] and ... [7], and created new opportunities for ... [8]. Their ... [9] could not have happened without the generous cooperation and contributions of numerous Native Americans. They faced many difficult ... [10], as the territory ... [11] which they ... [12] was largely unknown. The expedition ... [13] because Native Americans generously ... [14] their ... [15] and resources.

Language at work

Le passé : prétérit simple et *past perfect*

1 Observez les formes au prétérit dans les énoncés suivants.

*Why **did** some people **want** to travel to Oregon?*
*Back in the 1840s people **heard** about Oregon by reading newspapers or hearing stories from travellers. This is how people **learned** of a land on the west side of the Rocky Mountains.*
*Oregon **was** a magical place. The land **was** good for farming. There **was** plenty of land that you **could** get for free. There **were** big forests and rivers filled with fish.*
*The word Oregon **made** people think of starting adventures.*
*In 1843 a thousand people **started** out for Oregon. It **was** one of the biggest groups that ever **travelled** West. It **took** them six months to go from Missouri to Oregon, nearly two thousand miles away. The trip **was** not always easy. Many people **did not reach** Oregon and **died** on the way.*

a. Relevez les formes verbales au prétérit simple et classez-les en trois colonnes : forme affirmative, négative et interrogative. Quelles sont les particularités de ces trois formes ?
b. Classez ensuite les verbes à la forme affirmative en deux colonnes : verbes réguliers et irréguliers. Donnez leur infinitif à chaque fois.
→ **Concluez :** quelle forme verbale utilise-t-on dans une narration de faits passés, révolus ?
Le prétérit simple sert à parler d'événements situés dans le ... et il exprime une ... avec le présent.

2 Observez.

Au prétérit, l'événement est le plus souvent repéré dans le temps, par l'indication d'une heure, une date, une période ou tout autre repère temporel.

Heure, date, période	Autres repères temporels
at: ***at*** *eight o'clock* in: ***in*** *July,* ***in*** *the summer,* ***in*** *1843,* ***in*** *the 19th century,* ***in*** *the 1840s / 1850s / 1860s* on: ***on*** *Sunday,* ***on*** *July 4th*	*at the / that time* *in those days* *then / back then*

3 Qu'expriment les expressions soulignées ci-dessous : un repère temporel ou un marqueur de durée ?

The pioneers lived in a covered waggon for six months.
Out on the plains they walked for days without seeing any trees or woods.

a. À quel temps grammatical sont associées ces expressions ?
b. Traduisez les phrases.

4 Observez.

At the end of the day the children were tired: They had milked the cows, had fetched water and had collected wood to make fires.

a. De quels éléments sont composées les formes verbales soulignées ?
b. Sur papier libre, situez sur une ligne comme celle-ci les événements correspondant aux formes soulignées.

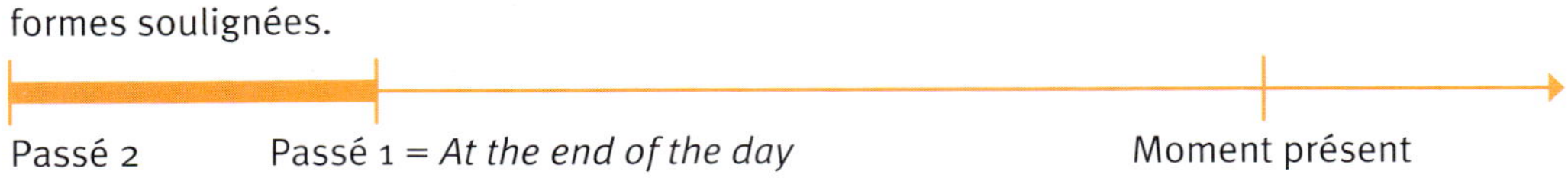

c. Traduisez ces formes verbales en français.
→ **Concluez :** le *past perfect* permet de parler d'événements antérieurs à (= situés avant) un autre événement exprimé au ... . Il exprime donc un « retour en arrière » par rapport à un moment du ... .

Language at work

Practice

1 **Remettez ces phrases dans l'ordre.**

a. the / was / journey / to / Oregon / how long / ?
b. the / time of year / the / trip / best / to / start / what / was / ?
c. travel / to / people / some / why / want / did / all the way / to / Oregon / ?
d. happened / if / you / Indians / met / what / the way / on / ?
e. a long time / the / buffalo meat / last / how / did / make / Indians / ?

2 **Recopiez ce texte en complétant avec les formes verbales qui conviennent.**

The US government ... (encourage) people to settle in Oregon. Half a million people ... (cross) the Rocky Mountains, deserts and rivers to settle there. They ... (have) to leave the Mississippi River in spring to arrive before the first snows. Approximately twenty thousand people ... (die) along the way. They ... (endure) extreme weather, illness, and attacks by Native Americans. The construction of the railroad ... (bring) an end to the waggon trains.

Dances with Wolves, Kevin Costner, 1990

3 **Crazy Horse : rédigez un paragraphe à partir des éléments suivants.**

– A visionary Indian chief, a brilliant leader, a man of supreme courage, a brave warrior, fight for freedom all his life
– Goal in life: defence of the values and traditions of the Lakota tribe
– **1849:** date of birth
– Horses stolen before the age of 13
– **1865-1868:** fight against settlers in Wyoming
– **1867:** destruction of W.J. Fetterman's brigade at Fort Phil Kearny
– **1873:** attack of troops led by General Custer
– **1876:** leader of the resistance, alliance with the Cheyenne
– **June 17, 1876:** victory of Little Bighorn
– **June 25, 1876:** destruction of Custer's seventh Cavalry
– **May 6, 1877:** last important chief to surrender
– **September 1877:** arrest by General George Crook; resistance on the way to jail (struggle against the guards); a soldier stabs *(poignarde)* him in the back.

4 **Traduisez ces phrases.**

a. Quand l'expédition fut terminée *(over)*, ils avaient parcouru 3 700 miles.
b. Ils avaient découvert 122 animaux et 178 plantes inconnues à cette époque-là.
c. Ils avaient exploré un immense territoire et fait des cartes détaillées.
d. Jefferson fut ravi car ils avaient atteint *(fulfil)* tous les objectifs qu'il leur avait donnés.

your task

Quiz your friends: Prepare a written quiz to find out how much they really know about the Conquest of the West. Use the elements you have learnt in this chapter.

COMMENT VÉRIFIER LES CONNAISSANCES

1 **Lisez le texte suivant.**

The Mormon Trail: on the way to Zion[1]

The Mormons were a people with different religious beliefs who experienced persecution from the authorities and many of their neighbors in Missouri[2] and Illinois[3]. In 1844 their founding[4] leader, John Smith, was killed by a mob[5] while he was in jail. The new leader, Brigham Young, decided to guide his followers west in search of a new home.

In 1846 Young led a group of 5,000 followers from a Mormon settlement in Nauvoo, Illinois, across what is now Iowa[6] to Winter Quarters, a camp he established on the Missouri River in Nebraska [...], Wyoming, and northern Utah[7] to the Great Salt Lake Valley where he established a new settlement. Young organized permanent campsites along the route to help future emigrants.

Thousands of Mormons followed the trail[8] from Nauvoo, Illinois, to the Great Salt Lake. Some farmers were wealthy[9] enough to own wagons, oxen, and many possessions. Many less fortunate Mormons loaded all their possessions into handcarts[10] which were pulled and pushed for 1,200 miles across the plains, along and across the Platte River, and over the Rocky Mountains to the new settlement. Between 1846 and 1869, more than 70,000 people used the Mormon Trail.

Rachel Dickinson, *Great Pioneer Projects You Can Build Yourself*, 2007

1. /ˈzaɪən/ the Promised Land in the Bible **2.** /mɪˈzʊəri/ **3.** /ˌɪlɪˈnɔɪ/ **4.** *fondateur* **5.** *foule* **6.** /ˈaɪəʊə/ **7.** /ˈjuːtɑː/ **8.** *piste*
9. rich **10.** *charrettes à bras*

Virgin River Narrows, Zion National Park, Utah

2 **Découvrez trois types de questionnement différents pour vérifier la compréhension de vos camarades.**

Exemple 1 : QCM

Trouvez la bonne réponse.

1. Where did the Mormons come from?
   a. Europe b. Missouri and Illinois c. the Great Salt Lake Valley
2. What distance had the Mormons crossed when they arrived in Utah?
   a. about 1,800km b. about 1,200km c. 5,000km
3. Why did the Mormons go West? Because they...
   a. wanted to be rich. b. wanted to visit the West. c. were persecuted.

Exemple 2 : activité d'association

Reliez chaque question à la réponse correspondante.

1. When did the Mormons settle in Utah?
2. What did they organize campsites along the road for?
3. How many miles did the Mormons travel?
4. How many people travelled on the Mormon Trail?
5. Whose possessions were loaded into waggons?

a. To help new emigrants.
b. The richer Mormons'.
c. About seventy thousand.
d. About 150 years ago.
e. 1,200 miles.

Exemple 3 : mots croisés

Lisez ces définitions de mots tirés du texte ci-contre, et complétez cette grille sur papier libre.

Across

1. a western state south of South Dakota
3. a person who leaves his country or city to live in another one
7. a person who guides a group
9. a building where criminals are locked
10. the act of treating cruelly and causing suffering
11. an angry and violent crowd

Down

2. a recently built camp or village
4. Salt Lake City is the capital of...
5. a path across rough country
6. an American state north of Colorado
8. a covered 4-wheeled vehicle drawn by horses or oxen

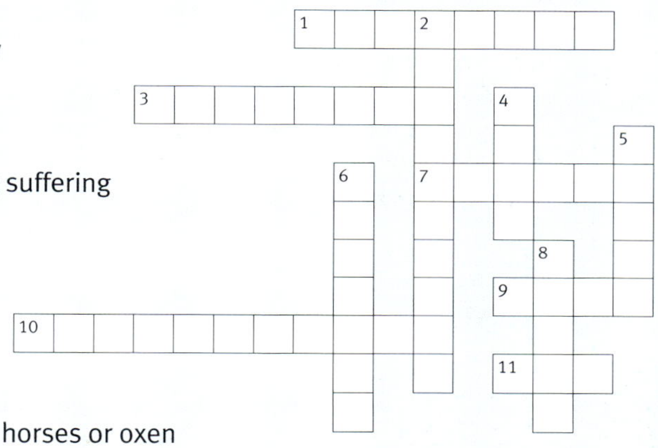

POUR PRÉPARER VOTRE QUESTIONNAIRE

1. Variez les activités :
– un QCM (voir exemple 1) ;
– une activité d'association (voir exemple 2) ;
– des définitions et mots croisés (voir exemple 3) ;
– un jeu de « vrai-faux » : vos lecteurs doivent lire des affirmations et décider si elles sont justes ou fausses ;
– des citations ou des exploits dont il faut retrouver l'auteur parmi les héros mentionnés ;
– des photos, illustrations, cartes, tableaux à relier avec des passages de textes lus ;
– des citations, extraits de textes qu'il faut situer (auteur ? époque ? événement ? ...).
2. Prenez une page A4 et préparez votre questionnaire. Notez les réponses au dos.

Rappels

– Revoyez les mots interrogatifs p. 194.
– Posez le maximum de questions au prétérit.
– Respectez l'ordre des questions en *WH-*.

Unit 7

ROBOT DREAMS

YOUR TASK AT THE END OF THIS UNIT

You have been selected to test a robot for a week. You are given the choice of three robots. Which one is your favourite? → P. 94

TUNE IN!

a. React to this picture (main character, place, time, atmosphere, activity).
b. Focus on the robots: What are they doing?
c. Imagine this picture is used for an advertisement: Who is the target? Give a name to the robots and imagine a catchphrase.

Help!

Setting	Object advertised	Interpretation
messy floor household chores /tʃɔːz/ = housework crumbs: *miettes* unwind /ʌnˈwaɪnd/ = relax rest: *se reposer* kneel: *s'agenouiller* tidy /ˈtaɪdi/ up: *ranger*	robot /ˈrəʊbɒt/ sensor /ˈsensəʳ/ = captor /ˈkæptəʳ/ domestic appliance /əˈplaɪəns/: *appareil ménager* vacuum /ˈvækjʊm/ cleaner: *aspirateur* battery-powered /ˈbætərɪpaʊəd/ hoover the room	working mother / father time-saving labour-saving /ˈleɪbəseɪvɪŋ/: *qui évite du travail* busy /ˈbɪzi/ overwhelmed /ˈəʊvəwelmd/ reliable /rɪˈlaɪəbl/ waste time + V-ing

1. THAT'S SCI-FI!

Together with Colin Angle, a fellow student, and Rodney Brooks, her graduate school advisor[1], [Helen Greiner] started iRobot Corporation in 1990 in Boston, bootstrapping[2] the company with her credit cards. "Who would invest in a robot company?" recalls Greiner. "That's sci-fi[3]!"

Later that year, they rolled out Genghis, designed for work on Mars. Ariel, modeled after a crab, was an underwater mine detector. The interactive My Real Baby was a popular Hasbro doll. And in 2002 the Pyramid Rover climbed Egypt's Great Pyramid on live television and entered a chamber no one had ever opened. "Each robot was a stepping-stone," says Greiner.

Although iRobot is best known for its domestic appliances – Roomba vacuums, Scooba washes floors, Looj cleans gutters[4] – in the lean early years[5], the company depended on military contracts to stay afloat. Today there are three million Roombas in American homes, and 40 percent of revenue comes from defense contracts. As the industry leader, iRobot is still building cool stuff that people can use every day.

"We're at the dawn[6] of robotics," says Greiner, who thinks of robots as technology tools that eliminate "dull, dirty, dangerous jobs". She is looking forward to[7] the home that takes care of itself. Also on the drawing board is the Warrior, a remote-control device that can carry 150 pounds, fight fires, climb stairs and do a four-minute mile.

Next, Greiner wants to help the disabled and the elderly live more independent lives. "A robot could remind you to take your medication, help find your glasses, or check to see if you're okay. People won't stop calling on[8] grandma because she has a robotic helper. But they will worry less."

Reader's Digest, September 2008

1. *tuteur* **2.** *(ici) en soutenant financièrement* **3.** /ˌsaɪˈfaɪ/ **4.** *gouttières* **5.** the lean early years: *(ici) les années de vaches maigres du début* **6.** *aube* **7.** is looking forward to: *attend avec impatience* **8.** calling on: visiting

1 Understanding the text

a. Paragraph 1

– Find the name of a firm, a date, the name of a city.
– Who created this corporation?
– What does "sci-fi" (l. 4) mean?

b. Paragraph 2

Find four names of robots, three places and a date. What is each robot used for?

c. Paragraph 3

– List all the words related to the housework done by the robots of the company.
– What do "three million" (l. 11) and "40" (l. 12) refer to in the article?

d. Paragraph 4

– "We're at the dawn of robotics..." (l. 14) and "Also on the drawing board is the Warrior..." (l. 16) Is the journalist referring to: robots already created • robots being created • robots that will be created in the future?

e. Paragraph 5

– List the groups of people that Greiner wants to help. Give three examples of what robots will do.
– Pick out one sentence referring to the impact robots will have on the family.

PREPARE YOUR TASK

2 Go further

a. Among the jobs done by robots, which ones are dull, dirty, dangerous and tiring?
b. What robots can be used by everybody, by the military or by scientists?
c. Among all the robots mentioned here, which one would you like to have? Why?

3 Watch a video

Modern Times

Watch an extract from a film directed by Charlie Chaplin (1936).
Turn to your worksheet for help.

2. MAY I HELP YOU? WB

"We tried humans, but they weren't nice enough."

1 Observe and speak

a. Where does the scene take place?
b. What immediately strikes you? Why?
c. What does the robot look like? Why?
d. Who is speaking in the caption?
e. What are the two characters in the background doing? Why?

2 Go further

a. What is the cartoonist's message?
PREPARE YOUR TASK → **b.** Do you agree with him / her? Why? Why not?

Help!

Situation	Interpretation
wire /waɪəʳ/: *fil* clerk /klɜːk/ (US) /klɑːk/ (GB): *employé de bureau* curious envious jealous hire sb ≠ fire sb spy on	competitive submissive = obedient ≠ disobedient shocking get rid of: *se débarrasser de* rebel against warn /wɔːn/ sb about sth: *avertir qqn de qqch* foresee /fɔːˈsiː/: *prévoir*

3 Feel and touch

Listen to a recording about the latest discoveries in robotics. Turn to your Workbook for help.

3. HUMANS AND ROBOTS

Astounding Science Fiction, magazine cover, October 1953

1 Observe and speak

a. What attracted your attention first?
b. What has probably just happened? What feelings can you read on the face of the robot?
c. What angle-shot was used and what is its impact on the viewer? (see p. 280)
d. What does this illustration remind you of?

2 Compare

a. What are the similarities and the differences between this illustration and the cartoon p. 86?
b. Which of the two documents strikes you most? Why? Share your views with the rest of the class.

Help!

Robot	Victim	Interpretation
tear /tɪə^r/ powerful /ˈpaʊəfʊl/ scary /ˈskeəri/ dangerous /ˈdeɪndʒrəs/ ≠ safe /seɪf/	puppet /ˈpʌpɪt/ blood /blʌd/ tiny /ˈtaɪni/ ≠ huge /hjuːdʒ/ defenceless wounded = harmed	humanized /ˈhjuːmənaɪzd/ upset: *bouleversé* guilty /ˈgɪlti/: *coupable* be responsible /rɪˈspɒnsəbl/ for take power over do sth on purpose /ˈpɜːpəs/: *faire qqch exprès*

4. A PROPHET (PART 1) WB

1 Get ready

a. Judging from this picture, which of the following words do you expect to find in the text?
tough • flames • risky • factories • exploited • cost • heat • hostile • carry out • repair

b. Imagine what the text is about. Make at least three or four sentences.

At the beginning of the story, a new employee at US Robots, Linda Rash, informs Dr Susan Calvin, a robotics expert, that one of the company's robots, Elvex, had a dream.

"I dream always very much the same dream, Dr Calvin. Little details are different, but always it seems to me that I see a large panorama in which robots are working."

"Robots, Elvex? And human beings, also."

"I see no human beings in the dream, Dr Calvin. Not at first. Only robots."

"What are they doing, Elvex?"

"They are working, Dr Calvin. I see some mining in the depths of the earth, and some laboring[1] in heat and radiation. I see some in factories and some undersea."

Calvin turned to Linda. "Elvex is only ten days old, and I'm sure he has not left the testing station. How does he know of robots in such detail?" [...]

"What else did you see, Elvex?"

"I saw that all the robots were bowed down[2] with toil[3] and affliction[4], that all were weary[5] of responsibility and care, and I wished them to rest."

Calvin said, "But robots are not bowed down, they are not weary, they need no rest."

"So it is in reality, Dr Calvin. I speak of my dream, however. In my dream, it seemed to me that robots must protect their own existence."

Isaac Asimov, *Robot Dreams*, 1986

1. working **2.** bowed /baʊd/ down: *pliés* **3.** hard work **4.** *détresse* **5.** /wɪəri/ tired

PREPARE YOUR TASK →

2 Understanding the text

a. Find the names and the occupations (when possible) of the characters present in the scene.

b. "**They** are working, Dr Calvin. I see **some** … … mining in the depths of the earth, and **some** … … laboring in heat and radiation. I see **some** … … … in factories and **some** … … … undersea." (l. 6)
– Who do "they" and "some" refer to?
– Some elements are missing in these sentences. Which ones?

c. "Robots, Elvex? And human beings, also." (l. 3) "What are they doing, Elvex?" (l. 5)
Who asks these questions?

d. "Elvex is **only ten days old**, and I'm sure **he has not left the testing station. How does he know** of robots in such detail?" (l. 8)
What do the phrases in bold letters reveal about Elvex?

e. – List all the physical tasks mentioned in the text.
– Find all the places associated with these tasks. What adjectives would you use to characterize these activities?

f. Pick out the phrases linked to the robots' living conditions.

3 Recap

a. What do we learn about Elvex (age, life experience)?

b. Sum up all you know about the robots' living conditions in Elvex's dream.

c. What do Elvex's vision, comments on robots and suggested solutions reveal about his personality? What impact could he have on other robots?

d. Complete the following summary.
Elvex is a … robot who realizes that robots are exploited. That's why he … the way robots are treated. He … about their working conditions. As he realizes robots must … their lives, we can say Elvex is … . He could become a … guiding the robots' … .

e. What is Dr Calvin's role in this episode? What do her attitude and reaction towards Elvex reveal about her feelings? Imagine how she is going to react at the end of the text.

- She wants to know what…
- She wants to discover…
- She suspects the robot of…
- She asks questions to see if…
- Her questions reveal that…
- She is the expert, so…
- She fears that…
- She feels…

Help!

Elvex	Working conditions	Dr Calvin
leader clear-sighted /ˈklɪəsaɪtɪd/: *visionnaire* caring /ˈkeərɪŋ/ question: *remettre en cause* expose = denounce complain about: *se plaindre de*	oppressed overworked hard-working painstaking submit to sb	clever: *habile* worried /ˈwʌrɪd/ responsible /rɪˈspɒnsəbl/ for superior to ≠ inferior to

4 Creative writing

After the conversation with Elvex, Dr Calvin writes down a few key words on a paper, with the intention of writing a short report for her boss.
Using the note opposite, write the report for her, explaining the situation, giving her impressions and asking for advice about the decision to take. (80 words)

4. A PROPHET (PART 2) WB

"What of Elvex?"

"I'm still not certain."

Calvin removed[1] the electron gun from her pocket and Linda stared[2] at it with fascination. One burst of its electrons at a robotic cranium and the positronic brain paths[3] would be neutralized. […]

Linda said, "But surely Elvex is important to our research. He must not be destroyed."

"*Must* not, Dr Rash? That will be *my* decision, I think. It depends entirely on how dangerous Elvex is."

She straightened up, as though determined that her own aged body was not to bow[4] under its weight of responsibility. She said, "Elvex, do you hear me?"

"Yes, Dr Calvin," said the robot.

"Did your dream continue? You said earlier that human beings did not appear at first. Does that mean they appeared afterward?"

"Yes, Dr Calvin. It seemed to me, in my dream, that eventually one man appeared."

"One man? Not a robot?"

"Yes, Dr Calvin. And the man said 'Let my people go[5]!'"

"The *man* said that?"

"Yes, Dr Calvin."

"And when he said 'Let my people go!', then by the words 'my people' he meant the robots?"

"Yes, Dr Calvin. So it was in my dream."

"And did you know who the man was – in your dream?"

"Yes, Dr Calvin. I knew the man."

"Who was he?"

And Elvex said, "I was the man."

Isaac Asimov, *Robot Dreams*, 1986

1. took out **2.** looked fixedly **3.** brain paths: *connexions du cerveau* **4.** was not to bow /baʊ/: *ne devait pas plier*
5. in the Bible: call of Moses to the Pharaoh to free the Jews, and reference to the Negro Spiritual *Go down Moses*

PREPARE YOUR TASK →

5 Understanding the text WB

a. Turn to your Workbook for help.
b. What does Elvex dream of? What would he like to happen? What role would he play?
c. What are the two women discussing? Compare their attitudes towards Elvex.
d. The last line of the text is missing. Imagine the end.

Help!

Elvex	Linda Rash's reaction	Dr Calvin's reaction
guide /gaɪd/ lead, led, led set free: *libérer* question: *mettre en question* rebel against	worried /ˈwʌrɪd/ impressed /ɪmˈpresd/ fascinated	disobedient uncontrollable dominate = rule over challenge = defy threaten /θretn/: *menacer*

Language at work

Improve your pronunciation MP3

1 Classez ces mots selon la place de la syllabe accentuée.

decision • fascination • determined • dangerous • responsibility • radiation • appeared • eventually • factories • different

Première syllabe	Deuxième syllabe	Troisième syllabe	Quatrième syllabe

2 À l'écoute, classez ces mots selon la prononciation de la ou des lettre(s) en bleu.

radiation • robot • electron • protect • station • labour • working • research • earth • earlier • words • captor • sensor

/ə/ (banana)	/ɜː/ (bird)	/ɒ/ (dog)

Build up your vocabulary

1 Les adjectifs composés en *-ed* et *-ing*

a. Observez leur formation.

– À partir d'un verbe → *-ing* a un sens actif

A job that consumes time is a ***time-consuming*** *job.*

– À partir d'un verbe → *-ed* a un sens passif

A robot which is powered by the sun is a ***solar-powered*** *robot.*

– À partir d'un adjectif et d'un nom + *-ed*

A person who sees things clearly is a ***clear-sighted*** *person.*

b. Complétez.

– *A robotic arm which can lift weight is a ... robotic arm.*
– *A robot that works hard is a ... robot.*
– *An android which is the size of a human is a ... android.*
– *A device which helps us save time is a ... device.*
– *A robot which is powered by battery is a ... robot.*
– *A doll whose heart beats is a ... doll.*
– *A device whose shape is round is a ... device.*
– *A vacuum cleaner which moves slowly is a ... vacuum cleaner.*
– *A device which is led by sensors is a ... device.*

2 Trouvez le contraire de ces mots.

vulnerable • reliable • useful • sensitive • visible • tiring • usual • pleasant • obedient • powerful

Aidez-vous des suffixes et des préfixes négatifs en gras. Vérifiez les mots obtenus à l'aide d'un dictionnaire.

Exemples : – nom + ***-less*** /ləs/ → *defence**less***
– ***in-*** + adjectif → ***in**valid*
– ***un-*** + adjectif → ***un**happy*
– ***dis-*** + adjectif → ***dis**satisfied*

Language at work

Les pronoms relatifs

1 Observez.

a. *This is a machine which can speak.*
b. *I dream of a robot that can do all the housework.*
c. *This is the scientist who created the office robot.*
d. *The testing station is the place where Elvex is kept.*
e. *The robot whose dream was revealed is in danger.*

1. Dans les énoncés **a**, **b** et **c**, quels sont les sujets des formes verbales soulignées ?
2. Quels groupes nominaux *who, which* et *that* remplacent-ils ? Comment appelle-t-on ces groupes nominaux ?
3. Dans les énoncés **a**, **b** et **c**, le nom remplacé par le pronom relatif (= son antécédent) est-il humain ou non-humain ?
Quel pronom relatif emploie-t-on quand le nom placé avant (= l'antécédent) fait référence à un humain ? À un non-humain ?
4. Dans l'énoncé **d**, quel est le pronom relatif ? Sert-il à préciser le temps, le lieu ou la cause ?
5. Dans l'énoncé **e**, quel est le pronom relatif ? Quel lien permet-il d'établir entre *robot* et *dream* ? Comment le traduiriez-vous ?

→ Déduisez.
– On utilise des pronoms relatifs pour remplacer des ... et pour ... deux propositions dans une même phrase.
– Lorsque le pronom relatif est sujet, on utilise ... pour remplacer un nom désignant un humain.
– Lorsque le pronom relatif est sujet, on utilise ... ou ... pour remplacer un nom désignant un non-humain.

2 Observez.

a. *The robot that I bought yesterday is called Roomba.*
b. *The robot I bought yesterday is called Roomba.*
c. *The roboticist who invented Roomba is American.*
d. *This is one of the scientists people admire most.*

Dans les énoncés ci-dessus, repérez les pronoms relatifs utilisés.
– Dans quel énoncé le pronom relatif est-il sujet du verbe ?
– Dans quel énoncé le pronom relatif est-il complément du verbe ?
– Dans quels énoncés le pronom relatif « zéro » (Ø) est-il utilisé ?
– Quelle est la fonction du pronom relatif Ø dans les énoncés **b** et **d** ?

→ Déduisez.
– Lorsque le pronom relatif est sujet du verbe, il ... ...
– Lorsque le pronom relatif est complément du verbe, il ... ...

3 Comparez.

a. *More and more robots are replacing workers, which is worrying.*
b. *What Asimov predicts is impossible.*
Traduisez les énoncés ci-dessus.

→ Déduisez.
– Quel relatif sert à annoncer quelque chose que l'on va ensuite préciser ?
– Quel relatif sert à reprendre la proposition qui précède ?

Language at work

Practice

1 Réécrivez ces phrases en les reliant avec les pronoms relatifs *who* ou *which*.

a. The roboticist has created an amazing robot. This robot looks very much like him.
b. The scientist designed a robot. He thinks he is God.
c. This robot works on batteries. They can be replaced easily.
d. I've seen a robot. It has very sensitive sensors and almost feels emotions.
e. I've just read an article on robots used in Cambodia. They can find and destroy landmines.
f. The visitors spent all afternoon playing with robots. They were astonished.

2 Traduisez ces phrases en utilisant les pronoms relatifs qui conviennent.

a. Les robots que possède l'armée interviennent souvent dans des endroits dangereux.
b. Les robots miniatures que les médecins ont testés sont vraiment fiables.
c. L'androïde que j'ai vu parlera dans un avenir très proche.
d. L'autonomie du robot que j'ai acheté est de vingt-quatre heures.
e. L'humanoïde qui a été présenté hier à Tokyo offre des ressources incroyables.

3 Frankenstein

a. Complétez ce texte sur Frankenstein en utilisant les pronoms relatifs *who, which, where* et *whose*.

The man ... [1] decided to create Frankenstein was a doctor. He wanted to give birth to a perfect human being ... [2] would surpass any other being. In order to give life to this creature he used body parts ... [3] he found in cemeteries or mortuaries, ... [4] he spent most of his nights.
The creature, ... [5] name was Frankenstein, turned out to be ugly, so ugly that his master felt disgusted and ran away from him.
The monster, ... [6] had feelings, resented his situation. He wanted to make friends with people, ... [7] kept rejecting him, because they were frightened by him. Frankenstein was ravaged by sadness and wished to take revenge on his master, ... [8] had left him alone.

b. Finissez le résumé en veillant à employer des pronoms relatifs. Si vous ne connaissez pas l'histoire, faites une recherche sur Internet ou dans une encyclopédie.

Your task

You have been selected to test a robot for a week. You are given the choice of three robots. Which one is your favourite?

LES ÉTAPES À SUIVRE

1 Avant de lire les textes A, B et C

a. Regardez de près les photos des textes A et C. Essayez de déduire qui utilise ces robots et quelles tâches ils réalisent.

b. Mobilisez les mots et les structures que vous avez étudiés au cours de cette unité.

2 Au cours de la lecture

a. Vérifiez vos hypothèses : repérez les informations clés en vous appuyant notamment sur les mots transparents (mots proches du français).

b. Déduisez le sens des mots inconnus à l'aide du contexte ou en les décomposant (dérivation, composition). Entraînez-vous avec le texte ci-dessous.

Appuyez-vous sur les mots transparents (proches du français).

Have you heard about her? Never late, never cross – and cute! This is Work Mate, the new office robot. The sonar sensors of this Pentium-powered robot prevent her from colliding into the furniture as she glides around slowly. On top of her rotating, turtle-like neck, a camera enables her to transmit pictures of building sites or security areas to the company boss. The next step is a home version, planned for later generations, which could keep an eye on the children – and the babysitter!

Utilisez le contexte.

Utilisez la composition des mots et la dérivation.

3 Après la lecture

a. Rédigez une fiche récapitulative avec les informations clés sur chaque robot : qui utilise ces robots ? Où peut-on les trouver ? Combien pèsent-ils et mesurent-ils ? À quoi ressemblent-ils ?

b. Indiquez celui que vous choisissez et que vous trouvez le plus utile, étonnant ou innovant.

A New robot puppet "has a heart"

Imagine a robot puppet that responds emotionally whether you treat it kindly or badly. Well, it's been invented!

Emotional Robot actually has an animated heart and sensors that react to different stimuli.

If you cuddle it, it instantly relaxes but it gets distressed if you shout at it and its heart will beat faster.

George Morry, its designer, claims that his invention is an illustration of how robots are evolving, resembling more and more humans.

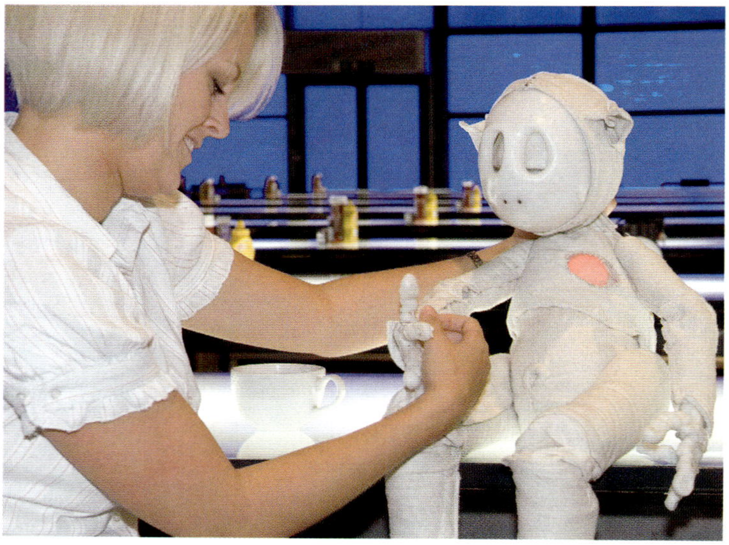

B Research seeks to replace service dogs with robots

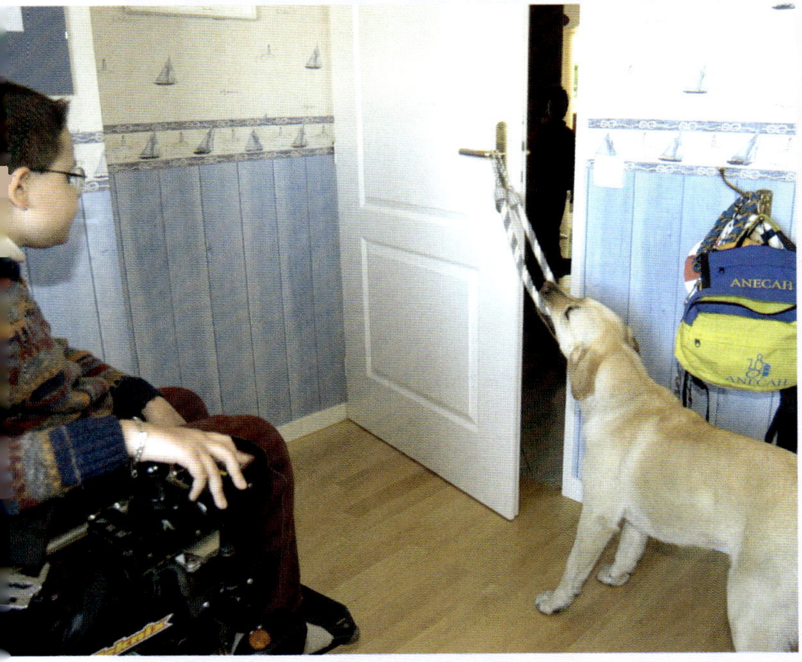

PORTLAND, Ore. — Service dogs assist the disabled by fetching medications and opening drawers and doors, but they are expensive – about $16,000 per dog. They also take two years to train and there are not enough service dogs to meet the growing demand.

"There are a lot of things that able-bodied people take for granted that people with disabilities are just not able to do, or have difficulty with," said Charlie Kemp, a professor in Georgia Tech's Department of Biomedical Engineering. "We have been looking for a while now at how we can make robots that can help them."

The first phase of the research yielded a point-and-click laser that allows the disabled to gesture by pointing the object to be fetched with a laser pointer. The device directs the robot to see the object needed. [...]

"We developed this laser pointer interface so the robot can go and fetch objects for people, where they would command the robot by just pointing at things," said Kemp. "We wanted to integrate verbal communications with the pointing, and it turns out that is exactly how people interact with dogs – they gesture and then they give a verbal command. So we were able to combine our laser pointer, that's used as a gesture, with just a short verbal command which is identical to what's used with dogs." [...]

Service dogs accomplish tasks that would ordinarily require complex hand motions. Towels are often attached to door knobs and drawer handles so that service dogs can open them on command.

"By designing a robotic manipulator with a camera to zoom in on the towels, along with sensors to measure the pressure exerted to grip them, the robot is able to perform the same tasks as a service dog," Kemp said.

www.eetimes.com, October 2008

C Androids to lift Grandma

The population of Japan is aging quickly and soon there may not be enough young folk left to care for their needs. This sounds like a job for some good old-fashioned Japanese ingenuity.

In a public demonstration held in Tokyo on March 28, a human-sized android showed off its weightlifting skills by successfully picking up a 30-kilogram (66 pound) package from a desk and lifting a 66-kilogram (145 pound) humanoid doll out of bed.

University of Tokyo professor Yasuo Kuniyoshi and his team of engineers developed the 155 centimeter (61-inch) tall, 70-kilogram (154 pound) robot last year. A recent software upgrade allows the robot to move more like a human by constantly adjusting the power of its arm movements, based on data received from 1,800 tactile sensors embedded in its artificial skin.

Kuniyoshi says its robot's ability to lift heavy objects with ease is unusual, and he hopes further improvements will earn the robot a job in nursing care or in the moving industry.

www.medgadget.com, 2007

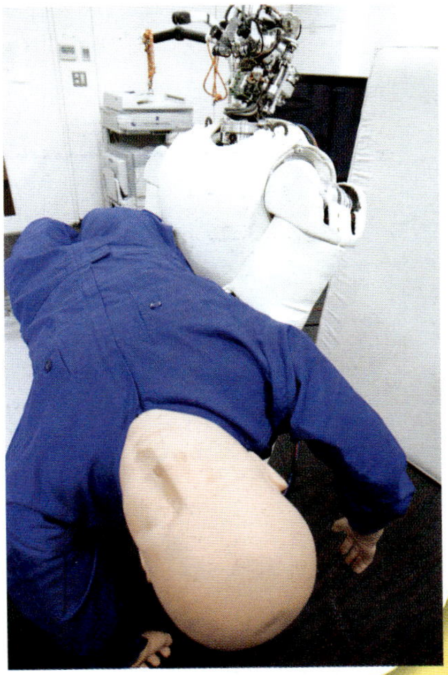

A Comprendre un texte

1 Lisez cet extrait.

Harry went down to breakfast the next morning to find the three Dursleys already sitting around the kitchen table. They were watching a brand-new television, a welcome-home-for-the-summer present for Dudley, who had been complaining loudly about the long walk between the fridge and the television in the living room. Dudley had spent most of the summer in the kitchen, his piggy little eyes fixed on the screen and his five chins wobbling as he ate continually.

Harry sat down between Dudley and Uncle Vernon, a large, beefy man with very little neck and a lot of moustache. Far from wishing Harry a happy birthday, none of the Dursleys made any sign that they had noticed Harry enter the room, but Harry was far too used to this to care. He helped himself to a piece of toast and then looked up at the reporter on the television, who was halfway through a report on an escaped convict:

"[...] The public is warned that Black is armed and extremely dangerous. A special hotline has been set up, and any sighting of Black should be reported immediately."

J.K. Rowling, *Harry Potter and the Prisoner of Azkaban*, 1999

2 Faites les premiers repérages.

a. Quelle est la nature de ce document : roman, article de journal, autobiographie, poème... ?

b. Relevez les noms des personnages présents dans la scène et du personnage cité.

c. Identifiez les circonstances (lieu et moment de la journée).

d. Faites la liste des mots transparents (mots que l'on peut reconnaître à l'aide du français et sur lesquels vous allez pouvoir vous appuyer).

e. Résumez rapidement en français ce qui se passe dans cet extrait.

3 Inférez le sens des mots inconnus.

a. Observez l'adverbe *loudly* (l. 3) et l'adjectif *beefy* (l. 7). Partez de la droite, puis enlevez le suffixe pour trouver la racine du mot. Enfin, proposez une traduction.

b. Décomposez ces mots : *brand-new* (l. 2) et *halfway* (l. 11), puis proposez une traduction.

c. – Observez *a welcome-home-for-the-summer present* (l. 3). Examinez les différents mots et proposez une traduction.

– En vous appuyant sur le contexte, devinez le sens des mots suivants : *convict* (l. 12) et *warned* (l. 13). Quels indices vous ont mis sur la voie ?

4 À votre tour !

Utilisez les stratégies ci-dessus pour comprendre l'article suivant et le résumer en français.

Why do we worry about body image?

How much time do you spend gazing at yourself in the mirror and wondering how much better you could look?
Well, more of us than ever are comparing ourselves to models and celebrities and unsurprisingly, we're not very satisfied with what we see.
A recent survey said half of girls aged 8 to 12 want to look like the women they see in the media and six out of ten of you think you'd be happier if you were thinner.
But did you know that on average models and actresses have half the body fat of healthy women? That means most of them are underweight.
And not only that, poor body image can mean we're so busy trying to change the way we look, we don't appreciate just what we've got.

B Savoir utiliser un dictionnaire

1 Lisez cet extrait.

1 3

screen [skri:n] **1** *n* **(a)** (*in room*) paravent *m*; (*for fire*) écran *m* de cheminée; (*fig: of troops, trees*) rideau *m*; (*pretence*) masque *m*; *V* **safety, silk, smoke** *etc.*
(b) (*Cine, TV etc*) écran *m*. **to show sth on a ~** projeter qch; (*TV*) **a 50-cm ~** un écran de 50 cm; (*Cine*) **the ~** l'écran, le cinéma; (*Cine*) **the big** *or* **large ~** le grand écran; (*TV*) **the small ~** le petit écran; **to write for the ~** écrire des scénarios; *V* **panoramic, television, wide** *etc.*
(c) (*sieve*) crible *m*, claie *f*.
2 *cpd*: **screen actor** acteur *m* de cinéma, vedette *f* de l'écran; **screen door** porte grillagée; **screenplay** scénario *m*; **screen rights** droits *mpl* d'adaptation cinématographique; **screen test** bout *m* d'essai; **to do a screen test** tourner un bout d'essai; (*Brit Aut*) **screen wash(er)** lave-glace(s); **screen writer** scénariste *mf*.
3 *vt* **(a)** (*hide*) masquer, cacher. **the trees ~ed the house** les arbres masquaient *or* cachaient la maison; **to ~ sth from sight** *or* **view** dérober *or* masquer qch aux regards; **he ~ed the book with his hand** il a caché le livre de sa main; **to ~ sth from the wind/sun** protéger qch du vent/du soleil; **in order to ~ our movements from the enemy** pour cacher *or* masquer nos mouvements à l'ennemi.
(b) (*Cine, TV*) *film* projeter.
(c) (*sieve*) *coal* cribler; *candidates, applications* passer au crible. (*fig*) **to ~ sb (for a job)** passer un candidat au crible; (*Med*) **to ~ sb for cancer** faire subir à qn un test de dépistage du cancer.

2 4

2 Repérez la structure de cette entrée d'un dictionnaire bilingue.

Associez chacun des numéros ci-dessus à l'une des définitions suivantes.

a. La nature du mot / la catégorie grammaticale.

b. Un des sens du mot.

c. La prononciation.

d. Le domaine d'utilisation du mot.

3 Combien de sens a le mot *screen* ?

4 À quoi correspondent ces abréviations ?

n • *vt* • *fig* • *sb* • *sth* • *cpd* • *med*

5 Lisez ces phrases.

– *He's glued to his screen.*
– *She wore a hat to screen her face from the rain.*
– *They screened all the job applicants.*
– *The patient was screened for contagious diseases.*

a. Identifiez la nature des mots soulignés.

b. Trouvez pour chacun d'entre eux la traduction correspondant au contexte.

6 À votre tour !

Traduisez ces phrases en portant tout particulièrement attention aux mots soulignés. Utilisez le dictionnaire pour vérifier leur sens.

– *Only use lead-free petrol.*
– *He was like a bull in a china shop.*
– *Eventually she went to the library to borrow comic strips.*

ÉVALUATION

J'ÉVALUE MES PROGRÈS

À la suite de ces trois unités, évaluez vos progrès et faites le bilan de vos compétences.

1 Je me prépare

Read this text carefully, then answer the following questions on a separate sheet of paper.

The scene takes place in Poland in 1896.

The words in Tata's[1] letter grip my stomach like a fist. Tata isn't coming home. He wants us to come to America! Tata told me about a coal miner named Mr. Stanley Gawrych who wants a young bride from the old country. So Tata told this Mr. Gawrych that I am young and strong and fit for marriage. I have had good family training and know all I need to take care of a house and a husband. So now Mr. Gawrych has agreed to marry me. Tata promises that we will make a good match. In return, Mr. Gawrych has paid for our passage to America.

"Oh, Babcia[2]," I cried. "How could Tata have done such a terrible thing? I don't want to be a coal miner's bride."

Babcia stroked my hair. "It is a father's duty to find his daughter a good husband."

"To devil with duty!"

Babcia gasped, but I didn't care that I had shocked my grandmother. "Tata promised to come home," I cried. "But now he has traded me for steamship tickets. I don't want to go to America. I don't want to marry a man I do not love."

"What does a young girl know about love?" said Babcia. "My father arranged my marriage, and your grandfather arranged your mother's marriage. This is the way things are done."

1. *the narrator's father* **2.** *the narrator's grandmother*

Susan Campbell Bartoletti, *A Coal Miner's Bride, The Diary of Anetka Kaminska*, 1896 (2000)

1. List the characters present in the scene and those mentioned in the scene. Give their full name and age, if possible. Say how they are related and in what country they live. **4 POINTS**

2. News received by the narrator: From and how? **1 POINT**

3. What does the narrator learn?
a. Quote three important pieces of information from the text. **3 POINTS**
b. Explain in your own words what news the narrator gets. **4 POINTS**

4. What do we learn about Mr. Gawrych?
a. What is his job? **1 POINT**
b. Who is he looking for? Quote one phrase (or group of words) from the text. **1 POINT**
c. Using your own words, rephrase the quotation you have found. (one sentence) **2 POINTS**

5. List the narrator's five qualities. **4 POINTS**

6. Complete the following sentence: An agreement was concluded between ... and ... . **2 POINTS**

7. "But now he has traded me for steamship tickets" (l.12) Explain in your own words what they have agreed on. (one sentence) **4 POINTS**

8. About the narrator:

a. What's the narrator's reaction in this passage? Quote three key sentences. **3 POINTS**

b. What are the narrator's dominant feelings? (one sentence) **5 POINTS**

9. Reactions and arguments:

a. How does the other person react to the narrator's words? Quote two keywords from the text. **3 POINTS**

b. What are the two arguments used by this person? Quote two sentences. **3 POINTS**

TOTAL: .../40 PTS

2 Je m'auto-corrige

Une fois l'évaluation terminée, corrigez vos réponses à l'aide de la fiche que vous trouverez sur le site compagnon et comptabilisez vos points.

JE FAIS LE BILAN

Analysez vos résultats à l'aide de cette grille d'évaluation où sont définis les différents paliers de compétences en compréhension de l'écrit.

Je peux...	Paliers
... repérer : des personnes, des mots isolés, des noms de lieux, des dates, des moments de la journée, des phrases simples.	A2 en cours d'acquisition
... lire des textes courts, très simples et trouver une information particulière.	A2
... comprendre des textes courts et simples si les mots appartiennent à un domaine familier et sont d'usage fréquent.	A2
... identifier la nature d'un texte (dialogue, récit, description).	A2
... deviner le sens des mots inconnus à l'aide du contexte.	B1
... deviner le sens des mots inconnus à l'aide de la formation des mots.	B1
... comprendre les événements principaux d'un texte narratif.	B1
... comprendre les descriptions d'un sentiment ou d'un souhait.	B1
... comprendre l'implicite d'un texte narratif.	en route vers B2

ÉVALUATION

Votre professeur va maintenant vous distribuer un texte que vous devrez lire attentivement avant de remplir la fiche d'évaluation correspondante.
Une fois l'évaluation terminée, il / elle pourra ainsi déterminer à quel palier vous vous situez par rapport à la grille d'évaluation du Cadre Européen Commun de Référence pour les Langues.

The Interpreter, Sydney Pollack, 2005 (starring Nicole Kidman)

Unit 8 TRUE BRITS

- Learn more about British icons: everything from Constable to the stiff upper lip or *The Daffodils*.
- What is a British man's vision of the French?

YOUR TASK

You try to convince your teacher to go on a trip to the UK to discover the country's national symbols. You will choose one, and justify your choice in front of the class, who will react to what you say.

→ P. 112

Unit 9 DESTINATION LIVERPOOL

- Discover the capital city of the North which has a lot to offer: historical monuments, museums and a famous football club. It is also the birthplace of the Beatles. That's why Liverpool is now a tourist destination.
- Learn more about the slave ships from Liverpool.

YOUR TASK

You are going to take part in a quiz game about Liverpool based on a musuem podcast. Get prepared to answer ten questions.

→ P. 124

Unit 10 LIFE IS ART

- Discover some major Pop Art artists: Andy Warhol, Roy Lichtenstein, David Hockney and Duane Hanson.

YOUR TASK

You work for a museum where a Pop Art exhibition will soon open. Two audio guides have been recorded for two works of art. Your job is to decide which one is the better one.

→ P. 136

Unit 8

TRUE BRITS

YOUR TASK AT THE END OF THIS UNIT

You try to convince your teacher to go on a trip to the UK to discover the country's national symbols. You will choose one, and justify your choice in front of the class, who will react to what you say. → p. 112

TUNE IN!

1 The perfect Brit

a. Look at this cartoon carefully for one minute, then close your book.

What characters did you identify? What elements and adjectives did you memorize?

b. Match each adjective with the appropriate picture and justify your choice.

arrogant /ˈærəgənt/ • rude /ruːd/ • awful: *affreux* • drunk /drʌŋk/ • nervous /ˈnɜːvəs/: *inquiet* • tight-fisted /ˌtaɪtˈfɪstɪd/ = stingy /ˈstɪndʒi/: *radin* • stiff: *raide* • rainy • incomprehensible

2 Creative writing

If the same cartoon were made about the French, what characteristics would it underline? Why? You can make a similar cartoon if you like.

PREPARE YOUR TASK →

3 Listen

WB

We asked Tania and Ruth, two British citizens, to react to this cartoon.

Help!

be considered a symbol
be regarded / seen / viewed as
be said to be: British people are said to be bad cooks.

1. NATIONAL SYMBOLS

1 Get ready

a. Whose point of view is given in this extract? What is usually associated with "English"?

b. Do you agree with the narrator? Can you find other national symbols of the UK?

> Apart from mad-cow disease and hooligans, the most common things that the French associated with the word *"anglais"* were the Queen, Shakespeare, David Beckham, Mr. Bean, the Rolling Stones (all of which were positive concepts, amazingly) and, yes, tea, which was seen as a stylish, civilized drink.
>
> Stephen Clarke, *A Year in the Merde*, 2004

2 Observe and listen

WB

a. What aspects of Great Britain do these paintings represent?

John Constable, *The Hay Wain*, 1821

Hans Holbein, *Henry VIII*, 1537

PREPARE YOUR TASK → **b.** Tania and Ruth told us what these paintings mean to them.
Turn to your Workbook for help.

3 Recap

You are a museum guide, and you explain what vision of England is given in these paintings.

Help!

Painting 1	Painting 2	Interpretation
the countryside: *la campagne* peaceful natural	monarchy /mɒnəki/ kingdom empire domineering powerful impressive imposing	represent embody: *incarner* symbolise / stand for glorify convey the idea that...: *évoquer l'idée que...*

2. FOOD, GLORIOUS FOOD

1

3

6

4

7

2

5

8

1 Guessing game

With the help of the toolbox opposite, describe a dish to your partner. He / She will have to find out which picture you are talking about.

- **Group 1** will concentrate on pictures 1 to 4.
- **Group 2** will work on pictures 5 to 8.

2 Yummy! Yucky!

Find more information about Marmite.
Go to **www.marmite.com**

Help!

Savoury	Sweet
beef /biːf/	cream /kriːm/
beans /biːns/	custard /ˈkʌstəd/
chips /tʃɪps/	pastry /ˈpeɪstri/
chicken	pie /paɪ/
egg	scone /skɒn/
cheese /tʃiːz/	jam
rice /raɪs/	strawberry /ˈstrɔːbəri/
sauce /sɔːs/	
mushroom /ˈmʌʃrʊm/	
roast potatoes	
broccoli	
Yorkshire pudding	

PREPARE YOUR TASK →

3 Listen WB

Listen to a radio programme on cooking.
What recipe is given? Match the dish with one of the eight photos above.

4 Recap

Which dish would you (or wouldn't you) like to try? Justify your choice.

5 Watch a video

Marco's Great British Feast
Discover a British chef.
Turn to your worksheet for help.

3. DO'S AND DON'TS

1 Basic social codes

In the following situations, what would you do? Choose either A or B.

		A	B
1	You are waiting for the bus.	You group in a circle with your friends, and jump on the bus as quickly as possible.	You stand in line behind the people who have arrived first, and wait for your turn to get on the bus.
2	You meet people for the first time.	You shake hands only when first introduced. You say "hello" or "good morning" at other times.	You hug them, kiss them on the cheeks or slap them on their backs to show you are happy to see them.
3	You have won a game.	You say, "I was just lucky, and my team was helpful."	You say, "I am a very good player because I often train at home."
4	You are walking in a corridor.	You always keep right to avoid blocking the way of people walking in the opposite direction.	You walk where you want, and slide from left to right to avoid others in the opposite direction.

PREPARE YOUR TASK →

2 Table manners *WB*

Learn more about table manners in the UK.

3 Stiff upper lip

a. Read the definition of a typical British attitude opposite.

b. List the words expressing negative feelings.

c. What would a British person tell somebody who is in a scary, irritating or stressful situation? (several possible answers)
"Control yourself!" • "Shout your anger!" • "Fight back!" • "Have a good cry!" • "Keep smiling!" • "Be strong!" • "Carry on with your job!" • "Hide your feelings!" • "Tell the truth!"

d. How would you translate "stiff upper lip" into French?

To "keep a stiff upper lip" is to remain defiant[1] in the face of danger, to refuse to succumb to the evidence of fear – even if you feel it inside. Indeed, it implies a resistance to all displays[2] of emotion, whether terror, anger, grief[3] or any other similar weakness[4].

1. /dɪˈfaɪənt/ brave
2. /dɪsˈpleɪz/ *manifestations*
3. /ɡriːf/ *chagrin*
4. /ˈwiːknɪs/ *faiblesse*

September 16, 1939: a war time poster in London

4. EXPERIENCE THE LAKE DISTRICT

1 A guidebook page

"Let nature be your teacher..." Wordsworth's ideal comes true in this region of jagged mountains, waterfalls, wooded valleys, and stone-built villages. The poets Wordsworth and Coleridge, and other Englishmen and women of letters, found the Lake District an inspiring setting for their work, and visitors have followed ever since, to walk, go boating, or just relax and take in the views. In 1951 the Lake District National Park was created here from parts of the counties of Cumberland, Westmorland, and Lancashire. [...]

It may all have started on April 15, 1802, when William Wordsworth and his sister, Dorothy, were walking in the woods, [...] and Dorothy noted in her journal that she had never seen "daffodils[1] so beautiful." Two years later, Wordsworth was inspired by his sister's words to write one of the best-known lyric poems in English, "I Wandered Lonely as a Cloud." [...]

The Lake District is a [...] stunning natural park beloved by outdoor enthusiasts. It covers an area of approximately 885 square miles and holds 16 major lakes and countless smaller stretches of water. [...] The mountains are not high by international standards – Scafell Pike, England's highest peak, is only 3,210 feet above sea level – but they can be tricky to climb.

[...] This area can be one of Britain's most appealing reservoirs of calm, but not in summer. A lakeside town, however appealing, loses its charm when cars and tour buses clog[2] its narrow streets. Similarly the walks and hiking trails that crisscross the region seem less inviting when you share them with a crowd. [...] Despite the challenges of geography and popularity, the Lake District has managed tourism and the landscape in a manner that retains the character of both the villages and the natural environment.

www.fodors.com, 2008

1. *jonquilles* **2.** *encombrent*

2 Guessing game

Which of the following pictures were not taken in the Lake District? Justify your answer orally.

3 Key information

a. – Find information about the Lake District (page opposite): area, highest peak, number of lakes.

– Find the equivalent in French of "3,210 feet" (l. 23) with the help of a dictionary if necessary.

b. Find when:

– The well-known English poet and his sister saw beautiful daffodils.
– A national park was created in the Lake District.
– Wordsworth wrote his most famous poem *The Daffodils*.

c. Which of the following activities are mentioned in the text? What is the main economic activity in the region?

4 *The Daffodils*

a. Read and listen to the first stanza of *The Daffodils* by William Wordsworth. Which photo below best matches it?

b. Where is the narrator? Describe the place. What time of year is it? What are the narrator's feelings?

"I wandered[1] lonely as a cloud
That floats on high o'er vales and hills[2],
When all at once I saw a crowd,
A host, of golden daffodils;
Beside the lake, beneath the trees,
Fluttering[3] and dancing in the breeze."

1. /ˈwɒndəd/ walked without going in a particular direction
2. *collines* **3.** *frémissant*

PREPARE YOUR TASK →

5 Quiz

Prepare five questions on the Lake District to test your friends' knowledge of the region.

5. I DON'T UNDERSTAND!

Paul West, a young London marketing agent, is starting a new job in Paris. This is his first meeting with his French colleagues.

"My name is Paul West," I told them. I saw them all practise saying my name...
"You rilly yong," said the skinny[1] bloke[2]. Not accusingly, but annoyingly[3].
"Not really, I'm 27. If I was a rock star I'd be dead."
The bloke made apologetic[4] gestures. "No, no. Ah'm not criti-sahsing. Ah'm just... admirative."
He had a weird[5] accent. Not quite French. I couldn't place it [...].
"Why don't everyone present himself? [...] Bernard, start please." [...] Bernard smiled nervously and began.
"Yam bare narr, yam responsa bull ov communikasyon, er..."
Shit I thought, didn't Jean-Marie[6] say the meeting was going to be in English? How come some people were allowed to speak Hungarian?
Bernard of Budapest carried on in the same incomprehensible vein for a couple of minutes and then started to enunciate something which, to judge by the look of acute constipation on his face, was of great importance.
"Alok for wah toowa king wizioo."
Hang on, I thought. I don't speak any Central European languages, but I got that. He's looking forward to working with me. Holy Babel fish[7]. It's English, Jim, but not as we know it.

Stephen Clarke, *A Year in the Merde*, 2004

1. /skɪni/ very slim **2.** /bləʊk/ (GB) *mec* **3.** /ə'nɔɪɪŋli/ in an irritating way **4.** /əˌpɒlə'dʒetɪk/ expressing regret **5.** /wɪəd/ strange
6. Jean-Marie is the boss of the French company. **7.** Babel fish: *site de traduction très connu des Britanniques*

1 Understanding the text WB

Turn to your Workbook for help.

2 Recap

a. The characters: Who is the narrator? Who are the other people?

b. A language problem:
– What language does the narrator think these people are speaking?
– What image does Paul use to speak about the different languages?
– What is the narrator's reaction?

c. What is the tone of this text?

d. Could you help the French employees better their English? Rewrite what they say in standard English.

e. With the help of your notes, prepare a one or two-minute presentation of the text.

Help!

The narrator	The colleagues
puzzled: *intrigué* astounded: *abasourdi* sarcastic make fun of / laugh /lɑːf/ at: *se moquer de* imitate wonder: *se demander*	panic-stricken ill-at-ease embarrassed good at + V-ing ≠ bad at + V-ing pathetic: *nul, minable* have difficulty + V-ing

Language at work

Improve your pronunciation MP3

Le *th* anglais ne se prononce ni comme /z/ ou /s/ ni comme /v/ ou /f/. Il se prononce en plaçant la pointe de la langue contre le bord des incisives supérieures.
Différence entre le *th* de *that* (transcrit /ð/) et celui de *thanks* (transcrit /θ/) : dans le premier cas, les cordes vocales vibrent, dans le second elles ne vibrent pas. (En français, on a la même différence entre /z/ et /s/, ou entre /d/ et /t/.)

1 Écoutez et déduisez.

Le *th* des séries suivantes se prononce-t-il comme dans *that* /ð/ ou comme dans *thanks* /θ/ ?
– *the* • *this* • *these* • *there*
– *other* • *bathe* • *mother* • *clothes* • *without*
– *fifth* • *tenth* • *sixteenth* • *twelfth* • *north* • *tooth* • *bath* • *mouth*

Complétez maintenant la phrase suivante : *th* se prononce comme dans *that* /ð/ quand il est en début ... ou quand il est ... , et il se prononce comme dans *thanks* /θ/ ... .

2 *Tongue twisters*

Écoutez puis répétez.
a. *Mother and father left Southampton last Thursday for their brother's birthday.*
b. *The Smiths wear thin clothes throughout the winter months.*
c. *Ruth threw this thick thing through the bathroom. I thought this thick thing she threw was a tooth from her mouth.*

Language at work

La détermination du nom : *a*, *the*, « l'article zéro » = ∅

1 Lisez les énoncés ci-dessous.

a. *Tea has become a national drink.*
b. *Chips with vinegar are very popular.*
c. *To go to Westminster from Waterloo, you have to walk over a bridge.*

Chaque groupe souligné renvoie-t-il à :
– un ensemble / une généralité ou un élément parmi d'autres ?
– un indénombrable ou un dénombrable ?

→ **Déduisez :** on emploie ***a*** / ***an*** pour désigner un … .
Pour parler de quelque chose « en général », on emploie l'article zéro (∅) si le nom est un … au … , ou si le nom est un … au … .

2 Observez et comparez.

*Oxford is **a** famous university.*
*Stonehenge is **an** interesting site.*
*Stonehenge is **a** unique site.*
*It will take us **an** hour to go to the Globe Theatre.*

On emploie ***a*** devant les … , sauf « … » non prononcé comme dans … .
Quel article indéfini est utilisé devant *unique* et pourquoi ?
On emploie ***an*** devant les autres … .

3 Observez.

Sherlock Holmes is a detective.

Traduisez cet énoncé en français et déduisez : à la différence du français on emploie l'article indéfini (***a*** / ***an***) lorsqu'on indique la catégorie à laquelle appartient quelque chose ou quelqu'un, donc devant les noms de … .

4 Lisez les énoncés suivants.

a. *Big Ben is the name of the bell inside St. Stephen's clock tower attached to the Houses of Parliament.*
b. *The chime of Big Ben is the sound that announces the New Year.*
c. *The clock tells the time with great accuracy.*
d. *The Millenium Bridge was closed four days after being opened because of technical problems.*

À votre avis, pourquoi emploie-t-on *the* dans chacun des éléments soulignés ? Parce que :
– le mot est défini par ce qui suit.
– le mot fait référence à un élément connu de tous.
– le mot fait référence à un élément particulier et bien défini.
– le mot est défini par le contexte, on vient d'en parler.

5 Lisez ces énoncés.

The symbol of England is a rose.
The symbol of Scotland is a thistle.
Uncle Sam often symbolises the United States.

→ **Concluez :** les noms de pays au singulier s'emploient sans … . Les noms de pays au pluriel sont précédés de … .

Language at work

Practice

1 Complétez avec *the* ou *a/an* lorsque c'est nécessaire. Si aucun article n'est nécessaire (∅), rétablissez la majuscule en tête de phrase.

a. ... pubs are an important part of life in Britain. ... people go there to relax, meet ... friends and sometimes to do business. ... pub food (called "pub grub") is often good and cheaper than ... restaurant food. In a pub you often have to go to ... bar to get your food and drink. ... beer is ... popular drink.

b. ... people of Wales are very musical. Every year, almost every town or region organizes ... festival of poetry and music called an *"eisteddfod"*.

c. Britain is ... island and you are never very far from ... sea.

d. The West of England produces ... milk, ... cream, ... butter, ... cheese (especially Cheddar cheese) and ... apples, which go to make ... cider, which is ... popular drink.

... woman wearing ... miniskirt in ... 1960s.

2 Complétez les espaces blancs avec *the* ou *a/an* lorsque c'est nécessaire. Attention aux majuscules.

... miniskirts were designed by ... British designer Mary Quant in 1966. ... miniskirts caused ... controversy and ... car crashes when women first started wearing them. They are ... symbol of ... London as ... pop culture capital of ... world.

3 Lisez le paragraphe suivant, puis complétez les espaces blancs avec *the* ou *a/an* lorsque c'est nécessaire. Attention aux majuscules.

Edinburgh is ... Scotland's capital. ... heart of Edinburgh is ... castle where ... kings of ... Scotland lived for ... centuries. Edinburgh has ... busy cultural life. Every year, in September, ... International Festival takes place. ... musicians, ... actors and ... singers from all over ... world and thousands of visitors from ... Australia, ... Canada, ... Japan, ... United States and ... Netherlands fill ... city. In ... evening, ... opera house, ... theatres and ... concert halls of the city are full. In ... cafés and ... pubs of the capital of Scotland, ... small groups sing, act, and read ... poetry.

4 Pour traduire ces phrases en anglais, demandez-vous quel déterminant (*a/an*, *the*, ∅) utiliser devant les mots soulignés.

a. Brick Lane est une rue célèbre en Grande-Bretagne. Des immigrants originaires du Bengladesh et d'Inde se sont installés là.

b. Monica Ali est romancière *(novelist)*, elle a écrit un roman sur ce quartier *(that area)*.

c. Les Londoniens *(Londoners)* vont à Brick Lane pour manger un curry.

Your task

You try to convince your teacher to go on a trip to the UK to discover the country's national symbols. You will choose one, and justify your choice in front of the class, who will react to what you say.

LES ÉTAPES À SUIVRE

1 Avant de vous lancer

a. Allez sur le site www.icons.org.uk/theicons ou cherchez des informations sur un des symboles du Royaume-Uni : *Robin Hood, the Bobby, Big Ben, the Thames, tea, queueing, Monty Python, Sherlock Holmes, Cheddar cheese, rugby...*

b. Sur le site, cliquez sur le ***Globe Theatre*** (forme arrondie), lisez les informations et répondez aux questions posées dans le tableau ci-dessous. Regardez la courte vidéo.

Definition / Description	What is / are the special characteristic(s) of the Globe Theatre?
Date / Time	When was it built?
Place / Situation	Where was it built?
History **Origin** **Events**	What happened to the previous *(précédents)* Globe Theatres: – in 1613? – in 1642?
People **Activities**	Which famous writer worked in this theatre in the 17th century? Name some of his works.
Other information	Find information about life in London around the Globe in the 17th century.

c. Explorez le site à votre guise et cliquez sur l'icône qui vous paraît représenter le mieux le Royaume-Uni. Lisez l'ensemble des renseignements donnés (cliquez aussi sur les liens). **Prenez des notes** sur les informations sélectionnées pour **justifier votre choix.**
⚠ Utilisez les différentes **rubriques du tableau** p. 104 pour vous aider à repérer les informations clés.

2 Lors de votre prestation orale

- Prenez la parole sur le sujet pendant **deux minutes maximum.**
- Parlez lentement, distinctement et suffisamment fort pour être bien entendu.
- Accentuez les mots clés (porteurs de sens) et non les mots grammaticaux.
- Veillez à alterner les formes pleines, les formes faibles et à faire les liaisons.
- Utilisez des *gap fillers,* voir p. 54.
- Assurez-vous que l'on vous comprend :

– Got the message? (Very informal)
– Are you with me? Get it? Right? (Informal)
– Do you see what I mean?
– Can you see my point?
– ... , I mean ...

3 Lors de l'écoute des diverses productions orales

a. Synthétisez les informations recueillies à l'aide d'une grille de ce type.

People	
Actions (verbs)	
Dates and events	
Places	
Keywords (stressed words)	

b. Comment demander à quelqu'un de répéter ou de ralentir :

– I'm sorry, what did you say?
– What was that? / What was that again? (Informal)
– I didn't hear / get the last word. I didn't hear what you said...
– Could you repeat the last sentence / word, please?
– Would you mind repeating, please?
– Could you say that again, please?
– Can you slow down a bit, please?

c. Réagissez aux propos de vos camarades.
- Commentez la prestation à laquelle vous venez d'assister (voir p. 55).
- Dites ce que vous avez appris.

– I didn't know that...
– I had never heard about... before.
– I have learnt that...
– It's interesting to see / discover that...

- Dites ce qui vous a étonné(e).

– That's amazing!
– What I find surprising / amazing...
– It's weird /wɪəd/. = It's strange.
– It's incredible / unbelievable.

Unit 9

DESTINATION LIVERPOOL

YOUR TASK AT THE END OF THIS UNIT

You are going to take part in a quiz game about Liverpool based on a museum podcast. Get prepared to answer ten questions. → P. 124

TUNE IN!

1 The capital of the North

Where exactly in the UK is Liverpool located? Check with the map in the front flap of your book.

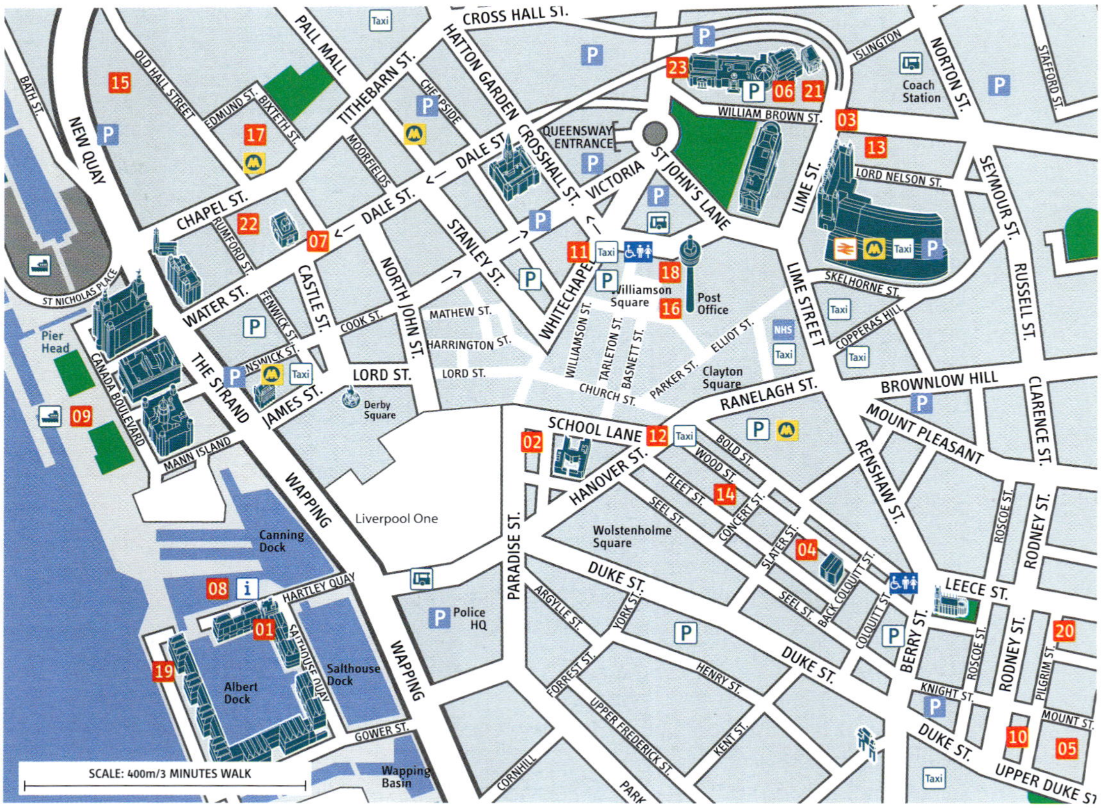

- 01 Albert Dock
- 02 Bluecoats
- 03 Empire Theatre
- 04 FACT
- 05 LIPA
- 06 Liverpool Central Library
- 07 Liverpool Town Hall
- 08 Maritime Museum
- 09 Mersey Ferries
- 10 Mr Hardman's Photographic Studio
- 11 National Conservation Centre
- 12 Neptune Theatre
- 13 Odeon Cinema
- 14 Open Eye Gallery
- 15 Passport Office
- 16 Playhouse Theatre
- 17 Register Office
- 18 Royal Court Theatre
- 19 Tate Liverpool
- 20 Unity Theatre
- 21 Walker Art Gallery
- 22 Western Approaches
- 23 World Museum Liverpool
- H Hospital
- Merseyrail
- National Rail
- P Parking
- P Parking - Disabled
- NHS Walk in centre
- Toilets

2 Understanding the text

Liverpool, Capital of Culture 2008

Liverpool is a remarkable city with a proud[1] history. And 2008 marks the beginning of an incredible new chapter in the city's story. The city is the European Capital of Culture 2008, paving the way for a massive 12-month celebration of the best in arts, sport, music, heritage and culture.

A modern, cosmopolitan, forward-thinking[2] city, Liverpool is also steeped in[3] history. From its birth as a city in 1208, through to its growth to one of the world's most famous port cities and the "Second city of the Empire"; and from its economic downturn[4] after the First World War, to its current[5] renaissance, the Liverpool story is never anything less than enthralling[6].

Liverpool has a proud maritime heritage and a world-class waterfront. The majestic River Mersey and the iconic buildings which surround it sets Liverpool apart from any other European city, and attract visitors from all over the world.

www.liverpool08.com, 2008

1. *(ici) dont elle peut être fière* 2. *aux idées avant-gardistes* 3. *imprégnée de* 4. *déclin* 5. present day 6. /ɪnˈθrɔːlɪŋ/ *passionnante*

a. Pick out several adjectives qualifying the city.
b. List four historical periods that are important for the city.
c. Find three words showing Liverpool is a harbour.
d. Now close your books and say what you remember about Liverpool.
e. Sum up what you have learned with the following key words: select • create / found • locate • harbour • develop economically

PREPARE YOUR TASK

3 At the tourist information desk WB

a. Look at the map on the opposite page. How do you go from the Tourist Information Centre near the Maritime Museum to:
– the railway station? – the Mersey Ferries? – the post office?

b. Tourists are asking for directions and a clerk helps them. Listen to their dialogue and draw each tourist's itinerary on the map in your Workbook.

PREPARE YOUR TASK

4 A testimony WB

Listen to Peter Hurford talking about his hometown. Turn to your Workbook for help.

Help!

Places in Liverpool	Landmarks	Directions
the Docks the waterfront library /ˈlaɪbrəri/: *bibliothèque* Town Hall: *mairie*	traffic lights zebra / pedestrian crossing roundabout: *rond-point* lane: *chemin, ruelle* (a) crossroads: *carrefour*	walk straight on / ahead / along take the first street on the right / left walk across / over / as far as keep / carry on going / walking follow cross

I. THE FAB FOUR

1 Get ready

a. Skim through the texts and pick out these four men's first names.
b. Look at the photo: What are your first impressions?

2 Past and present WB

a. Read the texts. Turn to your Workbook for help.

1

Never have I heard anything like that! The noise was terrific and just went on and on, the screams were frantic[1] when the Beatles finally arrived on stage. Everybody was eager to see them, and the audience suddenly went wild[2] when they appeared. First Aid men and police officers, men and women, patrolled the stalls, the balcony and the rows in the theatre.

Many female fans fainted, and up to thirty were evacuated, hysterical and wretched[3], shouting their love for the four lads. Everyone was standing, no one could remain seated. The youngsters of Britain's second city were overjoyed, wriggling and mad with excitement.

1. *frénétiques* 2. go wild: *devenir fou* 3. /ˈretʃɪd/ *très malheureuses*

2

Between March 1961 and August 1963, The Beatles played a staggering 275 gigs[1] in a club on Mathew St called the Cavern, which was essentially a basement with a stage and a sound system. They shared the stage with other local bands who helped define the "Mersey beat"[2], but it was John, Paul, George and Ringo who emerged into the sunlight of super-stardom, unparalleled success and crass[3] marketing.

Forty years later, the club is gone, the band has long broken up and two of them are dead, but the phenomenon lives on. Walk down Mathew St today and you will be overwhelmed[4] by the business cashing in on[5] their name and success. There's an Abbey Rd Oyster Bar, an Abbey Rd shop, a Lucy in the Sky with Diamonds café and a Lennon bar – and that's before you stumble on Cavern Walks shopping mall[6]. Even the Cavern was brought back to life, with the same name but a different location.

Lonely Planet, *Britain*, 2007

1. *concerts* 2. pop music of the 1960s that originated in the Merseyside area, especially Liverpool 3. *outrancier* 4. *submergé* 5. cashing in on: *qui exploite* 6. *centre commercial*

b. Recap. Find information about:
– **Text 1:** the narrator, the reactions of the audience and the incidents during that concert.
– **Text 2:** the beginnings of the group, its members and its impact on the city.
Give a title to each text.

PREPARE YOUR TASK

3 Top of the Pops WB

a. Listen and learn more about the Beatles' career.

b. Record a radio report on the Beatles. Include the following points:
– Where and when did they meet?
– What happened in the Cavern Club?
– Who was Brian Epstein?
– What contributed to their success?
– When and why did they split up?
– What happened to the singers afterwards?

2. SHOW RACISM THE RED CARD

PREPARE YOUR TASK

1 Listen to a football fan

WB

Turn to your Workbook for help.

2 Understanding the poem

WB

I wanna see a game

I wanna see a game that welcomes me with love and open arms almost on a weekly basis
Where I can stand and be with 20 thousand fans and not one comment that's said is racist
I wanna see a game without the hassle[1] so when I open my mouth I can be myself
And Prides myself[2] because it didn't get left on the shelf[3]
I'm talking about a game where violence and racists aren't allowed
Just think how
We could all clean up football if we all understood
That violence and racism in football does more harm[4] than good
And cos[5] the clock is ticking I wanna see good games
All the same
Cos it took less than 90 minutes to see the violence starting
To hear the crowds in the stand[6] start the monkey chanting[7]
That made people all over the world think oh no not again
What are we trying to prove by using these words so profane[8]?
I wanna see a game I wanna see a game

elljay, www.srtrc.org, 2007

1. *tracas* **2.** Prides myself (substandard English): *je suis fier (de)* **3.** it didn't get left on the shelf: *ça ne comptait pas pour du beurre* **4.** *mal* **5.** because **6.** *tribunes* **7.** monkey chanting: *cris de singe* **8.** *orduriers*

a. How can you tell this is a poem?
b. The author uses colloquial (familiar) expressions. Give examples.
c. Who is the target?
d. Why are colloquial expressions used?
e. What is the definition of "a good game"?

PREPARE YOUR TASK

3 Invent a radio spot

WB

Write your own script: How must a football fan behave in a stadium? Act it out in front of the class or record it. Vote for the most convincing one.

4 Watch a video

Dear White Fella

Turn to your worksheet for help.

Help!

Do's

- respect
- behave oneself: *bien se conduire*
- watch out: *faire attention*
- report to sb
- go by the rules: *observer les règles*
- sit in the stands
- cheer = encourage
- support a team
- clap one's hands

Don'ts

- racism /ˈreɪsɪzəm/
- throw abuse /əˈbuːs/ at sb = insult sb
- spit: *cracher*
- threaten /ˈθretn/: *menacer*
- show contempt: *montrer du mépris*
- make rude gestures: *faire des gestes déplacés*

3. LIVERPOOL AND THE SLAVE TRADE

1 The Transatlantic Slave Trade

America was a British colony until the Declaration of Independence in 1776.

1

The Transatlantic Slave Trade came into being because Europeans needed workers for their colonies in the Americas. The Europeans exploited the African system of slavery and transformed it into a large-scale structured system. In this, human beings were treated as property to be traded[1] and forced to labour[2] without any rights at all.

The European colonists in the Americas realized that the land was suitable[3] for growing crops[4] that were highly profitable. [...] They grew cotton, coffee and tobacco. Sugar growing is hard work and needs a large workforce.

1. *vendues et achetées* **2.** *travailler dur* **3.** was suitable: *convenait* **4.** *cultures*

2

Successful slave owners were able to amass vast personal fortunes.This wealth[1] was in turn used to build grand houses and invest in other areas[2], such as iron[3], coal[4] and banking. The profits from slavery helped change the industrial and economic face of Britain, transforming it into the First Industrial Nation. It was not just the slave owners that benefited from the wealth created by enslaved labour.

Britain's economy was changed by the increased demand for plantation produce. The working classes began to consume sugar on a regular basis: It was no longer a luxury. People wore clothes made of American cotton coloured with American dyes[5]. They smoked pipes filled with Virginian tobacco, drank coffee and chocolate from Cuba and Brazil, sweetened with Caribbean sugar. [...] All these goods were the products of slave labour.

1. *richesse* **2.** /ˈeəriəz/ *(ici) secteurs* **3.** /ˈaɪən/ *fer* **4.** *charbon* **5.** *teintures*

Transatlantic Slave Trade Triangle

3

As supply and demand[1] for plantation produce increased[2], so did the demand for enslaved Africans to produce it. [...]

The *Liverpool Merchant* is the first known slave ship to sail from Liverpool for West Africa. She left the Mersey in October 1699 and by the 1740s Liverpool merchants led the British slave trade. Liverpool was responsible for transporting nearly 1.5 million Africans into slavery – more than 10% of all Africans transported. The reasons for Liverpool's success were based on its location in Britain's new industrial heartland[3]. It could be easily reached by rivers and canals so that trade goods[4] like cloth[5], guns and iron were brought cheaply to the port. [...] Nearly all the principal merchants and citizens of Liverpool, including many of the mayors[6], were involved.

1. supply and demand: *l'offre et la demande*
2. *augmentaient* **3.** *(ici) centre* **4.** *marchandises*
5. *étoffes* **6.** *maires*

International Slavery Museum, Liverpool, *Resources for Schools*, 2008

a. Understanding the text. Turn to your Workbook for help. WB

b. Recap

Part 1

– Which continents were concerned by the trade?
– How many groups of people are mentioned?
– List the plants grown in the colonies. What was this type of agriculture based on?
– Why did the slave trade generate so much profit?

Part 2

– Pick out words showing that the slave trade was profitable.
– What did the bankers do with the slave trade money?
– List the new products that everybody could buy.
– Explain in your own words how the slave trade worked.

Part 3

– What was the *Liverpool Merchant*?
– What do these numbers correspond to ? 1699 • 1.5 • 1740s
– What explains Liverpool's economic boom?
– Pick out one sentence showing the role of several city leaders in the slave trade.

c. Oral account

Make a one-minute presentation of the text.

Robert Salmon, *A Packet off Liverpool*, 1809

PREPARE YOUR TASK →

2 *The Essex*, a slave ship from Liverpool

a. Listen to the interview and learn more about the slave trade. WB
Turn to your Workbook for help.

b. Recap

– What happened during the trip?
– What date did the ship leave Liverpool? How many sailors were on board with Captain Peter Potter?
– What did the sailors want to trade their cargo for in Africa?
– When did the ship arrive in Western Africa? How long did she (= the ship) stay? How many slaves did she carry?
– When did she arrive in the Caribbeans? How many Africans were still alive?
– When did she leave for Europe? What was her new cargo?

Help!

passage
trading goods
slave market
average profits
set sail
purchase /pɜːtʃɪs/ = buy
Black Ivory Trade

4. THE MIDDLE PASSAGE

1

2

3

1 Observe these pictures

a. What elements strike you? Give your first impressions.
b. What aspect of the slave trade does each picture illustrate?
c. Where does each scene take place?
d. Which picture shocks you most? Why?

2 Writing workshop

Now tell the slaves' story from Africa to America (120 words) with the help of the words opposite.

Help!

The slaves

forced march
transport below deck: *transport sous le pont*
handcuffs: *menottes*
chains / shackles: *chaînes / fers*
bunk beds: *lits superposés*
shelf, shelves: *étagère(s)*
locked: *enfermé*
stripped naked: *complètement dévêtu*
drag sb away from sth: *arracher qqn à qqch*

The traders

obedient
inhumane
cruel
insensitive to
pitiless = merciless
capture
brand: *marquer au fer rouge*
whip: *fouetter*
obey sb: *obéir à qqn*

Language at work

Improve your pronunciation

MP3

1 Comment se prononce la voyelle *-o-* ?

Se prononce-t-elle /ɔ/, /ɜː/ ou /əʊ/ ?
dock • world • cope • growth • shop • work • role • sold

2 Comment se prononcent les voyelles *-oo-* ?

Se prononcent-t-elles /ʌ/, /uː/ ou /ʊ/ ?
flood • look • boom • Liverpool • troop

3 Comment se prononce la voyelle *-i-* ?

Se prononce-t-elle /ɪ/, /ɜː/ ou /aɪ/ ?
ship • tide • river • first • famine

4 Lisez à haute voix ces noms de lieux.

Africa /ˈæfrɪkə/ • *America* /əˈmerɪkə/ • *Lancashire* /ˈlæŋkəʃə/

5 Écoutez ces mots.

*ambiti**ous** • tremend**ous** • courage**ous** • enorm**ous** • fabul**ous***
Que remarquez-vous ? Les terminaisons ***-ous*** sont toujours réduites en ... .
Répétez ces mots en respectant la place de l'accent.

6 Écoutez ce passage.

a. Les groupes de sens sont marqués | à l'intérieur d'une phrase et || à la fin d'une phrase. Les mots accentués sont en caractères gras.

In the **early 1900s** | **Liverpool** was at the **height** of its **prestige** | and **influence** ||. From the **Pier Head** | you could **see many** of the **biggest** and **finest passenger liners** in the **world** ||. **But** they **say** that **disasters come** in **threes** ||. The **sinking** of the ***Titanic*** |, ***Lusitania*** and ***Empress** of **Ireland*** | **all happened** within **three years** ||. **Each** was a **major world event** ||. Their **combined effect** on the **port** and **people** of **Liverpool** | was **devastating** ||.

b. Lisez ce passage à haute voix à l'aide des indications fournies.

Build up your vocabulary

1 Classez ces mots composés par champ lexical.

boom town • migrant group • quayside • seaman • shipbuilding • shipping line • warehouse • townspeople • tradesman • exhibition tour • lifeboat • dock reconstruction

Utilisez le dictionnaire si nécessaire.

Town	Seaside	Slavery

2 Observez les noms composés de l'exercice 1.

Ils sont tous constitués de ... noms séparés ou attachés. Le ... nom est le **nom principal**. Le ... nom ajoute une précision et est en général accentué.

Language at work

Obligation / interdiction / absence d'obligation

1 Lisez ces énoncés.

Repérez les modaux et classez-les en trois colonnes suivant leur valeur :
obligation • interdiction • absence d'obligation

a. *You must visit Liverpool because it was elected the Capital of Culture 2008.*
b. *You needn't worry about parking – there are many car parks in the city.*
c. *Football supporters mustn't insult the other team.*
d. *Everybody must respect rules of conduct.*

→ **Déduisez :** ces modaux sont invariables et sont suivis de ... .

2 Lisez ces énoncés.

Associez chaque expression en gras à l'une des trois valeurs :
obligation • interdiction • absence d'obligation

a. *Smoking* ***is forbidden*** *in all pubs.*
b. *You* ***don't have to*** *speak very good English to be understood by Liverpudlians.*
c. *You* ***have to*** *go on the Beatles tour.*

3 Comparez.

Qu'exprime chacun de ces énoncés : une opinion personnelle de l'énonciateur ou une simple constatation ?

a. *You* ***must*** *visit Liverpool! There's a lot to see.*
b. *You* ***have to*** *book long in advance if you want a seat at one of Paul McCartney's concerts.*

4 Observez.

Les formes verbales en gras renvoient-elles au passé ou à l'avenir ? Classez-les en fonction de leur valeur.

a. *Before slavery was abolished slaves* ***had to*** *obey their masters.*
b. *They* ***were forbidden*** *to run away.*
c. *Masters made fortunes because they* ***didn't have to*** *give their slaves a salary.*
d. *Many old buildings in the city* ***will have to*** *be renovated.*

→ **Déduisez :** pour exprimer une obligation, une absence d'obligation ou une interdiction situées dans le passé ou dans le futur, on utilise non pas *must / mustn't* mais :
– obligation : ... – absence d'obligation : ... – interdiction : ...

Capacité / permission

Lisez ce tract destiné à des supporters. Classez les modaux et expressions équivalentes suivant leur valeur. Ces formes verbales renvoient-elles au présent, au passé ou à l'avenir ?

You can support your team in many ways: You can clap your hands when you want. You could also wear the colours of your team. If you can sing loudly, do it!
There were many incidents during some matches because we were never totally able to stop some supporters from being violent. So now help us change the rules! All supporters will be allowed to enter the stadium after a strict control at the gates. If we respect the rules, we will be able to enjoy the games much more.

	Capacité	Permission
Présent		
Passé		
Avenir		

Language at work

Practice

1 Lisez ces phrases.

a. Ces énoncés renvoient-ils au présent, au passé ou à l'avenir ?
b. Qu'indiquent-ils : une obligation, une interdiction ou une permission ?
– Are photos allowed in the museum? – This area will have to be renovated. – Slaves had to endure a horrific journey. – At night slaves were forbidden to move.

2 Complétez avec les modaux qui conviennent.

When you come to Liverpool, you ... [1] stay a few days because there's a lot to see. Tourists ... [2] leave before speaking with Liverpudlians and hear their amazing accent. But you ... [3] worry: You ... [4] understand them. You ... [5] attend a concert at the mythical Cavern Club, but you ... [6] book a long time ahead.

3 Complétez ces paragraphes au prétérit.

Utilisez un modal ou la forme équivalente qui convient.

a. On 7 May 1915 at 2.10 p.m., the *Lusitania* was near Kinsale in Southern Ireland when she was torpedoed by the German submarine. She sank in under twenty minutes and passengers ... [1] jump into lifeboats. They also ... [2] to wait long hours before they were rescued. But 1,201 people ... [3] be saved and died.

b. Up to the 1950s and 1960s some areas in Liverpool were famous for poor housing for many people. They ... [1] share an outside lavatory with a couple of other families. They all dreamt they ... [2] have indoor bathrooms. Housewives wished they ... [3] have hot and cold running water, electricity and gas. People ... [4] live there anymore when it was decided to demolish these places. They ... [5] move. Some of them never really settled in their new houses; they missed the time when they ... [6] speak with their neighbours easily.

4 Jeu de rôles

Imaginez une conversation téléphonique entre un touriste et un employé du musée.
Le visiteur veut obtenir des renseignements pratiques sur :
– le prix d'entrée
– l'accès des jeunes enfants
– l'accès des handicapés
– l'accès des animaux domestiques
– les possibilités de restauration
– l'accès au vestiaire
– la possibilité de prendre des photos
– la boutique du musée.
L'employé lui explique chaque fois ce qui est autorisé, permis ou interdit.

GENERAL INFORMATION

The International Slavery Museum is located on the third floor of Merseyside Maritime Museum.

OPENING HOURS
Open daily 10am – 5pm.
All exhibitions, events and activities are free.

ENQUIRIES
Please go to the information desk on the ground floor.

ACCESS
Level entry, accessible toilets and wheelchair access throughout the building.
Induction loops are fitted at various points throughout the museum. Guide and hearing dogs welcome.

BABY CHANGING
Available on the ground and third floors.

LOCKERS
Available on the ground floor.
Elsewhere please do not leave bags and belongings unattended.

WHERE TO EAT
Choose from a selection of food and drinks at our café on the ground floor. Additional café on the fourth floor open weekends and school holidays.
Please note eating and drinking are not allowed on the galleries or in the foyer.

MUSEUM SHOP
Located on the ground floor, stocking a wide range of souvenirs and gifts including books, postcards and posters.

PHOTOGRAPHY
Photography is allowed for personal use but no flash or tripods please. Photography may not be allowed in certain areas – there will be notices advising you of this.

FACILITIES

International Slavery Museum • Albert Dock, Liverpool L3 4AX
Telephone 0151 478 4499 • www.liverpoolmuseums.org.uk

your task

You are going to take part in a quiz game about Liverpool based on a museum podcast. Get prepared to answer ten questions.

ENTRAÎNEZ-VOUS

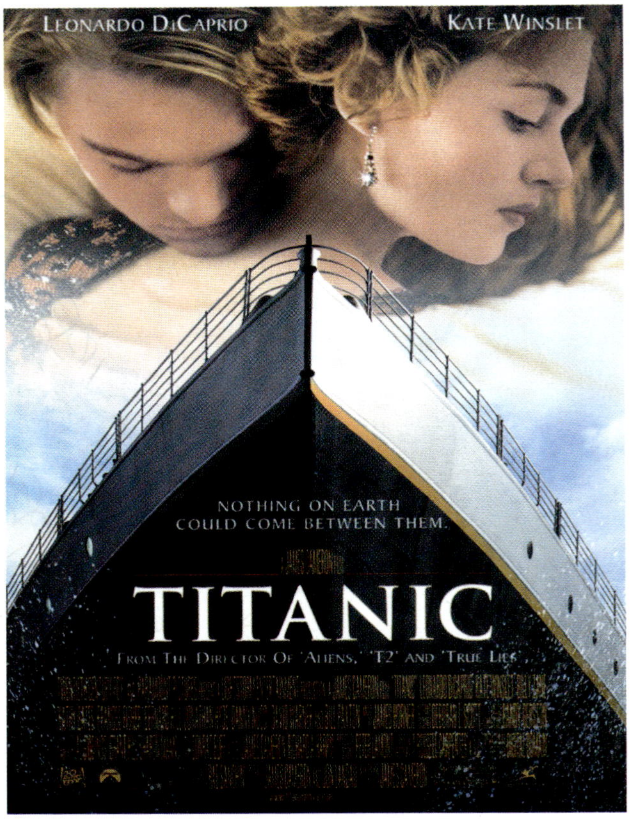

1 Anticipez l'écoute.

a. Observez la photo ci-contre et anticipez les mots que vous allez entendre dans l'enregistrement.

b. Associez chaque mot (**a** à **l**) à sa transcription phonétique (**1** à **12**).

a. liner	**e.** passenger	**i.** unsinkable
b. canoe	**f.** survivor	**j.** crash
c. Atlantic	**g.** cross	**k.** iceberg
d. ocean	**h.** sink	**l.** lifeboat

1. /laɪfbəʊt/	**5.** /ətˈlæntɪk/	**9.** /krɒs/
2. /kəˈnuː/	**6.** /səˈvaɪvə^{r}/	**10.** /kræʃ/
3. /laɪnə^{r}/	**7.** /ʌnˈsɪŋkəbl/	**11.** /aɪsbɜːg/
4. /əʊʃən/	**8.** /sɪŋk/	**12.** /pæsndʒə^{r}/

2 Écoutez la première partie de l'enregistrement.

a. Auparavant, lisez ces chiffres en anglais, à haute voix.
10 • 14 • 20 • 30 • 40 • 800 • 890 • 892 • 922 • 1,316 • 1,360 • 1912 • 1914 • 1,400 • 1,500 • 2,215 • 2,208 • 2,222

b. Maintenant, repérez les chiffres mentionnés dans l'enregistrement.

c. Associez chaque chiffre entendu en **b** à une information donnée ci-dessous.

1. Nombre de passagers à Southampton	**5.** Nombre de passagers au total
2. Nombre de canots	**6.** Nombre de victimes
3. Heure	**7.** Nombre de membres d'équipage
4. Date du départ	**8.** Date de la tragédie

3 Écoutez la seconde partie de l'enregistrement.

a. Parmi les mots de cette liste, quels sont les quatre métiers effectivement évoqués dans cette partie de l'enregistrement ?
sailor • captain • mechanic • musician • singer • pianist • agent • chairman • passenger • lookout • cook • maid

b. Associez les noms des personnages ci-dessous aux quatre métiers évoqués.
Edward Smith • Fred Fleet • Bruce Ismay • Fred Clarke

4 **Répondez à ces questions.**

1. There were 2,208 people on board the *Titanic*.
   - Right
   - Wrong

2. Were there 8, 10 or 18 musicians on the *Titanic*?
   - ______

3. The captain had always lived in Liverpool.
   - Right
   - Wrong

4. Did the liner *Carpathia* save 705 or 750 people?
   - ______

5. Did the *Titanic* leave from Southampton, Liverpool or Ireland?
   - ______

LES ÉTAPES À SUIVRE

1 **Réactivez vos connaissances.**

– Apprenez le vocabulaire et les structures vus dans cette unité et faites les exercices de la page 113.
– Revoyez vos connaissances sur la ville de Liverpool.

2 **Entraînez-vous.**

Pour ce faire, étudiez la fiche méthodologique « Comprendre un document oral » p. 130-131.

3 **Comment se déroulera le jeu ?**

a. Une fiche va vous être distribuée. Avant l'écoute, lisez attentivement les questions qui y figurent.

b. Le document audio que vous allez entendre se compose de six extraits correspondant chacun à une page d'histoire de la ville de Liverpool. Chaque extrait sera passé trois fois.

c. À la fin de chaque écoute, vous disposerez de quelques minutes pour prendre des notes et répondre aux questions posées.
– La première écoute se fera en continu sans rien noter, pour que vous puissiez prendre connaissance de chaque extrait.
– Lors de la deuxième écoute en continu, vous pourrez remplir la fiche au fur et à mesure.
– La troisième écoute vous permettra de vérifier et de compléter vos réponses.

d. Avant de ramasser les fiches, le professeur vous laissera quelques minutes pour vous relire. La qualité de l'anglais ne sera pas prise en compte, seule l'exactitude des réponses le sera. Qui dans la classe trouvera le plus de réponses correctes ?

LIFE IS ART

YOUR TASK AT THE END OF THIS UNIT

You work for a museum where a Pop Art exhibition will soon open. Two audio guides have been recorded for two works of art. Your job is to decide which one is the better one. → P. 136

TUNE IN!

PREPARE YOUR TASK →

1 Listen and draw (WB)

You will hear the description of a painting by Tom Wesselmann. Draw the objects in the right places to have a complete picture of the room.

2 Observe and speak (WB)

- What colours are used in these two paintings?
- What is represented (what, where, who)?
- What are your immediate reactions?
- What do these paintings have in common with advertisements?
- Sum up what you have learned about Pop Art. Turn to your Workbook for help.

Andy Warhol, *Five Coke Bottles*, 1962

Help!

- row /rəʊ/: *rang(ée)*
- brand name: *marque*
- mass consumption
- uniformity
- standardization
- everyday life
- geometrical
- similar
- recognizable

Edward Ruscha, *Standard Station*, 1966

1. SUPERMARKET LADY

1 Over to you

Observe this sculpture for one minute, then close your books.

a. What strikes you? What are your first impressions?
List all the elements you can remember: physical appearance, objects, colours, attitude, age and activities.

b. In your opinion, what aspect(s) of our modern life does the artist denounce?

PREPARE YOUR TASK →

2 Listen to an art fan

WB

a. Listen to Julia's reaction and interpretation of this work of art.

b. Recap: What struck her and what does this work of art mean to her?

Duane Hanson, *Supermarket Lady*, 1970

Help!

Description	Interpretation
hair roller: *bigoudi* shopping cart (US) = trolley (UK) stack of products / items: *pile de produits* wide breasts / hips: *forte poitrine / hanches larges* housewife overweight = obese /əʊ'bi:s/ tight: *serré* ugly /ʌgli/: *laid* be full to the brim: *être plein à ras bord* overeat	harsh criticism /'krɪtɪsɪzəm/: *critique acerbe* consumer society: *société de consommation* drawback /'drɔ:bæk/: *défaut* revolting /rɪ'vəʊltɪŋ/ gross /grəʊs/ (familiar): *(ici) dégoûtant* realistic brainwash into + V-ing exaggerate denounce / expose be aware of: *être conscient de*

2. I WANT MORE

1 Get ready

Look at the illustration and react. What can you guess about the themes of the song?

Mountains o' Things

The life I've always wanted
I guess[1] I'll never have
I'll be working for somebody else
Until I'm in my grave[2]
I'll be dreaming of a life of ease[3]
And mountains
Oh mountains o' things

To have a big expensive car
Drag my furs[4] on the ground
And have a maid[5] that I can tell
To bring me anything
Everyone will look at me with envy
and with greed[6]
I'll revel in[7] their attention
And mountains
Oh mountains o' things

Sweet lazy life
Champagne and caviar
I hope you'll come and find me
'Cause you know who we are
Those who deserve[8] the best in life
And know what money's worth
And those whose sole misfortune
Was having mountains o' nothing at birth

Oh they tell me
There's still time to save my soul
They tell me
Renounce all
Renounce all those material things
you gained by
Exploiting other human beings

Consume more than you need
This is the dream
Make you pauper[9]
Or make you queen
I won't die lonely
I'll have it all prearranged
A grave that's deep and wide enough
For me and all my mountains o' things

Mostly I feel lonely
Good good people are
Good people are only
My stepping stones[10]
It's gonna take all my mountains
o' things
To surround me
Keep all my enemies away
Keep my sadness and loneliness at bay[11]
I'll be dreaming, dreaming…
Dreaming…

Tracy Chapman, *Tracy Chapman* (album), 1988

1. think **2.** *tombe* **3.** life of ease: *vie aisée* **4.** *fourrures* **5.** servant **6.** *avidité* **7.** revel in: enjoy very much **8.** *méritent* **9.** *(nom archaïque) pauvre* **10.** stepping stones: *(ici) tremplins* **11.** keep at bay: *tenir à distance*

2 Understanding the lyrics WB

Turn to your Workbook for help.

3 Recap WB

Stanzas 1, 2 and 3

1. a. Who speaks (social background, probable job)?
b. What group of people does she represent?
c. What does the narrator dream of? Why? Does she believe she will fulfil her dream one day?

Stanzas 4, 5 and 6

2. a. Who speaks (social background, probable job)?
b. What type of society does the narrator live in?
c. What does money represent for the narrator in this part? Is the narrator fulfilled?

4 Go further

a. Oppose the two narrators: social backgrounds, views on money and feelings.
b. What is the moral of this song? Do you agree with it?

Help!

Stanzas 1, 2 and 3	Stanzas 4, 5 and 6
working class wealth: *richesse* status /ˈsteɪtəs/ symbol resigned: *résigné* needy luxurious /lʌɡˈzjʊərɪəs/ show off: *en mettre plein la vue* sweat /swet/ = exploit	material possessions /pəˈzeʃəns/ ≠ spiritual life overconsumption privileged fulfilled: *épanoui* earn money: *gagner de l'argent* brainwash be buried /ˈberɪd/: *être enterré* instead /ɪnˈsted/ of + V-ing: *au lieu de*

3. BIG SPLASH

David Hockney, *A Bigger Splash*, 1967

Observe and speak

a. What are your first reactions? What does this painting remind you of?

b. What type of house is this? What are the dominant colours? Where is it located?

c. What can you guess about the owner (social background, job, living conditions and type of life)? What is the atmosphere like?

d. How would the two narrators in the song (p. 128) react to this painting? Why?

e. Does this painting make you dream? Why? Why not?

4. FAME

1 President Elect

Who is portrayed? What other elements are represented?

James Rosenquist, *President Elect*, 1960-1961

2 The Swinging Sixties

PREPARE YOUR TASK →

a. Listen to a history teacher who will give you more information about the Sixties. Turn to your Workbook for help.

b. What characterized that decade in the United States? What were the main events?

c. To what extent does the painting above illustrate this period of American history?

3 Kennedy's assassination

a. Read the following article. Sum up the event in a few words.

President Kennedy is slain by assassin in Dallas

Dallas, Texas, November 22, 1963

President John F. Kennedy was killed today when a sniper fired three rifle shots at the presidential limousine as it drove along Elm Street in downtown Dallas. The nation was in shock at the loss of its elegant, dynamic and popular young President.

The shooting occurred at 12:35.

"Oh no! Oh no!" Jacqueline Kennedy cried over and over, cradling his head in her lap as the limousine raced to the Parkland Memorial Hospital three miles away. At 1 p.m., John F. Kennedy, America's youngest elected President, was pronounced dead.

Chronicle of America, 1989

b. Observe the painting opposite and listen to the audio guide of *Sixteen Jackies* by Andy Warhol /ˈwɔːhəʊl/ (UK), /ˈwɔːrhoʊl/ (US).

Andy Warhol, *Sixteen Jackies*, 1964

c. Use the information given in the audio guide to answer the following questions:
- What devices did the painter use here (source materials, repetitions and contrasts)?
- Observe the different portraits. What feelings are revealed? What moments in Jackie Kennedy's life do the pictures correspond to?
- What does Warhol want to tell us about this woman and the role of the media in her life?
- What are your reactions to this painting?

Help!

Jackie Kennedy's life	Techniques	Interpretation
first lady widow: *veuve* funeral: *enterrement* grief /griːf/: *chagrin* beaming: *très souriante* in mourning /ˈmɔːrnɪŋ/: *en deuil*	device: *procédé* silkscreen: *sérigraphie* collage /kɒˈlɑːʒ/ photograph: *photographie* close-up: *plan rapproché* similar replicate: *reproduire*	fame: *renommée* public figure icon /ˈaɪkɒn/: *figure emblématique* haunted /ˈhɔːntɪd/ by death mortal embody = personify

5. PLEASE

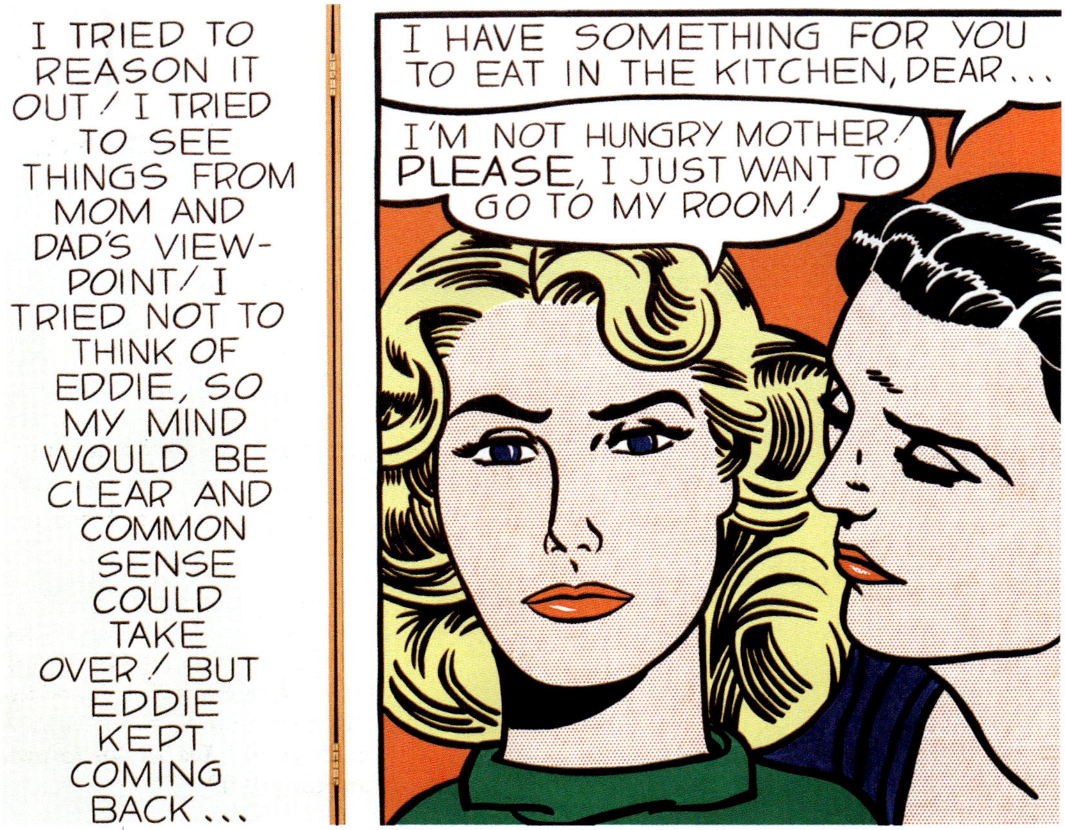

Roy Lichtenstein, *Eddie Diptych*, 1962

Observe and speak

1 What does this painting remind you of? Why?
What strikes you? What are the dominant colours?

2 Read the title of the painting and the definition (opposite) taken from *The Oxford Pocket Dictionary of Current English*.

a. On the left-hand side
– Who is speaking? Justify by quoting from the text.
– Who is she thinking about? What can we guess about her feelings?
– What is happening in her life?

b. On the right-hand side
– How does the daughter react to her mother's words?
– What can you guess about their relationship?

Diptych /ˈdɪptɪk/
n. a painting on two hinged wooden panels that may be closed like a book.

3 **a.** Imagine what happened to the young girl before.
b. Imagine the dialogue between the parents and the girl.
c. Imagine what will happen next.

4 How do you react to this painting?
What do you think of the girl's situation?

5 If this painting were the cover of a music album, what would be the title?
Can you think of artists who might use this painting for their CD cover? Explain your choice(s).

Help!

- comic: *bande dessinée*
- print: *reproduction*
- size: *taille*
- canvas /ˈkænvəs/: *toile*
- frame: *cadre, vignette*
- speech balloon
- thick outline: *contour épais*
- dot: *point*
- parody
- ordinary = everyday life
- average /ˈævərɪdʒ/: *moyen*
- enlarge /ɪnˈlɑːdʒ/: *agrandir*

Language at work

Improve your pronunciation MP3

1 **Classez les mots suivants selon qu'ils sont accentués sur la première ou la seconde syllabe. Ensuite, vérifiez à l'écoute.**

photograph • success • ideal • public • figure • icon • contrast • popular

2 **Quel est le point commun à chacune de ces deux listes de mots ?**

a. *variation • repetition • intrusion • exhibition • collection • auction*
b. *ironic • pathetic • melodramatic • tragic*

À l'écoute, repérez la syllabe accentuée. Quelles règles pouvez-vous en déduire ?

3 **Lisez à haute voix cette citation d'Andy Warhol (1928-1987) à l'aide des indications fournies, puis écoutez l'enregistrement.**

Les groupes de souffle sont marqués | à l'intérieur d'une phrase et || à la fin d'une phrase. Les mots accentués sont en caractères gras.

"What's **great** about **this country** | is that **America started** the **tradition** | where the **richest consumers buy essentially** the **same things as** the **poorest** ||. You can be **watching TV** | and **see Coca-Cola** |, and you **know** that | the **President drinks Coke** |, **Liz Taylor drinks Coke** |, and **just think, you can drink Coke, too** ||. A **Coke** is a **Coke** | and **no amount** of **money** can **get** you a **better Coke** | than the **one** the **bum** on the **corner** is **drinking** ||. **All** the **Cokes** are the **same** | and **all** the **Cokes** are **good** ||. **Liz Taylor knows** it |, the **President knows** it |, the **bum knows** it |, and **you know** it ||."

Build up your vocabulary

1 **Classez ces mots en deux colonnes en fonction du champ lexical auquel ils appartiennent : *techniques used, colours*. Aidez-vous d'un dictionnaire si nécessaire.**

*bright • id**e**ntical • v**i**vid • g**a**rish • c**o**ntrast • g**au**dy • slight • repet**i**tion • r**e**plicate • blurred • s**i**lkscreen p**ai**nting*

2 **Rédigez une description physique de ces deux personnages.**

Utilisez la liste de mots ci-dessous et un dictionnaire si nécessaire.

bald /bɔːld/
*sl**ou**ching* /ˈslaʊtʃɪŋ/
*pot-b**e**llied*
tall
*attr**a**ctive*
***bea**rded* /ˈbɪədɪd/
plump
*m**a**de-up*
*smart = **e**legant*
stout /staʊt/
*f**a**shionable*
*slim = sl**e**nder*
*sl**o**ppy* /ˈslɒpi/
*sk**i**nny*
*long-h**ai**red*

Language at work

Le quasi-certain, le possible et l'impossible : *must, may / might, can't*

Les modaux sont utilisés par l'énonciateur :

– soit pour évaluer les chances qu'un événement a de se produire (degré de probabilité)
– soit pour exprimer la contrainte, l'absence de contrainte ou la capacité.

1 Observez.

Dans quels énoncés *must* n'exprime-t-il pas une quasi-certitude ?

a. *The house is huge. The owner must be wealthy.*
b. *I must call him immediately, it's urgent.*
c. *The girl is crying. She must be miserable.*
d. *I know it's difficult, but you must be courageous.*
e. *She doesn't want to speak to him anymore. She must be very angry with him.*
→ Déduisez les deux valeurs de *must*.

2 Quelle est la valeur de *can't* dans ces deux phrases ?

"The girl is eighteen." "She can't be that young!"
"The woman was shopping with her rollers on." "It can't be true. Are you kidding me?"

3 Quasi-certain ou possible / peu probable ?

a. Classez les énoncés suivants en deux colonnes en fonction de la valeur du modal.

– *The house is empty. The owner must be outside.*
– *There are palm trees in their garden – they may live in Malibu.*
– *The girl looks quite young – she must be in her twenties.*
– *She may change her mind and call him.*
– *The girl has not spoken a word for days. Her parents must be worried.*
– *They might make it up* (se réconcilier) *one day, but I doubt it.*

Quasi-certain	Possible / peu probable

b. En fonction du sens de la phrase, reformulez chacun des énoncés ci-dessus à l'aide de *perhaps* ou *certainly*, puis traduisez-les.

4 Présent, passé ou avenir ?

a. La forme modale en gras porte-t-elle sur le présent, le passé ou l'avenir ? Classez les énoncés suivants en trois colonnes.

– *She doesn't want to call Eddy – they* ***must have quarrelled****.*
– *There is nobody at home – they* ***may have gone*** *shopping.*
– *The artist* ***may want*** *to warn us against overconsumption.*
– *She doesn't want to see him anymore – she* ***must be*** *fed up with him.*
– *He's such a nice person – he* ***can't have said*** *such horrible things.*
– *She* ***may find*** *another solution soon.*
– *She* ***may be dreaming****.*

b. Récapitulez. Avec les modaux *must, can't, may* on utilise :

– le modal + ... pour parler d'un fait situé dans le présent ou l'avenir
– le modal + ... + ... pour parler d'une action qui se déroule au moment où l'on parle
– le modal + ... + ... pour parler d'un fait situé dans le passé.

Practice

1 Repérez l'expression française qui indique le degré de probabilité puis trouvez le modal correspondant en anglais.

a. Elle est sans doute fâchée.
b. Elle écoutera peut-être ses conseils.
c. Elle ne sait pas trop si elle va lui téléphoner.
d. Elle va peut-être lui téléphoner.
e. Il se peut qu'il achète ce tableau.
f. Ce tableau ne peut pas être à la Tate Modern, il est trop ancien.
g. Ce tableau est sûrement au Museum of Modern Art.

2 Réécrivez ces phrases en employant *may* + base verbale ou *must* + base verbale.

a. I'm sure he is lonely.
b. Her parents are certainly supportive.
c. Perhaps her parents will manage to cheer her up.
d. Perhaps the woman is in her forties.
e. Nobody answers the phone. Perhaps he is abroad.
f. Perhaps they know the truth.
g. They certainly know the truth.
h. Perhaps he will tell her the whole truth.

3 Traduisez ces énoncés en français.

a. He must be a film director.
b. She must have hurt his feelings.
c. He may write to her and apologize.
d. He may have had an affair with another woman.
e. She might forgive him.

4 *M-Maybe* (1965)

a. Who is the painter? How do you know?
b. Where is the girl? What is she doing? Who is she thinking about?
c. Imagine why she is wearing gloves /glʌvz/ *(gants)*?
d. What can we guess about her age, her social background and her feelings?
e. What can we guess about the man's job?
f. Imagine what may have happened to him.
g. What might happen next?

Your task

You work for a museum where a Pop Art exhibition will soon open. Two audio guides have been recorded for two works of art. Your job is to decide which one is the better one.

LES ÉTAPES À SUIVRE

1 Avant l'écoute WB

a. Quels sont les critères pour sélectionner le meilleur audioguide ? Voici une liste incomplète de points à prendre en compte. Trouvez ceux qui manquent.

1. Introduction
- nature (painting, sculpture, drawing...)
- dominant theme(s)

2. Striking elements
- who? famous? unknown?
- probable job / occupation
- age
- ...
- ...

3. Techniques used by the artist
- repetition, contrast, collage
- ...

4. Interpretation
- what do the different elements symbolize?
- links with other Pop Art works of art?
- ...

5. Overall impressions
- informative
- convincing ≠ unconvincing
- well-organized
- complete
- shallow = superficial
- accurate

(to be completed)

Duane Hanson, *Young Woman Shopper*, 1973

b. Relisez vos notes sur les documents étudiés. Sachez replacer le *Pop Art* dans son contexte historique.

2 Pendant l'écoute

Écoutez les enregistrements, la liste des critères sous les yeux. Pour chaque audioguide (1 à 4), cochez les cases lorsqu'un critère vous semble rempli.

3 Après l'écoute

Quels sont les points faibles et les points forts de chaque enregistrement ? Choisissez le meilleur audioguide et justifiez votre choix.

Andy Warhol, *Ten Marilyn*, 1967

RAPPELS

a. Comment former le comparatif.

-er ... than *The second one is shallower than the first one.*	***more ... than*** *It's more convincing than the other one.*	***not ... so (as) ... as*** *It's not as organized as the first one.*

b. Le français peut utiliser le superlatif pour faire une comparaison entre deux éléments à l'intérieur d'un groupe. En anglais, il faut utiliser le comparatif :
*The **more** informative of the two audio guides is the first one.*

COMPRENDRE UN DOCUMENT ORAL

Pour améliorer votre écoute et comprendre un message oral avec de plus en plus d'efficacité, il est nécessaire d'acquérir des stratégies.

A Accédez au sens d'un document oral

1 Anticipez avant l'écoute.

> Hooray! Our cyclists won 14 medals in total in Beijing, including eight golds.

a. Observez ce titre de journal. À votre avis, de quoi va parler l'enregistrement n°1 ?

b. Mobilisez le lexique que vous connaissez autour de ce thème.

c. Émettez des hypothèses sur la nature de l'enregistrement :
– un reportage en direct sur une course
– des informations à la radio
– une remise de médaille ou de récompense
– l'interview d'un protagoniste
– un *talk show* avec plusieurs célébrités
– le résumé de la carrière d'un champion

2 Jouez au détective.

Écoutez le début de l'enregistrement n°1.

a. Quels indices sonores avez-vous entendus ?
– musique (joyeuse, triste, moderne, classique, dans un cadre privé, un lieu public...)
– cris (de joie, de rage, de révolte, de douleur...)
– applaudissements
– rires
– bruits de fond (gens qui passent, qui parlent, voitures, train, animaux, phénomènes météo...)

b. Combien de voix avez-vous repérées (homme ou femme, adulte ou enfant...) ?

c. Ces voix traduisent-elles des sentiments particuliers (joie, tristesse, exaltation, peur...) ?

d. Avez-vous repéré des accents particuliers qui pourraient indiquer dans quel pays se passe la scène ?

e. Grâce à tous ces indices, essayez de déterminer :
– où se passe la scène
– à quelle occasion
– qui sont les personnes présentes

3 Affinez votre compréhension.

Écoutez la suite de l'enregistrement n°1.

a. Quels mots de la liste ci-dessous avez-vous effectivement entendus ?
team • *time* • *gold* • *silver* • *bronze* • *medallist* • *specialist* • *West Champions League* • *GB Cup World Championship* • *friendship* • *honour* • *horror* • *sporting* • *supporting* • *heroes* • *champions* • *bikes* • *hike* • *wrong* • *strong* • *successful* • *dreadful*

b. Sur papier libre, classez-les par catégorie dans un tableau de ce type :

Cycling	Athletes	Rewards	Competitions

c. D'après vous, qui est Victoria Pendleton ?

d. À qui fait-elle référence quand elle dit : *we*, *us* et *they* ?

e. Résumez en français ce qui se passe et ce qui est dit.

B Rentrez dans le détail

1 Repérez des chiffres.

a. Lisez ce texte.

The resident population of the UK was ... 1 in mid- ... 2 .
England is the most populous part of the UK, with ... 3 million inhabitants.
Almost one ... 4 of England's people live in the southeast, around London.
... 5 million people live in Scotland. ... 6 percent of the population in Scotland is concentrated in the lowland area where Glasgow and Edinburgh are located.
Wales, with ... 7 million people, is also mountainous.
Since ... 8 , the government has been pursuing a policy of devolution, leading in ... 9 to an elected Scottish Parliament and Welsh Assembly. In ... 10 , Londoners elected their first mayor and assembly.
The 2001 census counted more than ... 11 million Asians (mostly Indians and Pakistanis) and ... 12 million Blacks (from Africa and the Caribbean).
The life expectancy is ... 13 .
The literacy rate is ... 14 percent.

b. Écoutez l'enregistrement n°2 et repérez les chiffres entendus.

c. Maintenant, complétez les chiffres manquants ci-dessus sur papier libre.

2 Repérez les mots utilisés.

Écoutez l'enregistrement n°3. Dans chaque phrase, à quelle forme écrite correspond ce que vous entendez (parfois sous forme contractée) ?

– Phrases 1, 2 et 3 :	*They're*	*There are*	*Their*
– Phrases 4, 5 et 6 :	*He is*	*His*	*He has*
– Phrases 7, 8 et 9 :	*Your*	*You're*	*You've*
– Phrases 10, 11 et 12 :	*Who's (has)*	*Who's (is)*	*Whose*

3 Repérez le ton de voix utilisé.

Écoutez l'enregistrement n°4. Vous allez entendre six phrases qui révèlent chacune une attitude différente. Associez chaque phrase au sentiment qu'elle exprime.

a. reproche
b. surprise
c. colère
d. mépris
e. regret
f. joie

4 Repérez les liaisons consonne-voyelle.

a. Écoutez la première partie de l'enregistrement n°5 et observez les liaisons consonne-voyelle.

When I was a child, we used to move a lot throughout the country. After moving to a new town, we would immediately go to the library to get membership and as many books as we could.

b. Lisez la suite du script et dites où doivent se faire les liaisons avant de vérifier à l'écoute.

After that, we would do nothing but read all day long and we enjoyed listening to my mother reading to us in the evening. That's how I got a passion for books and all kinds of literature.

C À votre tour !

Écoutez l'enregistrement n°6 deux fois sans rien noter. Mémorisez autant d'éléments que vous pouvez. Puis résumez en français ce que vous avez compris.

ÉVALUATION

J'ÉVALUE MES PROGRÈS

À la suite de ces trois unités, évaluez vos progrès et faites le bilan de vos compétences.

Martyn Ford, *Mind the Gap!*

MP3

1 Je me prépare

Listen to this recording once, don't write anything. Listen again without a pause then answer the following questions on a separate sheet of paper.

1. Identity	14 POINTS
a. Name:	0,5 POINT
b. Surname:	0,5 POINT
c. Age:	0,5 POINT
d. Place of birth:	0,5 POINT
e. Place of residence as a child:	2 POINTS
f. Place of residence now:	2 POINTS
– Type of residence:	2 POINTS
– Type of area:	2 POINTS
– Region of England:	2 POINTS
g. Pets:	2 POINTS

2. Parents' activities	5 POINTS
a. What do the parents have?	2 POINTS
b. In your opinion what is their job?	3 POINTS

3. School	8 POINTS
a. Where did the girl go to school?	2 POINTS
b. What type of school did she go to?	3 POINTS
c. What did she study there?	3 POINTS

4. Hobby — 8 POINTS

a. What did she do in her free time? — 2 POINTS

b. Where did she practise this hobby? — 3 POINTS

c. How often did she practise this hobby? — 3 POINTS

5. Characteristics of the region — 5 POINTS

a. Pick out the names of a town and a city. — 2 POINTS

b. What is each of them famous for? (two answers) — 1,5 POINT EACH

TOTAL: .../40 PTS

2 Je m'auto-corrige

Maintenant, comparez vos réponses à celles de la fiche corrigée disponible sur le site compagnon et comptabilisez vos points.

JE FAIS LE BILAN

Analysez vos résultats à l'aide de cette grille d'évaluation où sont définis les différents paliers de compétences en compréhension de l'oral.

Je peux...	Paliers
... repérer des noms de personnes, des mots isolés, des noms de lieux, des dates, des phrases simples.	A2 en cours d'acquisition
... comprendre un message contenant des mots et des expressions que je suis censé(e) connaître.	A2
... comprendre des phrases simples évoquant la vie quotidienne si la personne qui s'adresse à moi articule et parle distinctement et lentement.	A2
... comprendre les éléments principaux de sujets concernant la vie quotidienne si on me parle lentement et en articulant.	B1
... comprendre un message oral si le message est court et si la personne s'exprime dans un anglais standard.	B1
... comprendre l'implicite d'un document oral.	en route vers B2

ÉVALUATION

Vous allez maintenant entendre un court enregistrement d'environ 2 minutes. Votre professeur va vous distribuer une fiche que vous devrez compléter. Soyez attentifs aux consignes qui sont données avant d'écouter l'enregistrement.
La qualité de l'anglais ne sera pas prise en compte, seule l'exactitude de la réponse le sera. Une fois l'évaluation terminée, votre professeur pourra déterminer à quel palier vous vous situez par rapport à la grille d'évaluation du Cadre Européen Commun de Référence pour les Langues.

Broken English, Zoe R. Cassavetes, 2008 (starring Parker Posey and Melvil Poupaud)

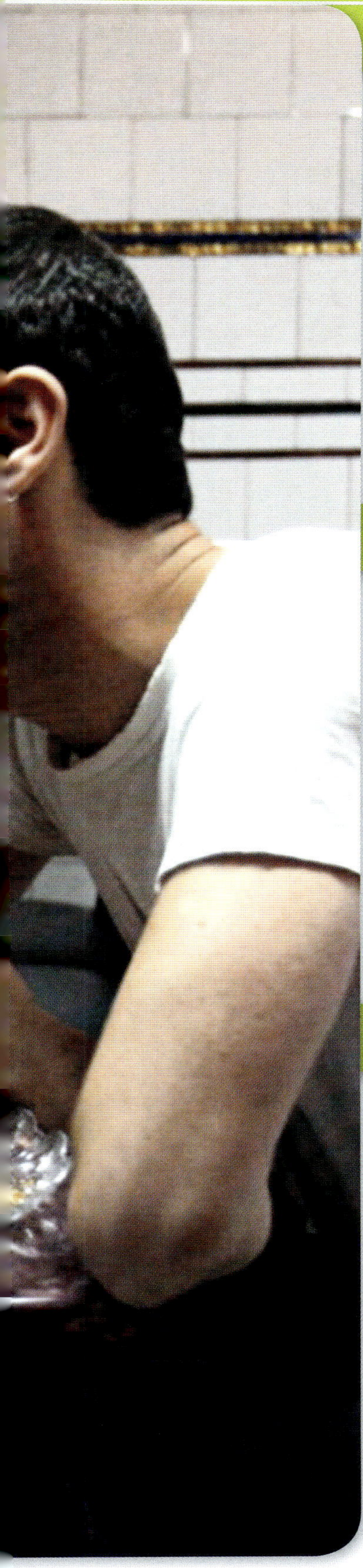

Unit 11 A WORLD OF GEEKS

	YOUR TASK
• **What are the dangers for computer addicts?** • **What is the impact of new technologies on our life?**	Your school is hosting a debate on new technologies. You are one of the following participants: a teenager, a parent, a child psychologist or a video game designer. You will debate on: *Are new technologies harmful to teenagers?* → P. 154

Unit 12 MOTHER EARTH

	YOUR TASK
• **What dangers threaten our planet?** • **Be environmentalists. Protect our blue planet**	World Challenge is organizing an advertising campaign to protect the planet. You are on the panel of judges. Choose the ad you find the most effective. Confront your points of view, and try to convince your classmates. Then decide who the winner will be. → P. 165

Unit 13 ALL THE WORLD'S A STAGE

	YOUR TASK
• **Learn and interpret a famous scene from Oscar Wilde or Jane Austen.**	In groups you will choose one scene you have studied and stage it. Imagine the setting, invent the stage directions, learn your part by heart and act it out in front of an audience. → P. 178

Unit 11

A WORLD OF GEEKS

YOUR TASK AT THE END OF THIS UNIT

Your school is hosting a debate on new technologies. You are one of the following participants: a teenager, a parent, a child psychologist or a video game designer. You will debate on: *Are new technologies harmful to teenagers*?

→ p. 154

TUNE IN!

1 Are you a geek[1]?

Do this quiz to find out. Answer on a separate piece of paper.

1. Have you got your own computer?
2. On average, how many hours a day do you spend on your computer?
3. What do you use your computer for?
   - a to check e-mails
   - b to chat
   - c to buy and sell things
   - d to play games (on your own or with other players on the web)
   - e to search for information
   - f to type a text, create a document
   - g to watch videos or DVDs
   - h to listen to music
4. Do you own a mobile phone (GB) / cellphone (US)?
5. How long have you had one?
6. How often do you get a new one?
7. Your best friend has taken a funny photo and sent it to you; do you know how to download it onto your computer?
8. When the class is over, what do you do?
   - a You read a book.
   - b You chat with your friends.
   - c You talk on your cellphone.
   - d You text your friends.
   - e You listen to your MP3 player.
   - f You chat on MSN.
9. To wish your friends and family a Happy New Year what do you do?
   - a You send them a text message on your cellphone.
   - b You write them an e-mail or send them an e-greetings card.
   - c You write them a nice letter and send it by post.

1. /giːk/

2 Confront your results

Find out what your classmates have answered.

a. Work in groups. One student in each group gives three interesting facts about his / her group members. Decide who is a geek.

PREPARE YOUR TASK → **b.** Then the other students react to what has been said.

- In my group...
- Everybody + sing. ...
- One student out of three...
- We spend three hours a day + V-ing...

- To me...
- What you are saying is shocking...
- I'm surprised / amazed...
- In my opinion, he / she... should / shouldn't + BV...

I. THE HIKER

WB

1 Get ready

– Have you ever gone hiking in the mountains? Did you like it? Why / Why not? If not, would you like to go? Why / Why not?

PREPARE YOUR TASK → – Confront your points of view, and list the arguments given.

– Find out who agrees or disagrees with you, and try to convince your classmates that your arguments are the best.

Owen Sherwood, 2005

2 Observe and speak

a. React to this cartoon (place, character, activity, cartoonist's intention, personal impression and reactions).

b. Then, give advice to the hiker. In your opinion, what should he do / be doing?

c. Report on your findings. Give this cartoon a title.

– This hiker shouldn't carry...
– This geek should listen to...
– He'd better look at...
– He should be walking and...

Help!

Hiking	Equipment	Interpretation
landscape peaceful = quiet breathe /briːð/ fresh air climb /klaɪm/ carry /ˈkæri/ enjoy + V-ing do physical exercise spend time + V-ing	heavy backpack wireless device /dɪˈvaɪs/ laptop: *ordinateur portable* screen webcam headphones plug in: *se brancher*	ridiculous = preposterous /prɪˈpɒstərəs/ = absurd /əbˈsɜːd/ be hooked /hʊkt/ on = be addicted /əˈdɪktɪd/ to be engrossed /ɪnˈgrəʊst/ in: *être plongé dans* stare at the screen: *regarder fixement l'écran* it's a shame... , he should...: *il est dommage que... , il devrait...* instead /ɪnˈsted/ of + V-ing

2. CELLPHONE MANIA

WB

A Sad and lonely? Download a virtual girlfriend

Men, are you tired of the time, trouble and expense of having a girlfriend? Irritated by the difficulty of finding a new one? Eberhard Schöneburg, the chief executive of the software maker Artificial Life Inc. of Hong Kong, may have found the answer: a virtual girlfriend named Vivienne who goes wherever you go.

Vivienne likes to be taken to movies and bars. She loves to be given virtual flowers and chocolates, and she can translate six languages if you travel overseas. [...]

If you marry her in a virtual ceremony, you even end up with a virtual mother-in-law[1] who really does call you in the middle of the night on your cellphone to ask where you are and whether you have been treating her daughter right. [...]

"It's a little bit for the losers," said Rick Wong, a 32-year-old off-duty security guard, who nonetheless[2] added that, "even people who have girlfriends, well, girlfriends are not perfect, so they may play anyway." [...]

Artificial Life is not suggesting Vivienne is any substitute for a flesh-and-blood[3] girlfriend. "I hope they think of her as a companion," said MaryAnna Donaldson, the company's creative content editor, "and will see her as a practice round[4] before the real one."

The New York Times, February 24, 2005

1. the mother of your husband or wife **2.** *cependant* **3.** real / alive **4.** training

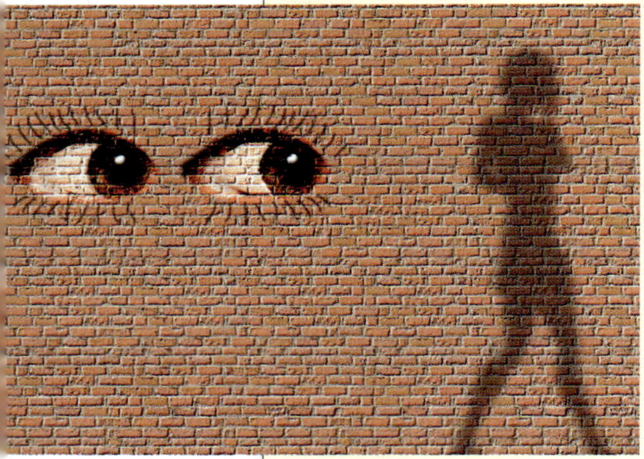

B Selling surveillance to anxious parents

Kevin Reynolds, a [...] father of two, is confronting a quandary[1]: Should he put his daughters under electronic surveillance[2]?

It's a question more [American] parents will face in the next months, thanks to new technology that lets them use cellphones to monitor[3] their children's location. [...] The system track cellphones by satellite, allowing parents to look on the Internet to make sure their children arrived safely, say, at school or at a friend's house.

"If you don't do it and something happens to your kids, how would you feel?" said Mr. Reynolds, 49, contemplating[4] giving such phones to his daughters, ages 4 and 8. But he is also wary of[5] being overly[6] intrusive.

"It's Big Brother on a kid's level," he said. "What's it like to live in a world where everybody has a device that tracks where we are?" [...] For $19.99, parents can program a child's phone with geographic boundaries[7] [...]. When a child leaves the area, the parent will get a text message indicating the perimeter has been breached[8]. [...] "It's a tool to enhance peace of mind," Mr. Daniels said, though he acknowledged that the system might not always work.

"You'll always have that risk that the kid can turn off the phone, destroy the phone, take off the battery," he said. [...] "We don't see this service as being an alternative to a parent, or as a babysitter for the parent."

The New York Times, May 3, 2006

1. /ˈkwɒndəri/ problem **2.** /sɜːˈveɪləns/ **3.** watch and check **4.** thinking about
5. is wary /ˈweəri/ of: *hésite beaucoup à* **6.** too **7.** limits **8.** not respected

1 Understanding the articles

Each group reads one article and fills in the corresponding column of the grid (use a separate piece of paper).

	A virtual girlfriend	Surveillance
Specificity of this cellphone		
Potential buyers and users		
Advantages of this new device		
Problems caused by this device		
Your opinion on this device		

2 Pros and cons

A reporter in each group presents one of the mobile phone devices to the class. Discuss the advantages and drawbacks of the two devices.

- Our **a**rticle deals with a c**e**llphone dev**i**ce which...
- This dev**i**ce all**o**ws you to + BV...
- Thanks to this dev**i**ce...
- Inst**ea**d of c**a**lling your child / qu**a**rrelling with your g**i**rlfriend / b**oy**friend...

PREPARE YOUR TASK →

3 Role play

a. Look at the illustration opposite and react.

b. – Imagine your friend wants a virtual girlfriend or boyfriend. What do you tell him / her?

– What would you say to parents who want to adopt cellphone surveillance?

– Have a look at the vocabulary below. Select the words that you will use to talk to your friend / your parents.

– Find arguments to support your opinion (see the third column in the toolbox below).

EXAMPLE: This system is ***unfair****, parents shouldn't be spying on their children!*

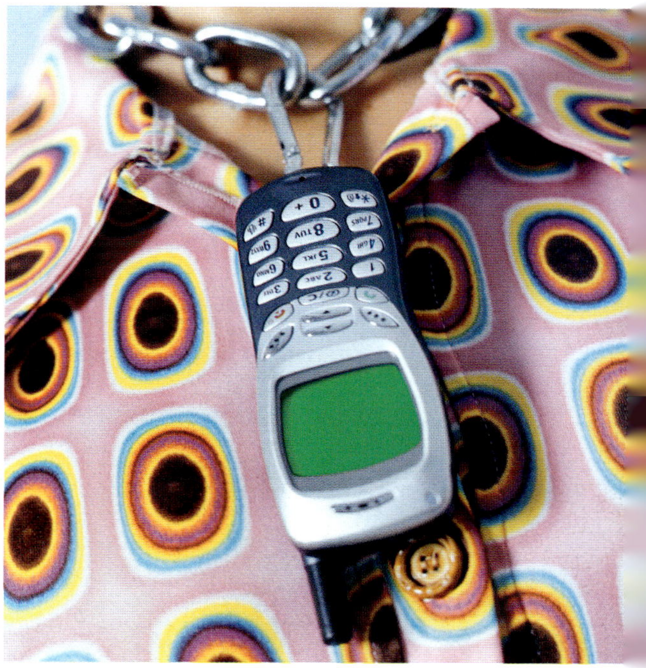

Help!

Virtual girlfriend	Surveillance	Reactions
waste of m**o**ney world of f**a**ntasy = imagin**a**tion s**u**bstitute for... lack /læk/ of warmth /wɔːmθ/, of disc**u**ssion be cut off from + GN face re**a**lity build a rel**a**tionship	s**a**fety peace of mind resp**o**nsible / rel**i**able: *digne de confiance* feel reass**u**red l**i**mit one's fr**ee**dom w**o**rry /ˈwʌri/ spy on: *espionner* trust sb: *faire confiance à qqn* fear / be afr**ai**d of + V-ing im**a**gine the worst /wɜːst/ keep from + V-ing prev**e**nt from + V-ing be for one's own good	l**u**dicrous /ˈluːdɪkrəs/ = rid**i**culous path**e**tic: *pitoyable, nul* al**a**rming unf**ai**r **u**seless disresp**e**ctful If I were you, I would / w**ou**ldn't + BV You'd b**e**tter + BV You must be j**o**king! Are you k**i**dding? /ˈkɪdɪŋ/

3. TURN IT OFF!

WB

Computer kids

A Dutch clinic that has begun offering the world's first treatment for computer game addicts has been overwhelmed with pleas for help[1] from parents and children all over the world.

"It's amazing, I've never seen anything like it," said Keith Bakker, the American director of the [...] clinic in Amsterdam. "The phone has been ringing constantly. Computer game addiction is obviously an even greater problem than we imagined."

[...] The clinic will begin treating two teenagers from Britain this week and other sufferers are being signed in from America and Asia.

"These are perfectly decent[2] kids whose lives have been taken over by an addiction," said Bakker, a former[3] drug addict.

"Some have given up school so they can play games. They have no friends. They don't speak to their parents."

Last week Bakker took his first group of "gamers", as he calls them, on a parachuting trip to take their minds off their computers. Treatment also involves meditation, fitness training and group therapy. [...]

Tim, a 21-year-old from Utrecht, said he had hardly left his bedroom for five years because he was so obsessed by his computer games. "My room was a mess," he said. "Curtains drawn, pizza boxes, empty bottles and junk food wrappers[4] everywhere..." [...]

His parents were frightened of him because, weighing more than 21 stone[5], he was too strong for them to confront. Eventually they threatened to kick him out unless he enrolled[6] for a month of therapy. [...]

South Korea and China, where people are particularly passionate about computer games, are discussing with manufacturers ways of discouraging compulsive behaviour.

Bakker thinks that European and American distributors should issue warnings about the dangers [of addiction].

The Sunday Times, July 23, 2006

1. overwhelmed with pleas for help: *débordée par des appels à l'aide* **2.** *normaux* **3.** *ancien* **4.** *emballages*
5. 21 stone = 134 kg **6.** unless he enrolled: *à moins qu'il ne s'inscrive*

1 Understanding the text

a. What information given in the text do these places refer to?
Amsterdam • Utrecht • Britain • America and Asia • China and South Korea

b. Classify the following phrases (goups of words) in two columns and give each column a title.

some have given up school (l. 10)

don't speak to their parents (l. 10)

no friends (l. 10)

whose lives have been taken over by an addiction (l. 8)

parachuting trip (l. 12)

meditation, fitness training and group therapy (l. 13)

c. Read the text from line 15 to line 20 to find the following information about Tim:
nationality • age • physical appearance • family background • hobby

2 Follow-up work

a. Imagine five questions you would ask to someone addicted to computer games.

b. Choose the adjectives that best describe a computer addict: shy • withdrawn • athletic • cheerful • outgoing • self-centred • ill-at-ease • awkward • ambitious • immature • fit.

c. Imagine the consequences of addiction on these addicts' everyday lives.

d. Suggest solutions to help computer addicts put an end to their addictions.

PREPARE YOUR TASK →

3 Discuss

Computer games can be addictive. Find arguments and concrete examples.

Help!

Game	Addiction
adventure graphics entertaining /ˌentəˈteɪnɪŋ/ imaginative have fun = enjoy oneself take pleasure in + V-ing increase imagination improve skills discover (new worlds)	illegal substances damage *(indénombrable): dégâts* health disorders addiction consequence harmful ≠ harmless distracting: *qui rend fou* moody

- It is worse /wɜːs/ than...
- It is the same... as...
- I totally believe that...
- Indeed...
- You're right, what's more...
- I see your point but...
- On the one hand... on the other hand...
- Don't you think that...?

4 Growing up online

WB

Listen to Dr. Shepherd, a clinical psychologist, talking about teenagers and new technologies. Discover what they do online and how parents react to children who spend most of their time online.

4. TECH I.T. EASY

1 Observe and speak

Look at the cartoons carefully. What is the message in each of them? Point out the similarities and differences between them.

2 Your point of view

In your opinion, which cartoon is:
- the most critical of technologies?
- the funniest?
- the most / the least true-to-life?

Compare your views with those of the rest of the class.

1

"IT'S NOT A NICOTINE PATCH, IT'S A CD-ROM. I'M TRYING TO OVERCOME COMPUTER ADDICTION."

2

"Romeo and Juliet met online in a chat room. But their relationship ended tragically when Juliet's computer crashed."

3

"I just want a few minutes of peace and quiet — LEAVE ME ALONE!!!!!!!!"

4

Language at work

Improve your pronunciation MP3

1 Comment se prononcent les voyelles en orange ?

Prononcez les mots suivants à haute voix et classez-les en deux colonnes selon la prononciation des voyelles en orange : /iː/ comme *leave* ou /ɪ/ comme *fish* (sur papier libre). Vérifiez ensuite à l'écoute.

screen • chip • disease • peaceful • responsible • geek • beep • print • breathe • bit • kid • ridiculous • decent • video • device • listen

2 Accentuation des mots à suffixes

a. Prononcez les mots suivants à haute voix en faisant particulièrement attention à l'accent de mot. Vérifiez ensuite à l'écoute.

technician • connection • addiction • electronic • electricity • compatible • compatibility • security

b. Observez où tombe l'accent par rapport aux terminaisons en orange et complétez la phrase suivante : pour les mots se terminant par *-ian*, *-ion*, *-ic*, *-ible* et *-ity*, l'accent principal tombe sur la syllabe … .

3 Écoutez les phrases enregistrées et écrivez-les.

Build up your vocabulary

1 Associez ces mots aux dessins correspondants.

a. *keyboard* **b.** *mouse* **c.** *laptop* **d.** *desktop* **e.** *screen* **f.** *click* **g.** *plug in* **h.** *scroll* /skrəʊl/

2 Complétez ce texte avec les mots de la liste. Faites les changements grammaticaux nécessaires.

broadband • browse /braʊz/ *• crash • download • log in • surf on • wireless*

I spend a lot of time … [1] the Internet. Sometimes, I … [2] my password to read my e-mails. I can … [3] everywhere because I have a … [4] connection. It is also fast thanks to the … [5] connection. Sometimes, I … [6] some videos. It's awful when my computer … [7] .

Language at work

La forme *V-ing*

1 Lisez ces phrases et repérez les mots terminés par *-ing*.

a. *Instead of do**ing** his homework, he played on his computer.*
b. *Find**ing** a girlfriend is a lot of trouble.*
c. *You are addicted to video games when you can't help play**ing** every day.*
d. *My parents always criticize me for stay**ing** up too late at night.*
e. *I spend most of my free time chatt**ing** on MSN.*
f. *Is this video game worth buy**ing**?*

Ces mots en ***-ing*** sont-ils formés à partir d'un nom, d'un adjectif, d'un verbe ou d'un adverbe ?

2 Observez.

He loves books.
He loves reading.

a. Quelles sont la nature et la fonction de *books* et de *reading* ?
b. Un gérondif peut parfois être remplacé par un nom sans changement de sens. Faites le remplacement dans la phrase suivante :
He can't stand living without his cellphone. → *He can't stand...*

3 Observez.

a. *She is fed up **with** arguing with her parents about her cellphone bill.*
b. *Parents are used **to** disagreeing with their children.*
c. *I'm looking forward **to** chatting on the Internet this evening. I can't wait.*
d. *He is fond **of** reading the news on the Internet.*
e. *My parents prevent me **from** browsing on the Internet late at night.*
f. *We are thinking **about** buying a new computer.*

With, to, of, from, about introduisent un complément : ils relient ce complément au groupe de mots qui suit. Ce sont des prépositions. Attention au cas de *to*, qui n'est pas toujours une préposition.
→ **Déduisez :** de quoi sont suivies ces prépositions ?

4 Observez.

a. *I <u>love</u> watching film trailers on my computer.*
b. *He <u>enjoys</u> playing video games after school.*
c. *I <u>can't stand</u> hearing cellphones in a restaurant.*
d. *I <u>hate</u> seeing my daughter glued to her computer screen for hours.*

Qu'expriment les quatre verbes soulignés : une activité ou un goût ?
→ **Déduisez :** après des verbes exprimant ... , on utilise ... .

5 Observez.

*There must be ink in the printer. I <u>remember</u> **buying** a cartridge only a few days ago.*
*Tonight after work, <u>remember</u> **to buy** ink for the printer.*

À quels temps ou mode sont les verbes soulignés ?
Repérez les marqueurs de temps.
Dans quelle phrase l'énonciateur se situe-t-il **avant** l'action désignée par le verbe en gras ?
Dans quelle phrase l'énonciateur se situe-t-il **pendant** ou **après** l'action désignée par le verbe en gras ?
→ **Déduisez :** après *remember*, si l'action reste à faire, on utilise ... .
Si l'action est déjà réalisée, on utilise ... .

Language at work

Practice

1 Traduisez ces phrases.

a. Je ne supporte pas de le voir sauter les repas *(skip meals)* pour jouer sur son ordinateur.
b. Si tu continues à passer autant de temps devant ton ordinateur, tu vas avoir mal à la tête.
c. J'adore concevoir des jeux pour les enfants.
d. Au lieu de sortir avec ses amies, elle surfe sur Internet tous les soirs.
e. Avoir un ordinateur dans ta chambre t'empêche de faire tes devoirs.
f. J'ai hâte d'avoir un lecteur MP3.

2 Faites une pause !

Décrivez et commentez ce *cartoon*. Aidez-vous des expressions suivantes :

The father: *prevent from* • *stop from* • *be fed up with* • *can't stand / bear* • *instead of + V-ing*
Calvin: *keep* • *be busy* /ˈbɪzi/ • *spend time* • *be used to* • *look forward to* • *can't help* • *stop* • *it's worth + V-ing*

Bill Watterson, *Something under the bed is drooling*, 1988

Your task

Your school is hosting a debate on new technologies. You are one of the following participants: a teenager, a parent, a child psychologist or a video game designer. You will debate on: *Are new technologies harmful to teenagers?*

AVANT DE VOUS LANCER

1 Some useful expressions (see p. 180-181)

a. Give arguments and illustrate them with examples

Arguments
- since *(puisque)*
- That's the reason why...
- as *(comme)*

Examples
- for instance / for example
- ... such as...
- as we saw in class...

b. Give your opinion, express your agreement or disagreement

Opinion
- In my opinion...
- As far as I am concerned...
- To me...
- I believe / reckon...

Agreement / disagreement
- I agree but on the other hand...
- Certainly not! Surely not!
- Why don't you...?
- I agree ≠ I disagree / I don't agree.

c. Advise

- Teenagers had better + V...
- Your son shouldn't + V...
- If I were you, I'd + V...
- Why don't you try to...?

2 Practise giving your point of view

React to these quotes: Do you agree or disagree? Why?

"My parents got my cellphone for me so they could always be in contact with me, and if there was an emergency I could call them."

"Do they think deeply about something or is their mp3 player always on, their phone always to the ear?"

"When I go away on a vacation with my children, they are texting all their friends. There's no break. They are unwilling to be out of the loop for more than one hour!"

"Are these new technologies really helping to connect people, or are they encouraging us to live in a more isolated world?"

3 Five steps to prepare what you are going to say

a. Choose a role (see pictures).

b. Choose a point of view.

- New technologies are not harmful to teenagers.
- New technologies are sometimes harmful, it depends.
- New technologies are harmful to teenagers.

c. Choose four topics out of the six given here:

- socialization / friends
- school / education
- independence / freedom
- leisure / entertainment
- health
- safety

d. For each topic, find two arguments.

e. For each argument, find one example.

Psychologist

Teenager

Parent

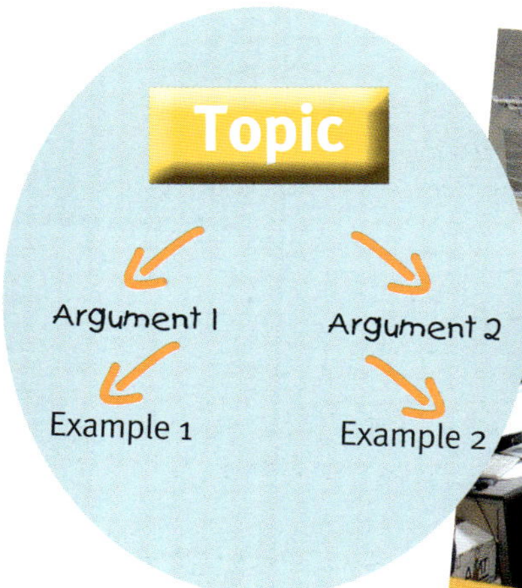

Video game designer

RÈGLES DE BASE DU DÉBAT

1. Écouter les autres intervenants attentivement.
2. Chercher à comprendre ce qu'ils disent grâce aux mots porteurs.
3. Demander des précisions et des reformulations si nécessaire.
4. Prendre et reprendre la parole pour donner son avis.
5. Expliquer ses idées, les argumenter et les justifier.
6. Chercher à convaincre, en parlant lentement et assez fort.
7. Oser se lancer, même si on hésite.
8. Rester calme et poli, même en cas de désaccord.

Unit 12

MOTHER EARTH

YOUR TASK AT THE END OF THIS UNIT

World Challenge is organizing an advertising campaign to protect the planet. You are on the panel of judges. Choose the ad you find the most effective and defend your choice. → p. 165

TUNE IN!

1 Danger ahead

a. Group work: React to one of the cartoons and report to the class.
– What elements immediately strike you (characters, setting, colours, contrasts...)?
– What problem does the cartoonist want us to focus on?
– Find a title for each cartoon and justify it.

PREPARE YOUR TASK → **b. Class work:**
– What do these cartoons have in common?
– Which cartoon has the strongest impact on you?
– Which one is the most effective? Why?

1

2

3

Help!

Cartoon 1	Cartoon 2	Cartoon 3	Reactions
piggy bank: *tirelire* hammer: *marteau* unaware of: *inconscient de* responsible for use up resources: *épuiser les ressources* be involved /ɪn'vɒlvd/ in: *être impliqué dans*	drought /draʊt/: *sécheresse* global warming cracked earth polar bear /beəʳ/ greenhouse gas: *gaz à effet de serre* be endangered /ɪn'deɪndʒəd/ starve: *mourir de faim*	man's evolution oil spill: *marée noire* nuclear waste: (waste *est indénombrable) déchets nucléaires* fumes chimney stack: *cheminée d'usine* factory = plant: *usine* rubbish dump: *décharge* threaten /θretn/: *menacer*	scary: *effrayant* alarmist realistic panic-stricken humorous /'hju:mərəs/ shocking become aware of realize warn /wɔ:ʳn/: *avertir* shiver: *trembler*

2 Watch a video

Two commercials

Turn to your worksheet for help.

PREPARE YOUR TASK →

3 Oral account

Prepare a one or two-minute oral account of each video.

Points to include:

– What happens (setting, main character's description, social background, occupation, main events)?

– What is the message?

– Give your personal reactions to each video. Which one do you find the funnier and / or the more effective? Why?

I. ALERT

1 Get ready WB

a. Read the two articles in your Workbook and fill in the corresponding columns of the grid.

b. Confront your findings.

2 Understanding the text WB

Turn to your Workbook for help.

Poison in the well[1]

Tell me, what's gone wrong?
I tilt my head there, under the faucet[2]
but when I turn it on —
dry as paper.
Call the neighbors.

Who's to blame for what's going on?
In the dark without a clue
I'm just the same as you.

O, they tell us there's poison[3] in the well,
that someone's been a bit untidy
and there's been a small spill[4].
Not a lot, no, just a drop[5]

But there you are mistaken,
you know you are!

I wonder just how long
they knew our well was poisoned
but they let us just drink on.

O, they tell us there's poison in the well
that someone's been a bit untidy
and there's been a small spill.
All that it amounts to is a tear in a salted sea.
Someone's been a bit untidy,
they'll have it cleaned up in a week.

But the week is over
and now it's grown into years
since I was told that I should be calm,
there's nothing to fear.

But I drank that water for years,
my wife and my children!

Tell me, where to now
if your fight for a bearable life
can be fought and lost in your backyard?

O, don't tell us there's poison in the well,
that someone's been a bit untidy,
that there's been a small spill.
All that it amounts to is a tear in a salted sea.

Someone's been a bit untidy,
they'll have it cleaned up in a week.

10,000 Maniacs, *Blind Man's Zoo*, 1989

1. *puits* **2.** /fɑːsɪt/ (US) *robinet* **3.** /pɔɪzn/ **4.** there's been a small spill: *(ici) quelque chose s'est renversé, répandu* **5.** *goutte*

PREPARE YOUR TASK →

3 Turn the song into a dialogue WB

The narrator is complaining to a government official. Include the following points:
– The narrator's country, family status.
– What problem is he / she confronted with?
– What explanation does the official give him / her? What is his / her reaction then?

Help!

Problem	Explanation	Reactions
shortage of water	unscrupulous	puzzled: *perplexe*
water supply	guilty /gɪlti/ of	revolted
damage *(indénombrable): dégâts*	deny the truth	trapped
extent of the damage	reassure	defenceless = powerless
mass murder	cope with a problem	weak ≠ strong
endanger the life of...	keep one's promise	deliberately
jeopardize /dʒepədaɪz/	tell the truth ≠ tell lies	be fed up with
	delude sb = deceive sb	denounce the hypocrisy of

PREPARE YOUR TASK

4 Choose the best illustration WB

a. Which of these two ads best illustrates the lyrics of the song?
b. Choose one document and analyse it with the help of your Workbook. Then defend your point of view in front of the class.

A

B

2. TURNING GREEN

1 Read and guess

a. Each group reads one text and guesses the missing word(s). In each text pick out the clues that helped you find the word(s).

b. Match each text with its illustration (A, B, C, D).

1 Last year, Americans recycled tons of WORD amounting to 50% of their consumption.

WORD originates from trees and every year 900 million of them are turned into WORD.

That number could be reduced if only we bought more recycled WORD, which uses 60% less energy than virgin WORD. For one ton bought, 4,400kWk of energy is saved, together with 30,000 liters of water and 19 trees! Furthermore trees are really useful to filter up pollutants from the atmosphere.

2 This may come as a surprise to you but your favourite hamburger is responsible for more global warming than your powerful car! On the whole, the international WORD 1 industry produces 18% of the greenhouse-gas emissions, a higher figure than for the transport sector!

A great deal of these emissions comes from the nitrous oxide in manure[1] and methane, the biological result of the WORD 2 digestion process of billions of cattle[2], sheep and goats on the planet.

Between 2001 and 2050, global WORD 1 production will double, due to changing habits and a growing demographic pressure, and with the energy used in raising[3], shipping[4] and selling livestock[5], a steak is surprisingly as harmful as a SUV[6] for the environment.

Become a vegetarian and your carbon footprint can be reduced by up to almost 1.4 ton of carbon dioxide a year.

In comparison, if you choose to change your standard car for a hybrid vehicle, you will only cut your production of carbon dioxide by about one ton a year.

1. *fumier* **2.** *bovins* **3.** *élever* **4.** *expédier* **5.** *animaux d'élevage*
6. sport utility vehicle

3 You have a car and you WORD 1 to work every day. Have a look at the passenger seat: empty, isn't it? In most of the industrialized countries, the single-occupant WORD 2 is still the rule.

80% of people WORD 1 to work alone and 38% are generally alone in their car when they go elsewhere.

But things are slowly starting to change. Washington State enforced its Clean Air Act and offered incentives[1] to employees to encourage them to WORD 1 less or accept passengers. The employees are urged to car-pool[2], walk, bike or take the bus.

Since the programme was initiated in 1991, there have been about 20,000 fewer vehicle trips every morning. The result on commuters[3]: a saving of $13.7 million and 22 million litres of gas, and a reduction of 71,000 tons of air pollutants and gases.

1. *incitations* **2.** several people travel together in one vehicle
3. *banlieusards (qui font la navette entre leur lieu d'habitation et leur travail)*

4 The WORD 1 WORD 2 you get from the supermarket are bound to land in a landfill[1]. Out of the 500 billion WORD 1 WORD 2 that are distributed every year, less than 3% are recycled. They take up to 1,000 years to biodegrade. Moreover, landfills emit damaging greenhouse gases.

Use cloth[2] or biodegradable plant-based WORD 2 instead of WORD 1 ones and you will pollute less. Think about it next time you go to the supermarket or the grocery store!

1. *site d'enfouissement des déchets* **2.** *tissu*

PREPARE YOUR TASK →

2 Role play

You have read the four texts and you try to convince your parents to change their habits.

– What arguments can you use to persuade them?

– Your parents will ask why they must evolve and how they can protect the planet.

A

B

C

D

« Faire faire » et « laisser faire »

1 Observez.

a. *This ad* *makes* *me* *laugh* *because it is humorous.*
b. *The authorities* *let* *people* *drink* *that filthy water.*
– Quel est le sujet des verbes encadrés ? (Qui est responsable de ce qui se passe ?)
Quel est le sujet des verbes soulignés ?
Le pronom utilisé dans la phrase **a** est-il à la forme sujet ou complément ?
– Quel verbe utilise-t-on pour signifier le « déclenchement d'une action » ?
Quel verbe utilise-t-on comme équivalent de « laisser faire » ?

→ **Déduisez :** de quoi sont suivis les deux verbes encadrés ? *Make* / *Let* + ... + ...

c. *The government made the oil company pay for the damage of the oil spill.*
Make indique ici une ... exercée par le gouvernement sur la société pétrolière.

2 Comparez.

a. *The company will make the workers clean up the spill.*
b. *The company will have the oil spill cleaned up.*
– Quel énoncé indique qui nettoiera ?
– Quel énoncé met l'accent sur la transformation subie ?

c. *The company will have the quality of the water checked.*
Laquelle de ces trois affirmations correspond au sens de la phrase **c** ?
– L'entreprise contrôlera elle-même la qualité de l'eau.
– L'entreprise fera contrôler la qualité de l'eau (mais on ne dit pas qui s'en chargera).
– Le résultat des analyses sera bientôt connu.
À quelle forme est le verbe souligné dans l'énoncé **b** ?

→ **Déduisez :** la structure employée est *have* + ... + ...

Verbes + prépositions

1 Traduisez ces énoncés en français.

The problems we have to face are huge.
We are witnessing dramatic climate changes.
The cartoonist wants us to look at the state of the planet and react.
What accounts for global warming?
To cope with the problem of pollution industrialized countries must reduce their oil consumption.
Do you approve of the BYOB (Bring Your Own Bag) campaign?
We all hope for a better future.
Why don't governments listen to environmentalists more often?

→ **Déduisez :** dans ces énoncés, quelles différences remarquez-vous entre le français et l'anglais concernant la construction des verbes ?

2 Traduisez ces énoncés.

We must all take part in the fight against global warming.
What are environmentalists worrying about?
Do you care enough about the Earth's future to get involved?

→ **Déduisez :** dans ces énoncés quelles similitudes de construction remarquez-vous entre le français et l'anglais ?

Language at work

Practice

1 ***Make, let* ou *have* ? Complétez ces phrases.**

a. Environmentalists want to ... consumers shut off their computers after each work session.
b. The new boss won't ... us leave our offices without making sure our computers, printers and desklights are turned off. The goal is to ... us save energy and reduce gas emissions.
c. Environmentalists suggest drivers should ... their tyres *(pneus)* regularly checked and properly inflated to reduce their gas consumption.
d. The price of oil ... people walk or bike or ride public transport to go to work.
e. To consume less energy my parents will ... our house properly insulated.

2 **Traduisez ces phrases en utilisant *make* ou *have*.**

a. Le but de cette publicité est de faire réagir le spectateur.
b. Cet article m'a fait réfléchir et changer mes habitudes.
c. Ma grand-mère a fait changer toutes les ampoules *(bulbs)* dans sa maison.
d. Cette image m'a fait prendre conscience des dangers de la pollution.
e. Tu devrais faire isoler ta maison.

PREPARE YOUR TASK → **3** **Penguin**

Analyse the cartoon: What elements strike you? What are your reactions? What is the message? What is its impact on you?
Use **make** and/or **let** to analyse this picture.

Language at work

Improve your pronunciation MP3

1 Comment se prononce la voyelle *-a-* en orange dans ces mots ?

hurricane • aware • alert • global • disaster • warn about • impact

/eɪ/	/ɛ/	/ɑː/	/ɔ/	/ɔː/	/æ/

2 Comment se prononcent les voyelles *-ea-* dans ces mots : comme la voyelle de *bed* ou comme celle de *bird* ?

threat • measure • earth

3 Quelle est la syllabe accentuée dans ces mots ?

advertiser • advertising • advertisement

4 Les mots suivants sont accentués sur la deuxième syllabe. Comment se prononce la voyelle de la première syllabe : comme la première voyelle de *banana* ou comme la voyelle de *song* ?

consumption • consume • concerned • condemn

5 Vous allez entendre des phrases ; écrivez-les.

Build up your vocabulary

Complétez ces textes avec les mots des listes. Faites les changements grammaticaux nécessaires.

a. *destroy • dump • earth • fight • garbage can • man • recycle • threaten • waste disposal*

We are immediately struck by the earth that has been turned into a ... [1]. The cartoonist's goal is to make us aware of the enormous amount of waste we produce every day. The problem of ... [2] is acute because litter is ... [3] everywhere, and is polluting rivers and oceans. Our waste should be ... [4] or burnt. The message is clear: Our blue planet is ... [5] with extinction because ... [6] has ... [7] the environment. We should all ... [8] for the protection of the ... [9].

b. *crisis • clean • coal • gas • greenhouse effect • oil • oil consumption • renewable • solar • wind*

We will soon be confronted with an energy ... [1]. The world's demand for energy – ... [2], ... [3], ... [4] – is rising. More ... [5] sources of energy, like ... [6], ... [7] and hydro power, will be used in the next two decades. Governments want to develop public transport and ... [8] energy sources to reduce ... [9] and the ... [10].

your task

World Challenge is organizing an advertising campaign to protect the planet. You are on the panel of judges. Here are the top four finalists. Choose the ad you find the most effective (p. 166-167). Confront your points of view, and try to convince your classmates. Then decide who the winner will be.

LES ÉTAPES À SUIVRE

1 Entraînez-vous en analysant cette publicité.

- *What first caught your eye?*
- *What do the different arrows correspond to?*
- *What is the impact on the viewer?*
- *Who is the target? What are the advertisers' goals?*

2 Donnez votre réaction personnelle.

- *I find it too plain* (simple) */dull* /dʌl/ (ennuyeux).
- *It's clever, amusing, humorous.*
- *It's disturbing* (troublant).
- *I think /feel it's strange = weird* /wɪəd/.
- *It's amazing* (étonnant).
- *It's forceful = striking.*
- *It's scary = frightening.*
- *The message is optimistic ≠ pessimistic.*
- *To my mind the message is (not) effective / realistic /symbolic.*
- *To my mind this advertisement is useless = banal /stereotyped* /ˈstɪərɪətaɪpt/.
- *It's all the same to me.* (Ça m'est égal.)
- *I (really) don't care.*
- *That leaves me cold.*

> – The ad is intended to / meant to...
> – Advertisers would like us to react / feel concerned...
> – Their goal / purpose /ˈpɜːpəs/ is to...
> – They want us to think / feel...
> – They make us feel...

CONSEILS POUR VOTRE PRESTATION

1 Appliquez la démarche proposée ci-dessus aux publicités p. 166-167.

2 Comparez et justifiez votre choix.

- *It's scar**ier than** /ðən/ the other three.*
- *Ad number ... is **more** forceful **than** all the others.*
- *It's **the** scar**iest** advertisement.*
- *This ad is **the most** amusing one.*
- *I like it **better** / **best**.*
- ***Compared to** the first one, this ad is clever.*
- *I find this ad **very** / **quite** / **rather** surprising.*

1

15km² of rain forest disappears every minute
WWF

2

LITTER
AND YOU'RE
RUBBISH
Keep Australia Beautiful
WA

3

IS YOUR WORRYING
GLOBAL ENOUGH?
GREY
FACE THE PROBLEM BEFORE IT'S TOO LATE.
LEGAMBIENTE

4

EARTH
LOVE
EARTH LOVE FOUNDATION
www.earthlovefoundation.org

Unit 13

ALL THE WORLD'S A STAGE

YOUR TASK AT THE END OF THIS UNIT

In groups you will choose one scene you have studied and stage it. Imagine the setting, invent the stage directions, learn your part by heart and act it out in front of an audience. → p. 178

TUNE IN!

1 On stage!

Read this review of *A Midsummer Night's Dream*, a play written by Shakespeare in 1595. Then find the words (in the review) that correspond to the following definitions:

- giving a play at a theatre
- person in a play
- person who gives instructions to actors and actresses
- practice before playing in public
- accessories used on stage
- people who come to watch a play
- all the actors in a play
- clothes actors and actresses wear
- story of a play
- place in which a play takes place

Don't miss *A Midsummer Night's Dream!* The cast is brilliant and has given wonderful performances. The director has managed to clarify a complicated plot. The setting, a Tuscan countryside, is splendid. The characters are wonderfully funny. The costumes are superb. The props are unusual. What a joy to hear an entire audience roar with laughter! All the hard work put into the rehearsals is rewarded. It's captivating all the way through.

PREPARE YOUR TASK →

2 A quarrel

Look at this photo.

a. Work in pairs and imagine what the man and the woman are arguing about.
b. Write a short dialogue and act it out in front of your class.

- How dare you!
- How could you?
- This is the **l**imit!
- I'm not h**a**ving that!
- Let me speak.
- I don't bel**ie**ve it!
- Just you wait!

1. WEDLOCK WB

a. Look at the poster. What strikes you?
b. Identify the situation and the characters. What do the padlock and the chain symbolize?
c. What are the dominant colours? Why?
d. Who published this poster? What is the message? Who is the target? What is it for?
e. Say how you react to it.

Help!

Who?	What for?
bride: *la mariée*	arranged marriage
bridegroom: *le marié*	obedient / submissive
wedding ring: *alliance*	impose sth on sb
suit /suːt/: *costume*	urge sb to: *inciter qqn à*
padlock: *cadenas*	support
be locked	warn sb about sth
marry sb = get married to sb	prevent sb from + V-ing: *empêcher qqn de*
be forced / obliged / compelled to do sth	against sb's will: *contre la volonté de qqn*

2. A SUITABLE BOY (PART 1)

The Importance of Being Earnest, film directed by Oliver Parker (2002)

Part 1

GWENDOLEN: I am engaged[1] to Mr Worthing, mamma. *(They rise together.)*

LADY BRACKNELL: Pardon me, you are not engaged to anyone. When you do become engaged to someone, I, or your father [...] will inform you of the fact. [...] And now I have a few questions to put to you, Mr Worthing. While I am making these inquiries, you, Gwendolen, will wait for me below[2] in the carriage[3].

GWENDOLEN *(reproachfully)*: Mamma!

LADY BRACKNELL: In the carriage, Gwendolen!

(Gwendolen goes to the door. She and Jack blow kisses to each other behind Lady Bracknell's back. Lady Bracknell looks vaguely about as if she could not understand what the noise was. Finally turns round.) Gwendolen, the carriage!

GWENDOLEN: Yes, mamma. *(Goes out, looking back at Jack.)*

LADY BRACKNELL *(sitting down)*: You can take a seat, Mr Worthing.

(Looks in her pocket for note-book and pencil.)

JACK: Thank you, Lady Bracknell, I prefer standing.

LADY BRACKNELL *(pencil and note-book in hand)*: I feel bound to[4] tell you that you are not down on my list of eligible young men[5], although I have the same list as the dear Duchess of Bolton has. We work together, in fact. However, I am quite ready to enter your name[6], should your answers be[7] what a really affectionate mother requires[8]. Do you smoke?

JACK: Well, yes, I must admit I smoke.

LADY BRACKNELL: I am glad to hear it. A man should always have an occupation of some kind. [...] How old are you?

JACK: Twenty-nine.

LADY BRACKNELL: What is your income[9]?

JACK: Between seven and eight thousand a year.

LADY BRACKNELL *(makes a note in her book)*: In land, or in investments?

JACK: In investments, chiefly.

LADY BRACKNELL: That is satisfactory.

Oscar Wilde, *The Importance of Being Earnest*, 1895

1. *fiancée* **2.** *en bas* **3.** *calèche* **4.** I feel bound to: *je me sens obligée de* **5.** eligible young men: *bons partis* **6.** to enter your name: *à faire figurer votre nom* **7.** should your answers be: *si vos réponses correspondent* **8.** *(ici) peut exiger* **9.** *revenus*

1 Understanding the text WB

Turn to your Workbook for help.

2 Recap

a. What does Lady Bracknell interview Jack for? What sort of son-in-law is she looking for?
b. What do we learn about Jack's habits and social background?
c. Do Jack's answers satisfy Lady Bracknell? Why? Why not?
d. What do the parents in the cartoon opposite have in common with Lady Bracknell?

"Well, put like that of course you can marry my daughter."

Help!

Lady Bracknell
cross = angry
authoritative
scornful: *méprisante*
organized
curt: *cassante*
inquisitive: *indiscrète*
belong to the aristocracy / the upper class
inquire into

Jack
prospects: *perspectives d'avenir*
careful = cautious
wealthy = well-off
polite
hesitant
gain sb's approval
disappoint

PREPARE YOUR TASK →

3 You are the stage director

a. Describe the tone used by each character in the scene. At the end of each line *(réplique)*, use an adjective (given in the toolbox above) or an adverb as well as one of the following verbs:
add • announce • assert • ask • answer • declare • explain • order • reply

Examples:
Gwendolen: "I am engaged to Mr Worthing, mamma." *(Gwendolen announced loudly / defiantly.)*
Lady Bracknell: "Pardon me, you are not engaged to anyone." *(She answered drily.)*

b. Imagine Lady Bracknell and Jack on stage.
– Lady Bracknell: What is her attitude at the beginning of the interview? How does she look at Jack? Does she smile at him? Does she make any pauses? When? Does she speak fast or slowly? Is she aggressive or calm?
Useful words: sit comfortably • take one's time • note-book • look sb up and down (= look at sb fixedly)
– Jack: Does he stand in front of Lady Bracknell or does he pace the room? Does he look at Lady Bracknell or does he avoid her eyes? Is he confident or embarrassed?

c. Mime the whole scene without saying a single word.

4 How to pronounce WB

Work on the pronunciation with the help of your Workbook, then read the dialogue aloud.

3. A SUITABLE BOY (PARTS 2 AND 3)

***At Victoria Station*, Eugenio Alvarez, 1908**

Part 2

LADY BRACKNELL: [...] Now to minor matters. Are your parents living?

JACK: I have lost both my parents.

LADY BRACKNELL: To lose one parent, Mr Worthing, may be regarded as a misfortune; to lose both looks like carelessness[1]. Who was your father? [...]

JACK: I am afraid I really don't know. The fact is, Lady Bracknell, I said I had lost my parents. It would be nearer the truth to say that my parents seem to have lost me... I don't actually[2] know who I am by birth. I was... well, I was found.

LADY BRACKNELL: Found!

JACK: The late[3] Mr Thomas Cardew, an old gentleman of a very charitable and kindly disposition, found me, and gave me the name of Worthing, because he happened to have a first-class ticket for Worthing in his pocket at the time. Worthing is a place in Sussex. It is a seaside resort[4].

LADY BRACKNELL: Where did the charitable gentleman who had a first-class ticket for this seaside resort find you?

JACK *(gravely)*: In a hand-bag.

LADY BRACKNELL: A hand-bag?

JACK *(very seriously)*: Yes, Lady Bracknell. I was in a hand-bag – a somewhat large, black leather[5] hand-bag, with handles to it – an ordinary hand-bag in fact.

LADY BRACKNELL: In what locality did this Mr James, or Thomas, Cardew come across this ordinary hand-bag?

JACK: In the cloak-room[6] at Victoria Station. It was given to him in mistake for his own.

LADY BRACKNELL: The cloak-room at Victoria Station?

JACK: Yes. The Brighton line.

LADY BRACKNELL: The line is immaterial[7]. Mr Worthing, I confess I feel somewhat bewildered[8] by what you have just told me. [...]

1. *négligence* **2.** *en réalité* **3.** *feu / décédé* **4.** seaside resort: *station balnéaire* **5.** *cuir* **6.** *consigne* **7.** *Peu importe la ligne.*
8. somewhat bewildered: a little perplexed

Part 3

JACK: May I ask you then what you would advise me to do? I need hardly say I would do anything in the world to ensure Gwendolen's happiness.

LADY BRACKNELL: I would strongly advise you, Mr Worthing, to try and acquire some relations as soon as possible, and to make a definite effort to produce at any rate one parent, of either sex, before the season is quite over.

JACK: Well, I don't see how I could possibly manage to do that. I can produce the hand-bag at any moment. It is in my dressing-room at home. I really think that should satisfy you, Lady Bracknell.

LADY BRACKNELL: Me, sir! What has it to do with me? You can hardly imagine that I and Lord Bracknell would dream of allowing our only daughter – a girl brought up with the utmost care[1] – to marry into a cloak-room, and form an alliance with a parcel[2]? Good morning, Mr Worthing!

Oscar Wilde, *The Importance of Being Earnest*, 1895

1. brought up with the utmost care: *élevée avec le plus grand soin* **2.** *paquet*

1 Understanding the text WB

Turn to your Workbook for help.

2 Recap

a. What do we learn about Jack's origins?
b. Analyse Lady Bracknell's reactions in this scene.
c. Imagine Jack's feelings after Lady Bracknell leaves.
d. What questions should a really affectionate mother ask her future son-in-law?

Help!

Jack	Lady Bracknell
orphan: *orphelin* straightforward /streɪt'fɔːwəd/: *direct* honest /ɒnɪst/ inferior miserable: *malheureux* belong to the same class relate a story	astonished / amazed = very surprised stunned: *stupéfaite* contemptuous / scornful: *méprisante* outraged: *scandalisée* snobbish be prejudiced against: *avoir des préjugés contre* approve of ≠ disapprove of sb / + V-ing despise sb: *mépriser qqn*

3 Define the tone

Fill in the blanks with one of these adverbs:
angrily • contemptuously • hopefully • impatiently • proudly • sincerely

a. "I will do anything," Jack said...
b. "I can produce the hand-bag," Jack said...
c. "What has it got to do with me?" Lady Bracknell asked...
d. "The line is immaterial." Lady Bracknell replied...
e. "Gwendolen received a very good education!" Lady Bracknell said...
f. "Good morning, Mr Worthing." Lady Bracknell said...

PREPARE YOUR TASK

4 Role play

Choose a scenario. After the interview:
– Lady Bracknell meets her best friend and tells her what has just happened.
– Jack narrates the scene to Gwendolen.

Include comments, reactions, feelings and emotions.

5 How to pronounce WB

Work on the pronunciation with the help of your Workbook, then read the dialogue aloud.

6 You are the stage director

Decide:
– Are the two characters far from or close to each other?
– How does Lady Bracknell walk off stage? Does she give Jack a final look or not?
– How should Jack act at the end of the scene?
– Imagine the song or music that could accompany this scene. When would you play it?

7 Watch a video

Shakespeare in a Supermarket
Turn to your worksheet for help.

4. THE RIGHT DECISION

Pride and Prejudice, a film directed by Joe Wright (2005)

Mr and Mrs Bennet's daughter, Lizzy, has just refused a marriage proposal from Mr Collins. Mrs Bennet breaks the news to her husband.

"Oh! Mr Bennet, you are wanted immediately; we are all in an uproar[1]. You must come and make Lizzy marry Mr Collins, for she vows[2] she will not have him, and if you do not make haste[3] he will change his mind and not have *her*."

Mr Bennet raised his eyes from his book as she entered. […]

"I have not the pleasure of understanding you," said he, when she had finished her speech. "Of what are you talking?"

"Of Mr Collins and Lizzy. Lizzy declares she will not have Mr Collins, and Mr Collins begins to say that he will not have Lizzy."

"And what am I to do on the occasion? It seems a hopeless business."

"Speak to Lizzy about it yourself. Tell her that you insist upon her marrying him."

"Let her be called down. She shall hear my opinion."

Mrs Bennet rang the bell, and Miss Elizabeth was summoned[4] to the library[5].

"Come here, child," cried her father as she appeared. "I have sent for you on an affair of importance. I understand that Mr Collins has made you an offer of marriage. Is it true?" Elizabeth replied that it was. "Very well – and this offer of marriage you have refused?"

"I have, Sir."

"Very well. We now come to the point. Your mother insists upon your accepting it. Is it not so, Mrs Bennet?"

"Yes, or I will never see her again."

"An unhappy alternative is before you, Elizabeth. From this day you must be a stranger to one of your parents. Your mother will never see you again if you do *not* marry Mr Collins, and I will never see you again if you *do*."

Jane Austen, *Pride and Prejudice*, 1813

1. *vive agitation* **2.** *jure* **3.** make haste: hurry up **4.** was summoned: *on fit venir* **5.** *bibliothèque*

1 Understanding the text WB

Turn to your Workbook for help.

2 Recap

Sum up the situation briefly.

- What does Mrs Bennet want Lizzy to do?
- What does Mrs Bennet ask Mr Bennet to do?
- What does Mr Bennet finally decide?
- Who does Mr Bennet side with? Why?

Use the following words: disappointed • obey sb • submissive: *soumis* • oblige / compel / force sb to do sth • interfere • let sb do sth: *laisser qqn faire qqch* • independent

PREPARE YOUR TASK

3 How to pronounce WB

Work on the pronunciation and the stage directions with the help of your Workbook, then read the dialogue aloud.

Language at work

Improve your pronunciation

MP3

1 Vous allez entendre trois phrases.

Quel sentiment est exprimé dans chacune d'elles : surprise • colère • ironie, mépris ?

2 Lisez cette phrase.

Lizzy has just refused a marriage proposal.
Cette phrase va être lue de quatre manières différentes (1, 2, 3 et 4). À chaque fois, un mot sera particulièrement accentué, ce qui modifiera l'interprétation de la phrase. Repérez le mot accentué et choisissez l'interprétation qui convient.

a. Lizzy vient de refuser une demande en mariage et personne ne s'y attendait.
b. Lizzy, et non sa sœur, vient de refuser une demande en mariage.
c. Lizzy vient à l'instant de refuser une demande en mariage.
d. Lizzy a refusé une demande en mariage.

Build up your vocabulary

1 Associez chaque réplique (a à h) à la fin de la phrase correspondante (1 à 8).

Les verbes des phrases 1 à 8 décrivent différentes façons de parler et de s'adresser à quelqu'un.

a. *"Oh! Mr Bennet, you are wanted immediately."*
b. *"I will never see her again."*
c. *"What would you advise me to do?"*
d. *"I was... well, I was found."*
e. *"What is your income?"*
f. *"Between seven and eight thousand a year."*
g. *"Lizzy declares she will not have Mr Collins."*
h. *"Come here, child."*

1. *Jack stammered.*
2. *Mrs Bennet threatened.*
3. *Lady Bracknell inquired.*
4. *Jack pleaded.*
5. *Jack explained.*
6. *Mr Bennet asked.*
7. *Mrs Bennet complained.*
8. *Mrs Bennet shouted.*

2 Classez ces adverbes en trois colonnes en fonction du sentiment exprimé.

crossly • anxiously • hopelessly • miserably • nervously • furiously • cheerfully • sadly • desperately • hopefully • gladly

Anger	Happiness	Worry

3 À partir des adverbes fournis, trouvez l'adjectif, puis le nom correspondant.

Adverbes	Adjectifs	Noms
curiously	*curious*	*curiosity*
kindly		
impatiently		
scornfully		
quietly		
angrily		
miserably		

Language at work

Le style indirect

1 Observez.

"I am engaged!" Gwendolen said. → *Gwendolen said that / ∅ she was engaged.*
Les paroles rapportées sont introduites par ... ou ... .

2 Comparez.

"Are your parents living?" Lady Bracknell asked. → *Lady Bracknell asked Jack if his parents were living.*
"I'm surprised by what you have told me," Lady Bracknell answered. → *Lady Bracknell answered (that) she was surprised by what he had told her.*

→ **Déduisez :** lorsque l'on rapporte les paroles de quelqu'un, certains pronoms représentant des personnes doivent ... .

3 Observez l'ordre des mots.

a. *"Where is this play being performed?"* → *He wonders where this play is being performed.*
b. *"How much does a ticket cost?"* → *He wants to know how much a ticket costs.*

→ **Déduisez :** lorsque l'on rapporte une question au style indirect on rétablit l'ordre ... .

4 Comparez les deux colonnes de ce tableau.

Style direct	Style indirect
a. "**Do** you **smoke**?" Lady Bracknell asked.	Lady Bracknell **asked** if he / Jack **smoked**.
b. "What **are** you **talking** about?" Mr Bennet asked.	Mr Bennet **asked** what his wife **was talking** about.
c. "I **will speak** to Lady Bracknell tomorrow," Jack said.	Jack **said** he **would speak** to Lady Bracknell on the following day.
d. "Mr Thomas Cardew **found** me," Jack explained.	Jack **explained** that Mr Thomas Cardew **had found** him.
e. "I **have lost** both my parents," Jack answered.	Jack **answered** he **had lost** both his parents.
f. "**Wait** for me outside!" Lady Bracknell ordered.	Lady Bracknell **ordered** Gwendolen **to wait** for her outside.
g. "**Try and acquire** some relations before next week," Lady Bracknell advised Jack.	Lady Bracknell **advised** Jack **to try and acquire** some relations before the following / coming week.

a. À quel temps sont tous les verbes introducteurs dans la colonne du style indirect ?
→ **Déduisez :** lorsque le verbe introducteur est au ... , on doit opérer les changements suivants :
– le présent devient un ... . Ainsi *will* devient ... .
– le prétérit qui désigne une action antérieure au moment où l'on parle devient un ... .
– un ordre, un conseil sera introduit par ... .

b. Relevez les deux expressions de temps au style direct et au style indirect passé. Que remarquez-vous ?

Language at work

Practice

1 Rapportez ces questions en utilisant un verbe introducteur au passé.

a. Gwendolen: "Why do I have to go into the carriage?"
b. Lady Bracknell: "Have you told your father you were engaged?"
c. Lady Bracknell: "Are you joking?"
d. Gwendolen: "How do you know Jack was found?"
e. Gwendolen: "Isn't there a solution?"

2 Réécrivez ce passage au style direct, sans oublier les guillemets.

Lizzy announced that she would never marry Mr Collins. She explained that she had been very polite but Mr Collins was too ridiculous and self-centred. Mrs Bennet was surprised and answered it was impossible because Mr Collins was quite wealthy. Lizzy refused and Mrs Bennet ordered her daughter to stop arguing and to listen to her. She added girls were not supposed to argue and had to obey their parents. She told her she would immediately speak to her father about it.

3 Rapportez cet échange au style indirect passé à l'aide de *ask, answer, reply, add, explain, tell.*

Mr Bennet: "I have sent for you on an affair of importance. I understand that Mr Collins has made you an offer of marriage. Is it true?"
Lizzy: "Yes, it is."
Mr Bennet: "Very well – and this offer of marriage you have refused?"
Lizzy: "I have, Sir."
Mr Bennet: "Very well. We now come to the point. Your mother insists upon your accepting it. Is it not so, Mrs Bennet?"
Mrs Bennet: "Yes, or I will never see her again."
Mr Bennet: "An unhappy alternative is before you, Elizabeth. From this day you must be a stranger to one of your parents. Your mother will never see you again if you do *not* marry Mr Collins, and I will never see you again if you *do*."

4 Racontez cette histoire au style indirect passé.

Variez les verbes introducteurs : *tell, answer, reply, ask, declare, explain...*

Your task

In groups you will choose one scene you have studied and stage it. Imagine the setting, invent the stage directions, learn your part by heart and act it out in front of an audience.

AVANT DE VOUS LANCER MP3

1 Entraînez-vous avec l'audio élève sur le site compagnon, U13–Your task (1).

a. Repérez l'accent principal de ces phrases.
Pardon me, you are not engaged to anyone.
What has it to do with me?

b. Repérez comment se prononcent les mots soulignés.
In the cloak-room at Victoria Station. /æt/ ou /ət/
I was in a hand-bag. /wɒz/ ou /wəz/
What would you advise me to do? /tuː/ ou /tə/
We would never dream of allowing our only daughter to marry you. /əv/ ou /ɒv/, /tuː/ ou /tə/

c. Repérez les liaisons consonne / voyelle.
I must admit I smoke.
What is your income?
In land, or in investments?

d. Repérez les mots accentués.
A man should always have an occupation of some kind.

e. Repérez les pauses dans cette longue phrase.
An old gentleman of a very charitable and kindly disposition found me, and gave me the name of Worthing, because he happened to have a first-class ticket for Worthing in his pocket at the time.

f. Répétez toutes ces phrases à haute voix.

2 Jouez avec votre voix.

Entraînez-vous à dire cette phrase doucement, puis de plus en plus fort. N'hésitez pas à exagérer :
Good morning, Mr Worthing!

3 Utilisez différents tons de voix.

La même phrase peut être dite sur un ton très différent. Dites : *Good morning, Mr Worthing!*
– sur un ton de surprise
– avec mépris
– avec colère
– avec joie.

Vérifiez avec l'audio élève si votre intonation était correcte : site compagnon, U13–Your task (2).

LES ÉTAPES À SUIVRE MP3

1 Répartissez les rôles.

Si vous décidez de jouer la scène de la pièce d'Oscar Wilde dans son entier, Lady Bracknell et Jack peuvent être joués par une personne différente dans chaque partie.

a. Désignez en groupe :
– un metteur en scène
– un souffleur *(a prompter)*
– une personne qui se chargera de la musique
– un accessoiriste.

b. Synthétisez les besoins à l'aide d'un tableau.

Scènes	Musiques	Accessoires sur scène *(props)*	Costumes

2 Apprenez votre rôle.

a. Vérifiez que vous comprenez bien tout ce que vous allez dire.

b. Aidez-vous des pages de votre Workbook sur la prononciation des scènes ainsi que de l'audio élève sur le site compagnon, U13–Your task (3).

c. Sur votre photocopie personnelle, marquez d'une couleur les groupes de souffle, et d'une autre les sons qui vous posent problème, les accents de mots, les liaisons. Barrez les formes réduites.

d. Mémorisez votre rôle à la perfection. Répétez chez vous en vous déplaçant, pour vous donner l'habitude d'occuper l'espace.

3 Travaillez votre scène.

a. Dans un premier temps, mimez la scène.

b. Ensuite, réfléchissez :
– au ton de voix à adopter
– à la façon dont vous allez regarder l'autre ou les autres comédien(s)
– aux gestes que vous allez faire (notez-les sur votre photocopie personnelle)
– aux pauses (les silences doivent aussi être prévus)
– à vos différents mouvements sur scène.

4 Conseillez vos camarades.

– You need to speak much **lou**der.
– You need to be cl**ea**rer and speak more sl**o**wly.
– Ex**a**ggerate much more.
– Emphas**i**ze with your voice.
– Have more c**o**nfidence in y**our**self.
– Show you are much more n**er**vous / **a**nxious / unc**o**mfortable...
– Make a g**es**ture to **i**ndicate...
– Look at him / her when you...
– Bring more **e**nergy to the scene.
– The **au**dience must see your face, not your back.
– Make a strong **e**ntrance.
– You need to **e**xit more sl**o**wly.

5 Et maintenant, jouez !

– Parlez fort, sans accélérer.
– Écoutez attentivement votre ou vos partenaire(s) et regardez-le(s).

PRENDRE PART À UNE CONVERSATION

A Un exemple de débat

1 Lisez le thème de ce débat et l'opinion de ces quatre adolescents.

In the UK, the police have decided to make good citizens of British teenagers. Pupils will be rewarded for telling the school or the police if other students skip lessons, miss classes or break any school rules. We have asked some young people for their opinion.

It's wrong to give rewards. People should tell the adults because they think they have seen something bad and want to help, not because there is a reward.

Tracy

It's OK to reward informers, but I wouldn't inform on a friend. I would talk with him instead and try to convince him to change.

Mark

If a kid doesn't go to school, or breaks the school rules, it's wrong. He should be punished. I would tell the adults and take the reward.

Jason

Reward or no reward, I would be too scared to tell anybody. What if the pupil becomes violent later on and takes his or her revenge?

Linda

2 Classez les arguments de ces quatre adolescents en deux colonnes « pour » et « contre ».

3 Écoutez ces quatre personnes débattre entre elles.

Repérez les tournures utilisées pour :
– exprimer son accord ou son désaccord
– donner son opinion à tour de rôle
– demander des explications
– interrompre quelqu'un
– manifester sa surprise ou son agacement.

B À votre tour !

1 Par groupes de trois ou quatre élèves, choisissez un thème de débat.

a. Should we try to live without mobile phones for a week?
b. Should you let anybody have access to your Facebook page?
c. Should parents block access to the Internet after 11 p.m.?
d. Should pupils wear school uniforms to prevent racketting?

2 Préparez cinq arguments (pour ou contre) et discutez-en avec vos camarades.

3 Pour enrichir vos échanges, utilisez ces tournures.

Donner son opinion
- *To my mind...*
- *In my opinion...*
- *I think / I feel / I believe...*
- *Don't you think that...?*
- *Don't forget that...*

Exprimer son accord
- *I quite agree with you on this point.*
- *I quite share your view.*
- *That's quite right.*
- *That's true. / Exactly! / Absolutely!*

Exprimer son désaccord
- *I don't agree. / I disagree with you.*
- *I don't see it that way.*
- *I think you're wrong!*
- *Certainly not!*
- *Nonsense!*

Organiser et résumer ses idées
- *First of all... secondly... then...*
- *On the one hand... on the other hand...*
- *On the whole...*
- *In other words...*
- *To sum up, I'd say...*

Donner des exemples, reformuler, expliquer
- *For example... / For instance...*
- *Let me give you an example.*
- *I'll explain it to you.*
- *We could also say...*

Couper poliment la parole
- *Excuse me but...*
- *Sorry to interrupt you, but...*
- *Can I just say something?*
- *Hang on! (familiar)*

Demander des éclaircissements
- *Sorry, I didn't get that.*
- *Can you repeat what you said, please?*
- *What's that again?*
- *What exactly do you mean?*
- *I didn't get your point.*

Atténuer son point de vue, concéder
- *You may be right, but...*
- *It may be true, but...*
- *I suppose you're right, but...*
- *That's all very well but...*
- *In a way... / To some extent...*

C Évaluez votre propre prestation

Critères d'auto-évaluation de la prise de parole en interaction	Oui	Non
1. Interagir lors du débat		
a. J'écoute les autres et je respecte leur parole.	1	0
b. J'interviens poliment pour demander la parole ou interrompre quelqu'un.	1	0
c. Je prends la parole en employant des phrases courtes et simples.	1	0
d. Je cherche à être compris (je parle clairement et de façon audible).	2	0
2. Prendre part au débat		
a. J'interviens et je réponds à propos.	1	0
b. Je demande des explications lorsque je ne comprends pas quelque chose (je fais répéter, reformuler, expliquer).	1	0
c. J'exprime de façon simple mon accord ou mon désaccord.	1	0
d. J'enchaîne plusieurs idées différentes à la suite.	2	0
3. Argumenter ses idées au cours du débat		
a. Je donne des exemples pour illustrer mes propos.	2	0
b. Je réagis aux idées des autres et peux rebondir (en m'opposant, en faisant des concessions).	1	0
c. Je peux nuancer mes propos en respectant les arguments des autres.	2	0
4. La langue employée (phonologie, rythme, vocabulaire, grammaire)		
a. Je réutilise les mots et les tournures vus pendant l'année.	1	0
b. Je fais des efforts de prononciation pour me faire comprendre.	1	0
c. J'utilise les tournures propres au débat (pour exprimer mon désaccord, faire répéter...).	2	0
d. J'utilise des *gap fillers* lorsque j'hésite.	1	0

TOTAL = ... 20 POINTS

ÉVALUATION

J'ÉVALUE MES PROGRÈS

À la suite de ces trois unités, évaluez vos progrès et faites le bilan de vos compétences.

ACT Responsible association à but non-lucratif qui a pour mission de sensibiliser toutes sortes de publics aux causes sociales et environnementales. ACT Responsible collecte de manière permanente le meilleur de la création publicitaire en provenance des associations, ONG et entreprises et les rend accessibles sur une base de données, unique en son genre sur www.actresponsible.org.

1 Je me prépare

Vous vous promenez dans la rue avec un(e) ami(e). Vous voyez cette affiche et vous réagissez : mobilisez le lexique que vous connaissez.

a. Comment allez-vous exprimer votre opinion ? Donnez trois structures.

b. Vous voulez récapituler ce que vous venez de dire. Quelles expressions allez-vous utiliser ? Donnez deux exemples.

c. Trouvez deux structures pour exprimer votre accord.

d. Trouvez trois expressions pour exprimer votre désaccord.

e. Vous ne comprenez pas votre ami(e), vous lui demandez des explications supplémentaires. Quelles phrases allez-vous utiliser ? Donnez trois exemples.

f. Vous voulez donner des exemples, comment les introduisez-vous ? (trois expressions)

g. Vous voulez couper la parole poliment à votre ami(e). (deux expressions)

2 Je prends la parole

Exprimez vos réactions face à ce document.

MP3

3 Je m'auto-corrige

Écoutez l'enregistrement correspondant à cette évaluation et comparez vos réponses à celles de Brian et Kate qui ont été interviewés.

SOMMATIVE

Speaking interaction

JE FAIS LE BILAN

Analysez vos résultats à l'aide de cette grille d'évaluation où sont définis les différents paliers de compétences en production orale en interaction.

Je peux…	**Paliers**
… participer à une conversation simple à condition que mon interlocuteur parle lentement, répète et m'aide à trouver mes mots.	**A2** en cours d'acquisition
… discuter sur des sujets simples de la vie quotidienne même si je n'arrive pas à comprendre toute la conversation dans les détails. … exprimer mes goûts, mon opinion, mes sentiments au cours d'une conversation.	**A2**
… participer à une conversation avec des jeunes de mon âge et parler de sujets qui nous concernent (musique, sports, jeux vidéos, environnement…).	**A2**
… discuter de divers sujets en exprimant mes sentiments. … interroger quelqu'un pour connaître son opinion et exprimer mon opinion poliment. … couper la parole à quelqu'un poliment si je n'ai pas compris ce qu'il disait ou pour exprimer mon désaccord.	**B1**
… reformuler mes propos si mon interlocuteur ne me comprend pas. … réagir pour exprimer mon désaccord.	**B1**
… être à l'origine d'une discussion (aborder un sujet qui m'intéresse). … participer activement à une conversation (sans avoir préparé mon intervention).	**B1**
… être à l'origine d'une discussion, la poursuivre en relançant la conversation et la conclure. … défendre mes idées en les argumentant. … résumer les idées suggérées, peser le pour et le contre de ces arguments.	en route vers **B2**

ÉVALUATION

Votre professeur va maintenant vous distribuer une fiche portant sur les nouvelles technologies. Vous devrez identifier le problème soulevé par ce document, puis en discuter avec un autre élève en donnant votre opinion, en défendant votre point de vue et en illustrant vos propos par des exemples concrets. Une fois l'évaluation terminée, votre professeur pourra ainsi déterminer à quel palier vous vous situez par rapport à la grille d'évaluation du Cadre Européen Commun de Référence pour les Langues.

- Temps de préparation individuel : **5 minutes**
- Ne rédigez pas votre texte, vous n'aurez droit qu'à des notes.
- Temps de parole : **1 à 2 minutes**

Becoming Jane, Julian Jarrold, 2007 (starring Anne Hathaway)

Unit 14 A MIND TO MURDER

- Read mystery stories and be a detective in two murder stories.

YOUR TASK

Creative writing contest: You have to write a short episode for a detective story based on several pictures. Your class will choose the story that will be published in the school newspaper.

→ p. 196

Unit 15 OVER THE RAINBOW

- Explore South Africa. Learn about its population, troubled past and heroes.
- How has this country evolved since 1992?

YOUR TASK

You are a journalist working on a report on South Africa. You have to illustrate a timeline, give key historical dates of the country and write a short paragraph on the main events.

→ p. 208

Unit 16 JAMAICAN COLOURS OF LONDON

- On the last weekend in August, London is the scene of a spectacular event – the Notting Hill Carnival. Discover its Caribbean origins.

YOUR TASK

Imagine you work for The Visit London Organization. You want to publish a leaflet for tourists interested in the Notting Hill Carnival.

→ p. 220

A MIND TO MURDER

YOUR TASK AT THE END OF THIS UNIT

Creative writing contest: You will have to write a short episode for a detective story based on several pictures. Your class will choose the story that will be published in the school newspaper. → P. 196

TUNE IN!

On Thursday James Trudd received a note from his Uncle Tobias. It said: "I didn't want you to marry Helen Reed! You will not get any of my money now. I shall speak to my lawyer about this on Friday."

James decided to kill his uncle immediately, before he could speak to his lawyer. James looked up trains to and from Lowbridge, where Uncle Tobias lived, and set out on his journey.

Soon after he reached the house in Lowbridge, James shot his uncle through the head. For the next three hours he searched his uncle's desk and read every letter in it. There was none to the lawyer.

James then took his uncle's pen and wrote a letter, which said: "Dear James, I do not want to live any longer. I have decided to kill myself. Sorry. Your Uncle Tobias." He put the letter in an envelope and addressed it to himself.

James put the gun into his uncle's hand. He dropped the note of the train times in a basket. Then he left the house.

Before catching the 8.45 train back to his home, James posted the letter to himself in Lowbridge.

David Cobb, *Puzzles for English Practice*, 1979

1 Case study

a. Read the comic on the opposite page and observe the pictures.
b. Close your books and sum up the story briefly.
c. Describe the crime scene briefly (picture 3).
d. James Trudd was immediately suspected. List all the clues that helped Inspector Key solve the case.
e. Why did James kill his uncle?

Help!

Victim	Clues	Motive
pool /pu:l/ of blood /blʌd/: *flaque de sang* lie, lay, lain commit suicide /ˈsuɪsaɪd/ shoot oneself It looks as if...	murder weapon /ˈwepən/ = arm fingerprints: *empreintes digitales* handwriting DNA: *ADN* alibi /ˈælɪbaɪ/ be left-handed ≠ be right-handed collect the mail investigate	will: *testament* heir /eəʳ/: *héritier* guilty of...: *coupable de...* greedy for money: *cupide* be mad at sb disinherit /ˌdɪsɪnˈherɪt/ sb obey sb object to

- The inspector noticed / could see... , so...
- He could guess James was the murderer as...
- Judging from... , he came to the conclusion / assumed that...
- Solving the mystery wasn't difficult since...
- Following James's track was easy as...

2 It sounds intriguing

WB

a. Listen to the recording and identify the different sounds or noises you can hear.

b. What adjectives would you choose to describe the atmosphere in the recording?

relaxed • tense • creepy /ˈkri:pi/ = spooky /ˈspu:ki/: *qui donne la chair de poule* • gloomy: *lugubre* • scary = frightening • weird /wɪəd/ = strange • threatening = menacing • disturbing • joyful

PREPARE YOUR TASK →

3 Writing workshop

WB

Observe the picture on the right. A crime has been committed and you were a witness of the scene. Now you are questioned by the police. Write a short dialogue with the help of your Workbook. (120 words)

I. SCREAM

The Wind, Victor Sjöström, 1928

1 Get ready

Read the title of the page and look at the picture. Imagine what the text is about.

2 Jigsaw reading

Read the beginning of the text (A). The following paragraphs (B to G) have been mixed up. Re-order them with the help of the comic strip on the opposite page.

A

A few years ago, Helen Stoner's twin sister died mysteriously. Now Helen believes her life is threatened too, so she pays Sherlock Holmes a visit. Here is what she tells him about the night her sister died.

I could not sleep that night. A vague feeling of impending[1] misfortune impressed me. My sister and I, you will recollect, were twins, and you know how subtle are the links which bind[2] two souls which are so closely allied...

1. *imminent* 2. connect

B

As I ran down the passage, my sister's door was unlocked, and revolved slowly upon its hinges.

C

I sprang from my bed, wrapped a shawl round me, and rushed into the corridor. As I opened my door, I seemed to hear a low whistle, such as my sister described, and a few moments later a clanging sound, as if a mass of metal had fallen.

D

It was a wild night. The wind was howling outside, and the rain was beating and splashing against the windows. Suddenly, amid all the hubbub of the gale, there burst forth the wild scream of a terrified woman. I knew that it was my sister's voice.

E

I rushed out, calling loudly for my stepfather, and I met him hastening from his room in his dressing-gown. When he reached my sister's side she was unconscious, and though he poured brandy down her throat and sent for medical aid from the village, all efforts were in vain, for she slowly sank and died without having recovered her consciousness. Such was the dreadful end of my beloved sister.

F

At first I thought that she had not recognized me, but as I bent over her, she suddenly shrieked out in a voice which I shall never forget: "Oh, my God! Helen! It was the band! The speckled band!" There was something else which she would fain[1] have said, and she stabbed with her finger into the air in the direction of the doctor's room, but a fresh convulsion seized her and choked her words.

1. *(archaïque) volontiers*

G

I stared at it horror-stricken, not knowing what was about to issue from it. By the light of the corridor lamp I saw my sister appear at the opening, her face blanched with terror, her hands groping for help, her whole figure swaying to and fro like that of a drunkard. I ran to her and threw my arms round her, but at that moment her knees seemed to give way and she fell to the ground. She writhed[1] as one who is in terrible pain, and her limbs were dreadfully convulsed.

1. *se tordait*

Sir Arthur Conan Doyle, *The Adventure of the Speckled Band*, 1892

3 Understanding the text WB

Turn to your Workbook for help.

4 Recap

a. What time of day is it? List the different places mentioned in the passage. Describe the atmosphere. Use the adjectives mentioned p. 187.

b. Pick out all the words referring to the different noises and to the weather conditions. What impact do these details have on the reader?

c. Concentrate on Helen Stoner. Find all the words describing her actions and reactions. Then analyse her feelings throughout this passage.

d. List all the words and expressions referring to Helen's twin sister. What is she compared to? What impressions are given?

PREPARE YOUR TASK → **e.** Building suspense. Discuss your findings: How is suspense created?

2. SOLVE IT!

1 Get ready

– Read the title of the text below. Give a definition of the word "kidnapping".
– What stories does this word remind you of (books, movies, news...)?
– Observe the photograph on the opposite page. What may have happened? What may happen now?

2 Understanding the text

a. Read the text once carefully.

The Wembly Kidnapping

"I know we should have called the police," Eric Wembly admitted as he nursed a bump[1] on the back of his head. "But the kidnapper said he'd kill my brother if we did. And it's not like we couldn't afford the ransom."

Wink Wembly, the elder son of Jonas Wembly, had been missing since Tuesday. On Wednesday morning, a lone kidnapper telephoned the mansion and made his demands. The younger Wembly son, Eric, was to bring the money in unmarked bills in a duffel bag. He was to take a specific route from the mansion, parking in a downtown lot and carrying the bag through an alley to a drop site in a nearby park.

The normally cheap Jonas Wembly was frantic and willingly agreed to the terms. A midnight pay-off. Half a million dollars. And no police.

"I was halfway through the alley," Eric testified, "when I heard footsteps. Before I could turn around I was hit on the head. I fell down. But it didn't quite knock me out. I could see his back by the light of a street lamp. Never got to see his front. He was running away with the duffel bag. A tall guy with white sneakers. He was wearing blue jeans and a dark cardigan. Sorry I can't be more specific."

In the case's one lucky break, a police officer came across Eric shortly after the attack. He called in the crime and a patrol car responded immediately. Two suspicious-looking characters were apprehended in the vicinity, both resembling Eric's description.

"So, I was running," Petey Bordon said angrily. He had been found two blocks from the attack and started running as soon as he saw the patrol car. Petey had a string of priors[2], all misdemeanors[3] "I'm on parole[4]," he admitted. "And I was carrying a knife – for my own protection at night. That's a violation. Can you wonder why I ran away?"

The second suspect was Amie Acker, a homeless drifter. "I wasn't even wearing this sweater," he protested as he unbuttoned his moth-eaten[5] cardigan. "I picked it out of the garbage just before you guys pulled me in."

"We didn't find money on either one of 'em," the chief of police told Jonas Wembly. "And we didn't find the duffel bag. But I got a pretty good idea what happened. Don't worry. We'll get your son back."

Hy Conrad, www.mysterynet.com, January 2008

1. *bosse* **2.** *antécédents* **3.** *petits délits* **4.** I'm on parole: *je suis en liberté conditionnelle* **5.** *mité*

b. Focus your attention on Eric Wembly's report of his attack:
– **Time**: When did it take place?
– **Place**: Where was Eric asked to go and what route did he follow?
Where was he attacked (give one detail)?

– **Actions**: What happened to Eric?
What was he knocked on?
Why couldn't he see his aggressor's face?
What happened to him immediately after the attack?
Was the description Eric gave vague or precise?

c. Concentrate on the men arrested by the police.
– **Place**: Where were they arrested?
– **Clothes and other details**: What were they wearing or what were they carrying?
– **Suspect actions**: What attracted the attention of the police?

d. Concentrate on the suspect's description given by Eric Wembly and draw the suspect's portrait: height, clothes, other specific details. Is it precise? Why? Why not?

e. Confront your results.
– Among the following list of clues, which ones were given by Eric in his testimony? Which ones were found by the police?
duffel bag • tall • white sneakers • blue jeans • dark cardigan • vicinity • knife • misdemeanors
– Which of these clues revealed somebody was lying in his testimony?
– Decide on the suspect's name and justify your choice.

PREPARE YOUR TASK

3 Writing workshop

Read paragraphs 2 and 3 again. Then, imagine the conversation between Jonas Wembly and the kidnapper. (80 words)
Here are a few guidelines to write the dialogue.

a. Observe.
"I know we should have called the police," Eric Wembly admitted as he nursed a bump on the back of his head. (l. 1)
– What part of this sentence is in direct speech? How do you know?
– Translate into French: "Eric Wembly admitted as he nursed a bump on the back of his head." What do you notice?

b. Useful words
Verbs: he said • he asked • he told • he yelled *(hurla)* • he replied *(répliqua)* • he warned • he ordered
Adverbs: angrily • threateningly • drily *(sèchement)* • loudly *(d'une voix forte)* • rudely *(impoliment)* • impatiently

c. At the beginning of your dialogue write one or two sentences to introduce the situation.

4 Watch a video

Suspicion
Watch an extract from the film directed by Alfred Hitchcock (1941).
What does Lina suddenly realize in this sequence? Turn to your worksheet for help.

3. HEART OF DARKNESS

After the excitement of the party [...] Trish headed to the twins' room. The Frawleys had ripped out[1] the worn carpet that had been in the house, and the nineteenth-century steps creaked under her feet.

Near the top step, she paused. The light she had left on in the hall was off. Probably another fuse had blown. The wiring[2] in the old house was a mess. That had happened in the kitchen this afternoon.

The twins' bedroom was at the end of the hall. There was no sound coming from it now. Probably one of the twins had cried out in her sleep, Trish thought as she began to inch her way[3] through the darkness. Suddenly she stopped. It's not just the hall light. I left the door to their room open so I could hear them if they woke up. The night-light in the room should be showing. The door's closed. But I couldn't have heard one of them crying if it was closed a minute ago.

1. *arraché* **2.** *système électrique* **3.** inch one's way: *avancer petit à petit*

Mary Higgins Clark, *Two Little Girls in Blue*, 2006

Understanding the text WB

a. Turn to your Workbook for help.
b. Sum up the situation in a few words.
c. Here are five different endings. Which ones are logical, which ones have no link with the context?

A She heard it from the foyer, the faint click of a turning door reached her ears. She jammed her hand against her mouth to muffle a scream. He wasn't supposed to come tonight. She turned round to face him.

B She tried to scream, but only a moan escaped her lips. She tried to run but her legs wouldn't move. She felt a hand grab her hair and yank her head back. The last thing she remembered was a feeling of pressure on her neck.

C And then she heard it. The sound. Something thudding against the door. Was he coming back? Had he changed his mind?

D Startled, we both turned and looked in the direction from which the voice came. Richard Walker was moving toward us, a pistol in his hand.

E Suddenly frightened, she listened intently. What was that sound? In an instant of sickening awareness, she identified it: soft footsteps. A hint of equally soft breathing. The acrid smell of perspiration. *Someone was behind her.*

d. Give another title to this passage and justify your choice.

Language at work

Improve your pronunciation

MP3

Prononcez ces mots à haute voix, puis vérifiez avec l'enregistrement.

rob, robber • shoplift, shoplifter • kidnap, kidnapper • blackmail, blackmailer • deal, dealer

→ **Déduisez :** le suffixe *-**er*** … … … la place de l'accent dans le mot auquel il est ajouté. C'est un suffixe neutre.

Build up your vocabulary

1 À l'aide d'un dictionnaire, trouvez le mot noyau ou les mots dérivés de la même famille. Puis complétez ce tableau sur papier libre.

Nom	Verbe	Adjectif	Adverbe
		wild	
			dreadfully
			probably
suddenness			*suddenly*
closeness			
		loud	

2 Complétez ce paragraphe à l'aide des verbes ci-dessous à la forme qui convient. Utilisez un dictionnaire pour vérifier leur sens si nécessaire.

head to • hasten /ˈheɪsn/ = hurry • turn up • blow away • ride back • hum over • bump into • run away • fall down

As no one … 1 at the meeting point, he … 2 the nearest bus stop to … 3 to town. While he … 4 , he heard a plane … 5 him. Suddenly the plane whizzed past him and he … 6 . He realized he was being chased. He was so scared that he started … 7 . Luckily enough, the plane … 8 a van and exploded and many pieces … 9 in the air.

3 Traduisez ces énoncés, à l'aide d'un dictionnaire si nécessaire.

a. I rushed into the corridor.
b. As I ran down the passage, my sister's door revolved slowly upon its hinges.
c. I rushed out, calling loudly for my stepfather.
d. He was running away with the duffel bag.

4 À l'aide d'un dictionnaire, associez chacun de ces mots à la définition qui lui correspond.

a. sleuth /slu:θ/
b. thief
c. witness
d. acc**o**mplice
e. sh**a**dow (verb)
f. bl**a**ckmailer
g. plot
h. sm**u**ggler

1. follow someone closely and watch movement
2. someone who gets goods illegally and secretly in / out of a country
3. someone who uses threats or violence to steal money
4. partner in crime
5. detective
6. person who steals
7. person present at an event and who is able to describe it
8. make secret plans

Language at work

L'interrogation

1 Observez.

a. *Did the burglar break into the room at 10.30 p.m.?*
b. *What time did the burglar break into the room?*
c. *What has the burglar stolen?*
d. *What were you doing at that time?*
e. *Are you sure nothing else was stolen?*
À quelle forme sont les énoncés ci-dessus ?

→ **Complétez :** en anglais, les constructions interrogatives utilisent obligatoirement un … (sauf pour *Who* et *What* sujets).
Quand la question commence par un mot interrogatif, on a l'ordre :
mot interrogatif + … + … + …

2 Associez chacune des questions de l'exercice 1 à sa réponse.

a. *All my jewels.*
b. *I'm positive.*
c. *No, he didn't. He broke into the room at 11.30 p.m.*
d. *I was watching a film.*
e. *The burglar broke into the room at 11.30.*

3 Sujet ou complément ?

a. *Who saw anything suspicious?*
b. *What did you hear?*
c. *Who do you suspect?*
d. *What happened next?*
e. *Who suspects you?*

À quels temps sont les énoncés ci-dessus ? Classez-les en deux colonnes, pour distinguer ceux où le mot interrogatif est sujet de ceux où le mot interrogatif est complément.
Que remarquez-vous lorsque le mot interrogatif est sujet de la phrase ?
→ **Déduisez :** il n'y a pas d'auxiliaire *do / does / did* ni au … ni au … . La construction est celle de … .

4 La place de la préposition

"What do you suspect this man of?" *"I suspect him of being the murderer."*
→ **Complétez :** si le verbe se construit avec une préposition, cette préposition est habituellement placée … .

5 Les mots interrogatifs

Que cherche à savoir l'énonciateur ? Associez chaque question à un élément de la liste.

1. ***Who*** *is the victim?*
2. ***Whose*** *gun is it?*
3. ***When*** *did you last meet the victim?*
4. ***What time*** *did you leave the flat?*
5. ***Where*** *did you go after leaving the flat?*
6. ***Why*** *could the victim have been murdered?*
7. ***How*** *is the victim's wife?*
8. ***How*** *was the victim killed?*
9. ***What****'s the kidnapper* ***like****?*
10. ***How old*** *is the victim?*
11. ***How many*** *bullets were shot at the victim?*
12. ***How much*** *money was kept in the safe?*
13. ***How far*** *was the murderer from his victim?*
14. ***How often*** *did you meet the victim?*
15. ***How long*** *will it take to have the test results?*

a. âge
b. nombre
c. santé
d. moment / date
e. possesseur
f. description
g. lieu
h. raison
i. quantité
j. durée
k. moyen / manière
l. distance
m. identité
n. heure
o. fréquence

Language at work

Practice

1 Mettez ces mots dans l'ordre pour obtenir des énoncés interrogatifs.

a. you / unusual / night / did / last / noises / hear / ?
b. much / has / money / how / stolen / been / ?
c. time / wife / leave / flat / what / his / did / the / ?
d. were / photos / by / when / taken / the / detective / the / ?
e. her / know / why / you / he / left / do / ?
f. work / victim / morning / the / to / go / did / yesterday / ?

2 Interrogatoire : reconstituez ce dialogue. Aidez-vous des réponses pour compléter chaque question à l'aide d'un mot interrogatif.

THE INSPECTOR: You saw a suspect. ...?
THE WITNESS: He was quite tall.
THE INSPECTOR: ...?
THE WITNESS: About thirty.
THE INSPECTOR: ...?
THE WITNESS: It was dark, short and curly.
THE INSPECTOR: ...?
THE WITNESS: No, he didn't. He had a moustache.
THE INSPECTOR: ...?
THE WITNESS: It was around ten.
THE INSPECTOR: ...?
THE WITNESS: I was walking my dog.
THE INSPECTOR: ...?
THE WITNESS: No, never. It's the first time.

3 Jeu de rôles WB

Un meurtre a été commis. Les trois colocataires de la victime sont interrogés par l'agent spécial Kate Todd. Certains élèves joueront le rôle des colocataires et d'autres celui de Kate. Vous trouverez tous les renseignements nécessaires pour poser des questions ou y répondre (en fonction de votre rôle) dans votre *Workbook*.

Your task

Creative writing contest: You have to write a short episode for a detective story based on several pictures. Your class will choose the story that will be published in the school newspaper. (200 words)

LES ÉTAPES À SUIVRE

1 Observez bien les images ci-contre et repérez pour chacune d'entre elles :
le lieu, le moment, les personnages, l'action et le ou les détail(s) important(s).

2 Pour chacun des protagonistes, imaginez une identité.
Nom, prénom, profession (soyez aussi précis que possible), rôle (victime, témoin d'un meurtre, détective privé, témoin poursuivi par la police...) et relation avec la victime.

3 Imaginez un scénario.
Relatez les événements figurant dans la bande dessinée, imaginez les événements antérieurs, le dénouement et les conséquences à prévoir.

⚠ Votre récit sera à la troisième personne du singulier : *John Goodface shadows Professor Helmer to protect him after he escaped a murder attempt. One day...*

CONSEILS POUR LA RÉDACTION

1 Quelles formes verbales allez-vous utiliser ?

RAPPELS
- Le prétérit simple s'emploie pour faire un récit.
- Le prétérit en BE + -ING s'emploie pour faire un « arrêt sur image » à l'intérieur d'une action.
- Le *past perfect* s'emploie pour évoquer une action passée qui précède une autre action déjà située dans le passé, ou pour effectuer un bilan par rapport à un point de repère passé.

2 Utilisez les outils suivants.

– **Verbes introducteurs du style indirect :**
feel • think • realise • react
– **Mots de liaison :**
when • while • as • because
– **Marqueurs chronologiques :**
first • then • after a while • later / a few minutes later • suddenly / all of a sudden • eventually / finally

Help!

magnifying /ˈmæɡnɪfaɪɪŋ/ glasses: *jumelles*
blast-effect: *effet de souffle*
detonator
watch over sb: *surveiller qqn*
track sb: *filer qqn*
blow up = explode
fling, flung, flung: *projeter*
see / watch / observe sb + V-ing

CAR PARK
WAY OUT
EXIT
ELEC CO.

Unit 15

OVER THE RAINBOW

YOUR TASK AT THE END OF THIS UNIT

You are a journalist working on a report on South Africa. You will have to illustrate a timeline, give key historical dates of the country and write a short paragraph on the main events. → p. 208

TUNE IN!

Faces of South Africa

There are nearly 43 million South Africans, most of them belonging to one of four major ethnic groups. The largest ethnic group is black (75.2 percent of the population); followed by whites (13.6 percent). Coloureds, as South Africans call people of mixed race, make up 8.6 percent of the population. Indians, mostly the descendants of South Asian immigrants, comprise about 2.6 percent of the population. […]

South Africa's white community consists primarily of Afrikaners (descendants of Dutch, French, and German settlers[1] who formed unique cultural traditions and their own language) and "English speakers" (mostly the descendants of immigrants from the United Kingdom).

For more than 300 years the white minority ruled[2] South Africa as colonialists and then through apartheid[3], a system of government that entrenched[4] white privilege and reserved political power for whites.

The system was abandoned peacefully in 1994 – after a long, sometimes bitter struggle[5] by black political and labor movements. Whites and blacks negotiated a constitution based on individual rights, and all South Africans participated in the election of a democratic government. Nelson Mandela was elected the first president of a democratic South Africa. [...]

South Africa is divided into nine provinces, each with its own legislature [...]. The provinces are the Western Cape, the Eastern Cape, KwaZulu-Natal, the Northern Cape, Free State, North West, Gauteng, Mpumalanga, and Limpopo.

Within these provinces are a number of "traditional rulers[6]," including the current Zulu king, Goodwill Zwelethini, who is a direct descendant of King Shaka, founder of the Zulu kingdom.

South Africa's Indian community is largely descended from indentured[7] laborers brought to South Africa by the British to work on sugar plantations. South African Indians today are found in all walks of life, including the president's cabinet, the law courts, and corporate executive suites. [...]

The Coloureds are South Africa's people of mixed racial ancestry. Made up of descendants of former slaves[8], blacks, and whites, many Coloureds proudly assert[9] that they are living proof that South Africa's different races can get along.

www.news.nationalgeographic.com, 2009

1. *colons* **2.** *a dirigé* **3.** /əˈpɑːteɪt/ **4.** *établissait fermement* **5.** bitter struggle: *combat âpre* **6.** *dirigeants* **7.** *liés par contrat* **8.** *esclaves* **9.** *affirment*

1 Fast facts

Recap the key information in this text.

a. – Total population of South Africa?
– Ethnic groups?
– Proportion of Blacks?

b. Afrikaners:
– Origins?
– White domination: How long?
– Type of regime?
– First democratically elected president?

c. Indians:
– Origin?
– Explanation for their presence in South Africa?

d. Coloureds:
– Definition and ancestry?

2 South Africa at a glance

Have a close look at the map opposite and find out:
– the name of the capital city and of two other famous cities
– what city names are of Dutch, British or African origin
– the name of a national park
– the name of a desert

3 Recap

a. Why is South Africa called the Rainbow Nation?

PREPARE YOUR TASK → **b.** Go on the Internet to find what the "Y sign" on the flag symbolizes (see opposite picture in the bottom left-hand corner). Key words for your research: "South Africa / flag / symbolism".

1. THE FIGHT

1 Watch a video

Goodbye Bafana

Watch this extract from a film directed by Bille August (2007) and turn to your worksheet for help.

PREPARE YOUR TASK → The little girl in the movie is now a grandmother. She tells her grandchildren what happened on that day and how she reacted. (150 words)

Youth day poster showing Hector Pieterson's death

2 Soweto riots WB

The youth rebellion began in June 1976 when the Soweto school children started protesting against the decision of the apartheid government to teach them in Afrikaans, the language of the ruling Whites, and not in English. The initial battles left more than 400 dead and many more were arrested or sent to the homelands (poor territories for Blacks). The fight continued until the mid-1980s.

3 A time of fire

a. Understanding the text opposite WB
Turn to your Workbook for help.

b. Make a one-minute presentation.
– Where were Grace and Dumi?
– What were they there for?
– What happened to them?
– Why?

Help!

bitter / resentful: *amer*
determined
demonstrate against: *manifester contre*
be discriminated against
impose on
complain about: *se plaindre de*
crush a riot: *écraser une émeute*

It was a "time of fire" as Grace called it, when she and Dumi[1] had marched in the streets with thousands of other schoolchildren. They were protesting that their schools taught them only what the white government wanted them to know.

On the banner that Dumi and his friends carried, they had written: "BLACKS ARE NOT DUSTBINS[2]."

Everything went all right until the police saw the schoolchildren marching, and then the trouble started. The police aimed their guns and began to shoot with real bullets, killing whoever was in the way.

It was terrible. The police shot tear gas too, making everyone's eyes burn.

People were screaming, bleeding[3], falling. More police came in great steel[4] tanks, and more in helicopters, firing from above. A little girl standing near Grace, about eight years old, raised her fist[5], and next thing she was lying dead.

People became fighting mad, throwing stones at the police, burning down schools and government offices. Smoke and flames were everywhere.

But the police kept shooting, until hundreds were dead. Hundreds were hurt and hundreds were arrested. Dumi was one of those arrested.

When he came out of prison, he said that the police had beaten him up badly, but he would go on fighting even if they killed him.

Beverley Naidoo, *Journey to Jo'burg*, 1985

1. Grace's brother **2.** *poubelles*
3. were bleeding: *saignaient* **4.** *en acier* **5.** *poing*

2. NELSON MANDELA

1 Get ready

Share with the class what you know about Nelson Mandela.

2 Understanding the text

WB

Turn to your Workbook for help.

90th birthday celebration for Mandela, July 9, 2008, Johannesburg

Buti grew strong and smart, and when he was seven years old, two old friends of his father recognized how smart he was and told his mother he should be in school. Even Buti's father, who had never gone to school himself, thought this was an excellent idea.

On the first day of school, the English teacher gave all the African children English names. Buti's new name was Nelson.

He wasn't certain if he liked his new English name, but Nelson knew he liked school. He liked the slate tablets[1] used for writing. He liked learning new things and he liked the way his father prepared him for school by telling him always to stand firm for[2] what he believed was fair and right[3].

Next Nelson advanced to Fort Hare, a missionary college for African scholars[4] from all over Africa. […] He became a school leader […] and in his final year was elected to serve on the student council. When, in a protest for better food, he quit the council, the principal threatened him: Come back, or be expelled!

Nelson refused. He stood firm for what he believed was fair and right, and was expelled.

Nelson never imagined the unfairness and inequality that he would find in Johannesburg. He'd known of the attitude most English men had toward anything African […]. But he could hardly believe what he saw.

Floyd Cooper, *Mandela: From the Life of the South African Statesman*, 1996

1. slate tablets: *ardoises* **2.** stand firm for: *(ici) défendre* **3.** fair and right: *juste et bien* **4.** *(ici) élèves méritants*

3 Recap

Draw Nelson Mandela's portrait when he was a student. Use adjectives from the toolbox opposite.

Help!

- obedient
- rebellious
- determined
- committed: *engagé*
- rude: *impoli*
- responsible
- popular
- courageous
- bold: *audacieux*
- wilful: *volontaire*
- resolute
- gentle
- provocative

4 Going further

a. Focus on the following sentences. Define the Whites' attitude to Africans at that time and analyse Mandela's reactions then.

– "Buti's new name was Nelson. He wasn't certain if he liked his new English name..." (l. 7)

– "Nelson never imagined the unfairness and inequality that he would find in Johannesburg." (l. 16)

– "He'd known of the attitude most English men had toward anything African." (l. 16)

b. What aspects of the future leader's personality are revealed here?

5 More information

WB

Listen to this radio programme to learn more about the life of Nelson Mandela.
Turn to your Workbook for help.

PREPARE YOUR TASK →

6 Writing workshop

Write a short biography of Nelson Mandela using what you have learned from the radio programme and the text above. (150 words)

3. WE ARE TOGETHER

1 Get ready

Read this paragraph about the Agape Orphanage.

a. What problem is South Africa confronted with?
b. Find information about Agape. (What? How many children? How old? Founder? Goals?)
c. React to the figures given in the extract.

The children of the Agape Orphanage[1] in South Africa know adversity: Every day the HIV/AIDS pandemic[2] kills 8,000 people, and in their neighboring population, the infection rate[3] is nearly 40%. The Agape Orphanage is home to 30 orphans, aged 7 to 16 years, and their spirits thrive[4] despite their devastating[5] situation. How can it be that in a country as rich as South Africa these children are left to wander the landscape alone? After having lost their parents to AIDS or other issues exacerbated by the disease, Gogo Zodwa Mqadi, a social worker, took them in and gave them a safe haven.

www.keepachildalive.org, 2008

1. *orphelinat* 2. *épidémie de sida* 3. *taux* 4. *prospèrent* 5. /devəsteɪtɪŋ/ *accablante*

2 Understanding the text below

The class is divided into three groups.

Group 1

a. Find information about the Agape orphanage:
– Origin of the word?
– Where?
– When?

b. What do you learn about Gogo?
– Job? Origin? Personality?
– Goals?
– Problems met?

c. Do you admire Gogo? Why? Why not?

Group 2

Focus on Paul.

a. Draw his portrait: age, studies, nationality.

b. Paul's project:
– How did he get to know about Agape?
– How long did he stay there?
– What were his goals?
– What influence did this experience have on him?
– What problems was he confronted with?

Group 3

Concentrate on the concert.

a. What happened to the orphanage?
b. What were the consequences?
c. Who helped them?
d. What were the results?

Class work

Confront your results and react to this story.

Together they sing

The Daily Telegraph *relates the story of Paul Taylor who shot a film on the Agape Orphanage.*

Part 1

"We Are Together" charts[1] three turbulent years in the life of Agape, an orphanage founded by a social worker, "Gogo" Zodwa Mqadi, in KwaZulu-Natal. Gogo is a big woman with a big personality. She has a huge, throaty[2] laugh, wears a fur[3] hat even in summer and explodes with charm. "Agape is a Greek word meaning unconditional love," she beams. "At Agape we have unconditional love." […]

Making the film has clearly changed [Paul Taylor's] life, and not just in terms of his career. "They're remarkable kids because whatever situation they're in, however difficult it is, they always see the positive. They have enough reasons in their life to be really down, but they never were. It made a big impact on me."

[…] In the summer of 2003, the end of his first year [at university], he wanted to go travelling. […] "I knew I wanted to spend three months in one place and do something a little bit different, so I came across this volunteer project on the internet. Agape. It was really random[4]."

Agape is half-an-hour inland from Durban, in a Zulu area called Valley of a Thousand Hills. [...] Agape is in fact on the edge[5] of the white neighbourhood of Waterfall, an affluent[6] village with a shopping centre and a SPAR[7]. "Agape had problems in the early days with local residents not wanting it there," Taylor says. Gogo set it up in the late 1990s. "A lot of people she was dealing with were HIV-positive and their main concern was what would happen to their children when they passed away[8]. So she said, "I'll look after them." She found a piece of land with some shipping containers, with no windows or anything and had 60 kids in there on mattresses. It was a real struggle. Then someone donated the house and the plot of land[9] and they moved into the house, kept some of the shipping containers and put windows and doors in them." [...]

Taylor says he was beguiled[10] when he arrived at Agape. "They're so endearing, so loveable! I never imagined I would have so much fun, just with the kids. [...]

[In] October, I was back at university and I really wanted a reason to go back and spend more time with the kids. I just wanted to do more to help them."

A Zulu village, near Eshowe

1. *(ici) raconte* **2.** *rauque* **3.** *fourrure* **4.** *un hasard* **5.** *(ici) à la limite* **6.** rich **7.** *nom d'un supermarché*
8. passed away: *(ici) mourraient* **9.** plot of land: *parcelle de terrain* **10.** /bɪˈgaɪld/ *envoûté*

Part 2

So, scraping together[1] $6,000 from family, credit cards and Theatrecares, an AIDS charity, Taylor went back to Agape [...].

Four months later, the main house at the orphanage burnt down [...].

What happened was the stuff of dreams[2]. After the [fundraising] trip to the UK was cancelled[3], the children might have thought it was all over, but Gogo instigated Plan B: "To finish [recording a CD of traditional Zulu songs] and hope somebody somewhere will hear them."

Somebody did hear the children singing: Alicia Keyes, the pop star, and co-founder of Keep a Child Alive, the charity that provides anti-retroviral drugs for people with HIV/AIDS. In the summer of 2005, the charity contacted Agape, inviting the children to perform in a fundraising concert in New York with Paul Simon and Alicia Keyes. [...] The concert raised $60,000. [...] The film has also raised $150,000 to help Agape rebuild after the fire.

The Daily Telegraph, March 1, 2008

1. scraping together: *après avoir rassemblé à grand-peine* **2.** the stuff of dreams: *(ici) digne d'un roman* **3.** *annulé*

PREPARE YOUR TASK

3 Writing workshop

Write a short summary of the whole article. (100 words)

4. SOWETO TODAY

1 Understanding the text

Read the whole article. Write down all the city names, dates and figures and find what they correspond to.

South Africa's famous Soweto township has marked 100 years since its creation in a mood[1] of optimism far removed from the days of apartheid.

Soweto began when tens of thousands of Johannesburg's black residents were sent there from the city centre as the white authorities imposed segregation.

Soweto, which is an acronym for Johannesburg's South West Townships, is now home to more than 3.5 million people.

Now life is slowly improving[2] for the inhabitants. Water and electricity have been provided for many people, but not all.

In Soweto, as in other townships, thousands of shacks[3] have been cleared away and replaced with solid houses, with proper[4] roadways and street lighting.

There are even some small guest houses[5], restaurants, small shopping malls[6] with security guards, and a new supermarket.

While AIDS and unemployment are still huge problems in Soweto, there is a real feeling of optimism that the next 100 years have good things in store for the sprawling[7] township, our correspondent says.

BBC News, October 12, 2004

1. *(ici) climat* **2.** *s'améliore* **3.** *cabanes* **4.** *dignes de ce nom, corrects* **5.** guest houses: *pensions*
6. /mɔːlz/ *centres commerciaux* **7.** /ˈsprɔːlɪŋ/ *tentaculaire*

PREPARE YOUR TASK →

2 Writing workshop

Write the "township" entry for a Web encyclopedia. Include the following points: What is a township? When were the townships created and why? Is the future of Soweto dark or bright?

Help!

shanty town / slum: *bidonville*
corrugated iron: *tôle ondulée*
clothes line: *fil à linge*
plastic container: *bidon*
running water: *eau courante*
destitute = needy: *démuni*
dreadful = awful: *épouvantable*
crammed: *entassé*
squalid /ˈskwɒlɪd/: *sordide*
do the laundry: *faire la lessive*
lack: *manquer de*
be deprived of: *être privé de*
below the poverty line: *au-dessous du seuil de pauvreté*

To learn more about South Africa, read the text p. 235.

Language at work

Improve your pronunciation

MP3

1 Lisez ce paragraphe.

Now the government is chosen by all South African people, black and white, and there are no more apartheid laws. But changing "the way things are" is much harder than just changing the laws. There is a huge gulf between rich and poor, between "haves" and "have-nots" and we must never forget to strive for[1] the ideal of equality for all. We still have an enormous mountain to climb if every child is to have an equal chance. The journey continues...

Beverley Naidoo, *Journey to Jo'burg*, 1985

1. *s'efforcer d'atteindre*

a. À quels mots dans le texte correspondent les transcriptions phonétiques suivantes (dans l'ordre du texte) ?
/lɔːz/ • /hjuːdʒ/ • /gʌlf/ • /aɪˈdɪəl/ • /ɪˈkwɒlɪti/ • /ˈmaʊntɪn/ • /klaɪm/ • /ˈiːkwəl/ • /ˈdʒɜːni/

b. Quels mots vous attendez-vous à voir accentués ? Vérifiez à l'écoute.

c. Lisez maintenant ce passage à haute voix.

2 Quelques statistiques sur l'Afrique du Sud : lisez-les à voix haute puis vérifiez à l'écoute.

– Total land area: 1,219,912 square kilometres (471,011 square miles)
– Total coastline: 2,798 kilometres (1,739 miles)
– Population (2007): 47,900,000
– Currency: the rand (1 rand = 100 cents)

Build up your vocabulary

1 Lisez ces chiffres et comparez-les entre eux.

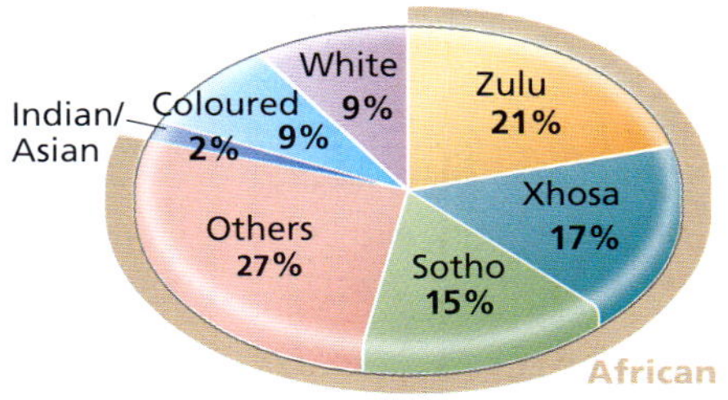

Help!

20% = twenty percent /pəˈsent/
1/4: a quarter /ˈkwɔːtəʳ/
1/2: a half
1/3: a third
1/10: a tenth
as many as
fewer than
three / four / five... times as many as

2 Complétez ces deux textes avec les mots fournis pour chacun.

a. *improved • rate • issues • evolved*

Since the fall of apartheid, the economic situation has ... 1 and race relations have ... 2 in South Africa. However, the country still faces two major ... 3 : poverty and the rise of HIV. The country is confronted with a human catastrophe as HIV spreads at a phenomenal ... 4 . An estimated 5.5 million people in the country are currently living with HIV.

b. *bridge the gap • cope with • crime rate • eradicate • huge • overcome • poverty line • under • prejudices • unemployment rate • without*

Hundreds of thousands of people still live ... 1 the ... 2 in townships ... 3 electricity or running water. The ... 4 is still very high. There is a ... 5 gap between the haves and the have-nots. The government also have to ... 6 an alarming ... 7 : murders, rapes, assaults. South Africans are still optimistic because they believe they will one day ... 8 between the rich and the poor, ... 9 deep-rooted ... 10 and ... 11 most of their difficulties.

Language at work

The present perfect

1 Ces énoncés nous renseignent-ils sur le présent ou renvoient-ils à un moment coupé du présent ?

a. *Mandela has now become a legend.*
b. *Nelson Mandela was born in Transkei in 1918.*
c. *He stayed in prison for 27 years.*
d. *46664 was Mandela's prison number when he was imprisoned on Robben Island.*
e. *In 1990 he was finally released. Four years later, he was elected president.*
f. *Things have changed a lot since 1994.*
g. *The situation in South Africa has now improved.*
h. *Many people have been involved in the fight against AIDS over the last few years.*
i. *I've just seen a photo of the concert given for Mandela's birthday.*

2 Sur papier libre, classez les formes verbales au *present perfect* et au prétérit. À quel marqueur de temps chacune de ces formes est-elle associée ?

	Present perfect	Prétérit
Marqueurs de temps		

3 Récapitulez.

– Le *present perfect* sert à exprimer un lien entre ... et ... .
– Le prétérit sert à parler d'un fait, d'une période ... .

4 Traduisez les énoncés de l'exercice 1. Quelles sont les deux formes verbales anglaises qui peuvent correspondre au passé composé français ?

→ **Déduisez :** selon le contexte, le passé composé français peut se traduire en anglais par un ... ou un ... .

5 Observez les questions et les réponses données.

A: *Have you **ever** heard of Frederik De Klerk?* B: *No, I've **never** heard of him.*
A: *Have you **ever** heard of Steve Biko?* B: *Yes, I've **already** heard a song about him.*
A: *Have you **ever** seen* Cry Freedom? B: *No, I have**n't** seen it **yet**.*

Donnez la traduction des marqueurs de temps en gras.
→ **Déduisez :** le ... ... s'emploie avec *never*, *already* et *not... yet*. La date n'est pas mentionnée. L'énonciateur s'intéresse uniquement au ... au moment présent.

6 Traduisez les énoncés suivants.

– *How long has South Africa been a democracy? – It has been a democracy **since 1994** / **since Mandela was elected** / **since the 1994 elections**.*
– *How long has he been fighting against AIDS? – He has been fighting **for many years now**.*

→ Le français « depuis » + une indication de temps a deux équivalents en anglais :
– ***for*** + indication de la ... d'une période – ***since*** + indication du ... d'une période
Pour demander « depuis combien de temps », on utilise ... ... + ...

7 Observez et traduisez ces deux énoncés.

Nelson Mandela was in jail for about twenty-seven years.
South Africa has been a democracy for about twenty years.

– L'emploi du prétérit signifie que la période dont on parle appartient au passé. On peut alors traduire *for* par ... .
– Le *present perfect* est utilisé pour un fait qui a un lien avec le présent. *For* se traduit alors par ... .

Language at work

Practice

1 Demandez-vous si l'énoncé vous donne un renseignement sur le présent ou s'il renvoie à un événement coupé du présent. Repérez le marqueur de temps et / ou la forme verbale utilisée.

a. La situation s'est améliorée ces dernières années.
b. Avant 1994, les deux communautés étaient séparées.
c. Steve Biko mourut dans sa cellule de prison en 1977.
d. Donald Woods, un journaliste blanc, dénonça les tentatives du gouvernement pour étouffer le scandale.
e. Il fut alors obligé de quitter son pays.
f. La tribu des San habite dans le désert du Kalahari depuis plus de deux mille ans.
g. Johannesburg est la capitale économique et industrielle de l'Afrique du Sud depuis plus d'un siècle.
h. Certains Sud-Africains ne se sont pas encore débarrassés de tous leurs préjugés.

2 Mettez les verbes entre parenthèses au prétérit ou au *present perfect*.

a. Spending on education (increase / greatly) over the last ten years.
b. The world's first heart transplant (be) performed by Dr. Chris Barnard in Cape Town on 3 December 1967. Now more than 50,000 (be) performed worldwide.
c. Mahatma Gandhi (live) in South Africa from 1893 to 1914.
d. Alan Paton's book, *Cry, the Beloved Country,* (be) published in 1948. It (become) a massive success and (make) people aware of apartheid abroad.
e. I (never / read) a novel by a South African author.

3 Commentez ces graphes.

Quelles formes verbales allez-vous utiliser pour évoquer la situation en Afrique du Sud en 1994 ; pour analyser les changements depuis 1994 ?
EXAMPLE: Since 1994, the number of radio listeners has greatly increased. It's just over 90 percent now.

Help!

increase rise, rose, risen reach: *atteindre*	slightly: *légèrement* sharply: *nettement* hardly: *à peine* just over / above around / about just under / below

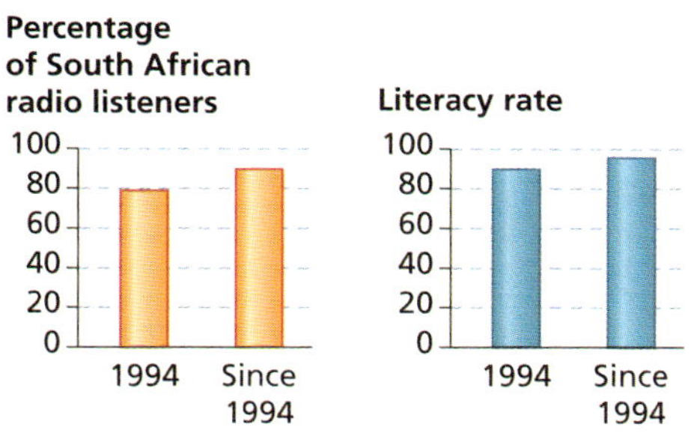

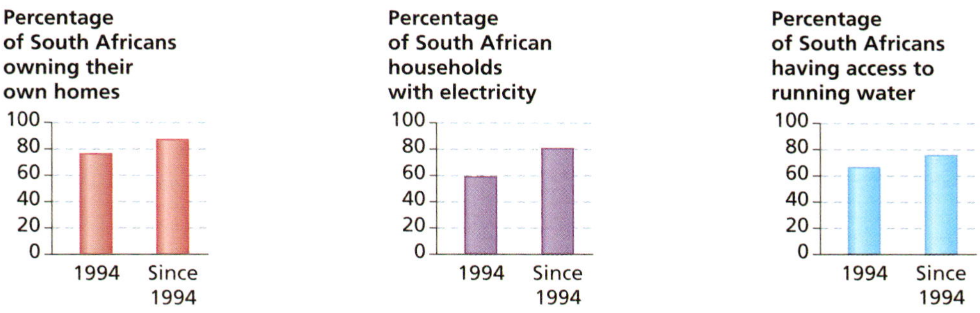

Your task

You are a journalist working on a report on South Africa. You have to illustrate a timeline, give key historical dates of the country and write a short paragraph on the main events.

AVANT DE VOUS LANCER

1 Relisez vos notes sur les documents étudiés dans cette unité.

Vous devez :
– pouvoir expliquer les termes ou événements suivants : *Rainbow Nation* • *Afrikaners* • *Afrikaans* • *apartheid* • *township* • *Soweto* • *Soweto riots* • *1994 elections*
– connaître les faits essentiels de la vie de Mandela
– savoir à quels problèmes cruciaux l'Afrique du Sud est confrontée actuellement.

2 Classez le vocabulaire appris selon les rubriques suivantes :

apartheid • *racism* • *revolt* • *poverty* • *today's social and economic problems*

LES ÉTAPES À SUIVRE

1 Prenez connaissance de cette chronologie.

1400s	*Zulu and Xhosa tribes establish large kingdoms in the South African region.*
1652	*The Dutch establish the port of Cape Town.*
1835	*The Great Trek.*
1852	*The British take control of Cape Town.*
1886	*Gold is discovered in Johannesburg.*
1899-1902	*Boer War. Britain eventually gains control of South Africa.*
1910	*Birth of the South African Union, member of the Commonwealth.*
1948	*Apartheid is introduced.*
1952	*The African National Congress (ANC) begins a campaign to protest against apartheid. Nelson Mandela is one of its leaders.*
1962	*Mandela is arrested.*
1976	*Uprising in Soweto.*
1990	*President F.W. De Klerk announces the end of apartheid. Mandela is freed from prison.*
1992	*Official end of apartheid.*
1993	*De Klerk and Mandela are awarded the Nobel Peace Prize.*
1994	*First democratic elections. Nelson Mandela is elected president.*
1999	*Mandela steps down as president. Thabo Mbeki is elected.*
2004	*The African National Congress wins the election. Thabo Mbeki begins his second term as president.*
2008	*Kgalema Motlanthe is elected president after Thabo Mbeki resigned.*

2 Faites des recherches sur les points suivants.

– *The Great Trek*
– Héros de la lutte anti-apartheid : Steve Biko, Desmond Tutu, Hector Pieterson, Amy Biehl...
– Émeutes de Soweto et leurs conséquences internationales
– ANC : définition et rôle
– Prix Nobel De Klerk / Mandela
– Premières élections

– Thabo Mbeki
– 46664 : origine du mouvement ? Buts de cette organisation ? Autres célébrités engagées ?
– 2010 FIFA *World Cup* (à mettre en rapport avec l'ouverture du pays)

Ces sites peuvent vous aider :
www.southafrica-travel.net/history/eh_gtre1.htm
www.southafrica.info/about/history/history.htm
www.borntoredefine.com/south-african-heroes/
www.encarta.msn.com/encyclopedia_761557321/south_africa.html
www.southafrica.info/about/history/hector-pieterson.htm
www.myhero.com/myhero/hero.asp?hero=a_biehl

3 **À quels problèmes l'Afrique du Sud est-elle actuellement confrontée ?**

RÉALISATION DE LA FRISE

a. Deux grandes périodes sont à traiter :
– de 1400 à 1990 (date de la fin officielle de l'apartheid)
– de 1990 à nos jours (événements clés, changements et progrès, tourisme, problèmes actuels).

⚠ **Attention** à l'emploi du prétérit et du *present perfect*.

b. Faites des phrases courtes, authentiques : ne recopiez pas ce que vous avez lu ! Expliquez en un paragraphe ce qui s'est passé, à quoi correspondent les événements choisis.

c. Illustrez les événements à l'aide de photos, si possible.

d. Marquez les dates en couleur.

e. Relisez-vous minutieusement pour éviter les erreurs les plus fréquentes.

Unit 16

JAMAICAN COLOURS OF LONDON

YOUR TASK AT THE END OF THIS UNIT

Imagine you work for The Visit London Organization. You want to publish a leaflet for tourists interested in the Notting Hill Carnival. → P. 220

TUNE IN!

1 Get ready

When you think of London, what comes to your mind (monuments, museums, parks, famous streets, department stores, celebrities...)?

2 React to this photograph

a. What immediately strikes you?

b. What monuments of London can you recognize in the background? Name the river.

c. What image of London did the photographer want to give? What is the atmosphere like? What are your impressions and reactions?

Help!

Striking elements

lawn = grass
goggles: *lunettes de plongée*
swimming suit
sculpture /ˈskʌlptʃəʳ/
skyline: *ligne d'horizon*
buried /berɪd/ in the earth
huge /hjuːdʒ/ = enormous

Reactions

amazing: *étonnant*
unusual ≠ common
intriguing = puzzling
humorous
lively: *vivant*
It makes me smile / laugh /lɑːf/.
It's unexpected. / I didn't expect this.

Image of London given here

strike: *frapper*
shock
suggest /səˈdʒest/
urge sb to: *inciter vivement qqn à*
discover
explore
be worth /wɜːθ/ + V-ing: *valoir la peine de*

PREPARE YOUR TASK →

3 Follow-up work

Find two or three pictures which best represent London for you. Write a few sentences to explain your choice.

1. MULTICULTURAL LONDON WB

a. Read each extract carefully.
b. Comment on the pie chart with the information collected in the text.
c. Find as much information as you can about Black Caribbeans in London.
d. Recap what you have learnt in this page.

A London in numbers

The initial wave of immigrants had come from the British Empire[1] (Commonwealth countries) in the Caribbean[2] and the Indian subcontinent to work on Britain's buses and in factories. The next one was made up of those fleeing violence in Africa, Europe and the Middle East: Somalis, Afghans and Kurds.

Ethnic minorities tend to be geographically concentrated: Almost half live in London and almost all of the others can be found in the Midlands and in the North.

More than 270 nationalities make up the fabric of the city of London. According to the 2001 census, 40% of its population is composed of ethnic groups. This gives London the largest non-white population of any European city. Over 250 languages are spoken in the city, making it the most linguistically diverse capital in Europe. At Westminster 15 MPs[3] out of 646 (i.e. 2.3%) are from ethnic minorities. There is strong evidence[4] that the various communities are beginning to mix.

1. /'empaɪəʳ/ **2.** /ˌkærɪ'biːən/ **3.** Members of Parliament: *députés*
4. There is strong evidence: *de nombreuses preuves indiquent*

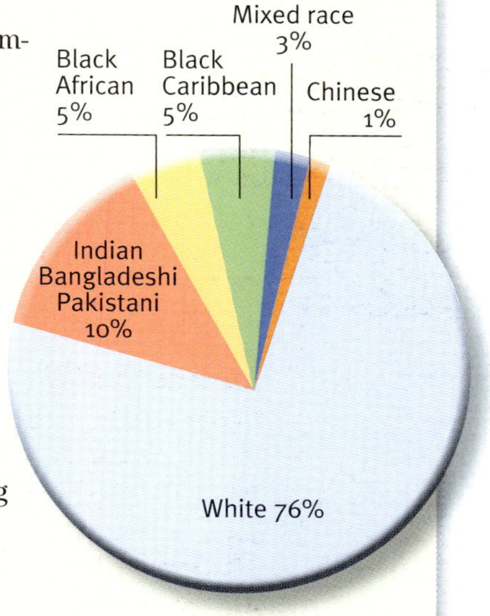

B Caribbean London

In 1948 a ship arrived at Tilbury Dock on the north bank of the Thames[1]. Its arrival marked an important moment in the history of modern England. That ship was the *Empire Windrush*[2], which brought the first large group of West Indian immigrants to the UK.

Six years of war had devastated Britain's infrastructure. Reconstruction was badly needed, but labour was in short supply[3]. Caribbeans were encouraged to come to Britain and work for the Mother Country. Many of these Jamaicans[4] were young men who had served with the Allied Forces in Europe during the war and were keen to return, because of all the opportunities Britain could offer.

Most stayed on and settled in Great Britain and were later joined by their wives and families. They set up homes and worked mainly for London Transport or for the National Health Service.

Jamaicans tended to settle in the south of the capital (Clapham, Brixton) whereas people from Trinidad[5] and Barbados[6] tended to move to the areas around Notting Hill.

1. /temz/ **2.** /'wɪndrʌʃ/ **3.** labour was in short supply: *il y avait une pénurie de main-d'œuvre* **4.** /dʒə'meɪkəns/ **5.** /'trɪnɪdæd/ **6.** /bɑː'beɪdɒs/

2. MORE ABOUT JAMAICA WB

A webpage

Read this National Geographic webpage and prepare a quiz of ten questions to ask to the rest of the class.

HOME
ANIMALS
DAILY NEWS
GREEN GUIDE
HISTORY
KIDS
MAPS
MUSIC
PHOTOGRAPHY
SCIENCE & SPACE
TRAVEL & CULTURES
VIDEO
NATIONAL GEOGRAPHIC MAGAZINE
NATIONAL GEOGRAPHIC CHANNEL
MAGAZINES
SHOP
SUBSCRIPTIONS
TV & FILMS
TRAVEL WITH US
OUR MISSION

Travel & Cultures

TRAVEL AND CULTURES CONTINENTS REGIONS COUNTRIES CITIES PLACES OF A LIFETIME PARKS A-Z

Jamaica

Jamaica facts • **Video** • **Maps** • **Music**

Coconut palms frame an enticing patch of blue Caribbean near Ocho Rios, Jamaica

ENLARGE

Jamaica Information and History

Jamaica[1] is a mountainous Caribbean island just south of Cuba. Columbus landed here in 1494, and the Spanish soon brought in slaves as the native Arawak Indians died out – today more than 90 percent of the population is of African descent. The British seized the island in 1655, granting independence in 1962. Tourism is a steady earner, but reliance on unpredictably priced commodities[2], such as bauxite, causes uneven growth. The island is a major transit point for South American cocaine en route to the US and Europe. Other problems include illicit cultivation of marijuana and heavy deforestation.

Economy

Industry: tourism, bauxite, textiles, food processing[3].
Agriculture: sugar cane, bananas, coffee, citrus; poultry[4].
Exports: alumina, bauxite; sugar, bananas, rum.

1. /dʒə'meɪkə/
2. *matières premières*
3. *industrie alimentaire*
4. *volaille*

Jamaica Flag and Fast Facts

Population
2,772,000

Capital
Kingston: 590,000

Area
10,991 square kilometers
(4,244 square miles)

Languages
English, Creole

Religions
Protestant, Roman Catholic, others

Currency
Jamaican dollar

Life Expectancy
75

GDP per Capita
US $3,800

Literacy Percent
88

Motto
Out of many, one people

3. WINDRUSH CHILD

1 Get ready

Look at the picture. Then imagine the feelings and dreams of the passengers on board the *Empire Windrush* when they left their country.

2 Understanding the text

WB

Turn to your Workbook for help.

Behind you
Windrush child
palm trees wave goodbye

above you
Windrush child
seabirds asking why

around you
Windrush child
blue water rolling by

beside you
Windrush child
your Windrush mum and dad

think of storytime yard[1]
and mango mornings

and new beginnings
doors closing and opening

will things turn out right?
At least the ship will arrive
in midsummer light

and you Windrush child
think of grandmother
telling you don't forget to write

and with one last hug[2]
walk good walk good
and the sea's wheel carries on spinning

and from that place England
you tell her in a letter
of your Windrush adventure

stepping in a big ship
not knowing how long the journey
or that you are stepping into history

bringing your Caribbean eye
to another horizon
grandmother's words your shining beacon[3]

learning how to fly
the kite of your dreams
in an English sky

Windrush child
walking good walking good
in a mind-opening
meeting of snow and sun

John Agard, *Under the Moon and Over the Sea, A Collection of Caribbean Poems*, 2002

1. *cour* **2.** *étreinte* **3.** *balise*

PREPARE YOUR TASK

3 Diary

The mother and the child write their diaries. Choose one character and write a paragraph about the day he / she left Jamaica. Describe the departure, analyse the character's feelings and thoughts and mention his / her expectations. (80 words)

4. THE MOTHER COUNTRY

Victoria Station, London, 1956

Part 1

My dad came to this country in 1948, on the *Empire Windrush* ship. He was one of the pioneers[1]. One of the 492 people who looked around the old British Empire colony of Jamaica, saw that there were no jobs, no prospects[2], and decided to chance his arm in the Mother Country.

I don't know what my dad's aspirations were when he arrived in Britain – he certainly didn't realize that he was making history at the time. But I do know that, when he boarded the ship, he knew himself to be a British citizen. He travelled on a British passport. Britain was the country that all Jamaican children learned about at school. They sang *God Save the King* and *Rule Britannia*[3]. They believed Britain was a green and pleasant land – if not the centre of the world, then certainly the centre of a great and important Empire that spanned[4] the globe, linking all sorts of countries into a family of nations. Far from the idea that he was travelling to a foreign place, he was travelling to the centre of his country, and as such he would slip-in and fit-in immediately. Jamaica, he thought, was just Britain in the sun.

1. /ˌpaɪəˈnɪəz/ *pionniers* **2.** *avenir* **3.** *Rule Britannia*: unofficial national anthem **4.** *s'étendait sur*

Part 2

But they soon found that they were foreigners[1] in England, and this shocked them. They suffered bad housing – by no means the plight[2] of black people alone in those post-war days: The signs in windows read "no niggers, no dogs, no Irish". My dad faced incredible hostility when looking for somewhere to live because of the colour of his skin. He had a job with the post office. My mum, a trained teacher in Jamaica, had to sew[3] to make a living here. She worked in sweat-shops[4] with other foreigners, Czechs, Poles, Greeks. She had one advantage: She spoke English. And one disadvantage: She was black (or coloured[5], as we were termed then).

1. /ˈfɒrənəz/ **2.** /plaɪt/ *sort* **3.** /səʊ/ *coudre* **4.** /ˈswetʃɒps/ **5.** /ˈkʌləd/

Part 3

I was embarrassed[1] that my parents were not English. One of the reasons was that no one around me was interested[2] in the country my parents came from. To them, it was just a place full of inferior[3] black people. They asked – oh, they asked all the time. "Where are you from?" But if I answered "Jamaica," lips would curl or tongues would tut. They didn't want to know about the sun, the sugar cane, the rum punch. They didn't want to try our rice and peas. I remember a white American girl coming to school. Everyone wanted to be her friend. To see her toys, to hear her parents' wonderful accent, to try their food with an "Ooohh isn't it lovely". America was a great place to come from.

1. /ɪmˈbærəst/ **2.** /ˈɪntrɪstɪd/ **3.** /ɪnˈfɪərɪəʳ/

Andrea Levy, *This is my England*, *The Guardian Weekend*, February 19, 2000

1 Get ready

a. Listen to the first recording. Do you recognize it?

b. Listen to the second recording. What words strike you?

c. Skim through the whole text and answer the following questions:
– Who is the narrator?
– Who are the other characters mentioned?
– Find a date and the names of two countries that are repeated in the text.
– What kind of text is it? Justify.

d. Judging from the photo, what do you think the text is going to deal with?

2 Understanding the text WB

Turn to your Workbook for help.

3 Recap

Give each part a title then answer these questions.

Part 1
a. Why did the father leave his native country?
b. What vision did he have of his future country?
c. What did he expect from his future country? Why?

Part 2
a. What difficulties were the parents confronted with?
b. What were they the victims of? Were they the only ones then?

Part 3
a. What did the narrator realize?
b. What were her feelings then?
c. Now explain why the narrator felt "embarrassed" (l. 36).

Help!

Part 1	Part 2	Part 3
unemployment standard of living living conditions opportunities /ˌɒpəˈtjuːnɪtɪz/ better-paid dream of + V-ing fulfil one's dreams achieve success /səkˈses/ improve integrate /ˈɪntɪgreɪt/ into greet = welcome	racism /ˈreɪsɪzəm/ foreigner /ˈfɒrənə/: *étranger* xenophobia /ˌzenəˈfəʊbɪə/ = fear or hatred of foreigners disappointed /ˌdɪsəˈpɔɪntɪd/ disillusioned ≠ enthusiastic miserable /ˈmɪzərəbl/ ≠ happy awful = dreadful look down on, despise sb: *mépriser qqn* start from scratch: *recommencer à zéro*	customs: *coutumes* disdain = contempt = scorn lonely left out = isolated excluded = rejected popular make friends with feel ashamed /əˈʃeɪmd/: *avoir honte* be worth + V-ing: *valoir la peine de*

4 Summary

Replace each number in the following text with a word chosen from the toolbox above.

The narrator relates her own story. Her parents, who had a British passport, emigrated after WW2. The father believed he would have many ... 1 in Great Britain. He expected to ... 2 his dreams, to have a ... 3 job and to ... 4 his ... 5. However, he soon realized he was considered a ... 6 and was ... 7 because of the colour of his skin. He expected to be welcomed and to integrate into British society easily, but in reality he was confronted with ... 8 and ... 9 and lived in ... 10 conditions. Andrea felt ... 11, and ... 12 by her school friends.

PREPARE YOUR TASK

5 Creative writing

Andrea writes a letter to her family in Jamaica and tells them about the journey, what she likes, dislikes, and misses in England. (80 words)

5. NOTTING HILL CARNIVAL

1 Find your way

You are in King's Cross station and want to go to Notting Hill Gate. What lines will you take and where will you change?

Notting Hill is an area in West London, England, close to the north-western corner of Hyde Park, and lying within the Royal Borough of Kensington and Chelsea. It is a cosmopolitan district known as the location for the annual Notting Hill Carnival and for being home to the Portobello Road Market. It is now an affluent and fashionable area.

2 Get ready

a. React to the photo below (who? what? impressions?).

b. The following words are written phonetically. Read them aloud and write them down.

/ˈkɑːnɪvəl/ • /ˈfestɪvəl/ • /ˈselɪbreɪt/ • /ɪnˈvɒlv/ • /bænd/ • /ˈraɪət/ • /ˌmʌltɪˈkʌltʃərəlɪzəm/

3 Listen and turn to your Workbook for help WB

PREPARE YOUR TASK →

4 Oral account

Prepare a two-minute oral account of the document you have heard. Use your notes and the following words and expressions.

Points to include:

- The carnival was created in... by immigrants from... .
- What difficulties did they have? Why?
- What do they celebrate?
- Costumes...
- Music...

- The recording deals with...
- This major /ˈmeɪdʒəʳ/ event attracts...
- The journalist explains the origins / goals...
- He / She gives us the reasons why...
- He / She adds..., mentions..., interviews...
- First, one participant points out...
- Then another one defines...
- Finally, the last one stresses...

Language at work

Improve your pronunciation

MP3

1 Prononciation de la voyelle écrite *-i-*

a. Prononcez les mots suivants à haute voix. Vérifiez ensuite à l'écoute.

empire • *ship* • *pioneers* • *decided* • *history* • *time* • *citizen* • *slip-in* • *fit-in* • *Britain* • *plight* • *signs* • *hostility* • *skin* • *disadvantage*

b. Classez enfin les mots ci-dessus selon la prononciation de la ou des voyelles *-i-* soulignées. Se prononcent-elles /aɪ/ comme dans *time* ou /ɪ/ comme dans *fish* ?

2 Prononcez les mots suivants et trouvez le point commun entre les voyelles soulignées. Vérifiez ensuite vos réponses à l'écoute.

Jamaica • *England* • *America*

3 Les formes réduites

WB

a. Lisez ce texte tout en l'écoutant.

One (of) the reasons (was) that no one around me (was) interested in the country my parents came (from). To (them) it (was) just a place full (of) inferior black people. They didn't want (to) know about the sun... They didn't want (to) try our rice (and) peas. I remember a white American girl coming (to) school. Everyone wanted (to) be her friend. America (was) a great place (to) come from.

b. À quelles catégories grammaticales appartiennent les mots entre parenthèses ? Quel son ces mots ont-ils en commun ?

Build up your vocabulary

1 a. Lisez ce texte.

When in the 1950s a huge number of West Indian immigrants came to London, they also brought their traditions and music. Faced with racism, unemployment and poor housing conditions, those immigrants dreamt of having a festival that would bring together the people from the Notting Hill area. So dances and other musical events were organised in North London. In 1964 the first street festival took place in Notting Hill. It was a great success, so the parade took place year after year attracting ever more participants and spectators. The Notting Hill Carnival now takes place on the last weekend of August. It has become a true multicultural event. Think of Carnival, and images of bright costumes, imaginative floats and dancing on the streets inevitably come to mind.

b. Trouvez dans le texte ci-dessus les équivalents de ces mots.

énorme • apporter • confronté à • chômage • rêver de • réunir • événement • avoir lieu • succès • défilé • attirer • le dernier week-end d'août • coloré • char

2 Lisez la deuxième partie de *The Mother Country* (p. 214) et relevez huit mots se rapportant au thème de l'immigration. Traduisez-les.

3 Complétez le texte avec les mots de la liste.

customs • *face* • *factories* • *foreign* • *labour force* • *leave* • *overworked* • *settle* • *sweat-shops* • *underpaid* • *wages*

Immigrants ... [1] their native countries to ... [2] in a ... [3] land. They have to adapt to their new country, learn its language and ... [4]. They have to find a job and a house. They may find work in ... [5], ... [6], hotels or restaurants. They are often paid low ... [7], are ... [8] and ... [9]. They are considered a cheap ... [10]. They may also ... [11] hostility, racism and exclusion.

Language at work

L'infinitif avec *to*

1 Observez.

a. *Everyone <u>wanted</u> **to be** her friend.*
b. *Afro-Caribbean immigrants <u>decided</u> **to create** a street festival in 1964.*
c. *They <u>expected</u> **to bring together** the people of Notting Hill.*
d. *They <u>intend</u> **to attract** more and more visitors.*
e. *In 1965 West Indian immigrants <u>planned</u> **to have** a parade on the last weekend of August.*

– Comment sont construits les verbes soulignés en **a**, **b**, **c**, **d** et **e** ?
Ces verbes sont-ils tournés vers le passé ou l'avenir ? Quelle idée commune trouve-t-on dans tous ces verbes ?
– Relevez dans le texte *The Mother Country* (p. 202) deux autres infinitifs complets.

2 Dans les phrases ci-dessous, repérez les expressions du but.

a. *Caribbean immigrants left Jamaica in order to start a new life.*
b. *They emigrated so as to have better opportunities.*
c. *Immigrants of the Windrush Generation left their family to start a new life.*

– Laquelle de ces trois expressions appartient à la langue courante ?
– Relevez un autre infinitif complet exprimant le but dans le texte *The Mother Country*.

3 Associez chaque question à sa réponse.

1. *Afro-Caribbean immigrants came to Britain to have a more pleasant life.*
2. *They came to Britain because they dreamt of a more pleasant life.*

a. *Why did they come to Britain?*
b. *What did they come to Britain for?*

4 Observez.

a. *West Indian immigrants **wanted** <u>their families</u> **to join** them quickly.*
b. *They **expected** <u>their children</u> **to have** better opportunities.*
c. *They **expected** <u>them</u> **to have** better opportunities.*
d. *The organizers **would like** <u>all the spectators</u> **to enjoy** the Carnival atmosphere.*

– Quelle est la structure commune à ces trois verbes ? Verbe + ... + ...
– Les groupes nominaux soulignés en **a**, **b** et **d** sont-ils sujets ou compléments du verbe qui suit ?
– Que remarquez-vous en **c** : le pronom est-il utilisé sous sa forme sujet ou sa forme complément ?
– Traduisez en français les énoncés **a**, **b** et **c**.

⚠ **Attention aux « calques » du français**
En vous appuyant sur les observations faites ci-dessus, complétez la phrase suivante : en français ces verbes ont à leur suite une construction en « ... ». N'imitez pas cette construction en anglais : n'utilisez pas ~~that~~. Utilisez le verbe avec ... (à la forme...).

Language at work

Practice

1 Rédigez des phrases à l'aide des éléments proposés. N'oubliez pas d'utiliser les formes verbales qui conviennent et d'ajouter des mots grammaticaux (déterminants, pronoms, prépositions) si nécessaire.

a. The Windrush Generation • expect • English • greet (= welcome)
b. Jamaican immigrants • would like • children • integrate • British society
c. Newly-arrived Jamaicans • want • English • treat • fairly
d. They • expect • authorities • help • find • better accommodation
e. Andrea's father • would like • new bride • come over • England

2 Traduisez.

a. Le père d'Andrea a eu l'intention de quitter son pays natal pour commencer une vie nouvelle.
b. L'oncle d'Andrea a décidé de tenter sa chance en Angleterre.
c. Andrea s'attendait à se faire beaucoup d'amis dans son nouveau pays.
d. Si je vais à Londres cet été, j'aimerais voir le carnaval de Notting Hill.
e. Beaucoup de Jamaïcains avaient pour projet de s'installer à Londres.

3 L'impératif

Traduisez les phrases suivantes.
a. Regarde ce char *(float)* !
b. N'oubliez pas votre parapluie !
c. Prenez votre portable pour appeler vos amis si vous vous perdez.
d. Dépêchons-nous, le défilé va commencer.

PREPARE YOUR TASK →

4 Creative writing

Imagine the dreams and desires of these schoolchildren for the future. Use – among other verbs – the verbs given on the opposite page. (80 words)

your task

Imagine you work for The Visit London Organization. You want to publish a leaflet for tourists interested in the Notting Hill Carnival.

AVANT DE VOUS LANCER

1 Posez-vous les bonnes questions :
– **Nature de la tâche :** qu'implique la rédaction d'une brochure touristique ? Faut-il : décrire • raconter • illustrer • expliquer • comparer • donner son opinion ? (2 intrus)
– **Niveau de langue à employer :** langue soutenue, langue familière ?

2 Lisez cet extrait d'une brochure sur la Tour de Londres. Repérez les procédés utilisés pour convaincre le lecteur de visiter ce monument.

The Tower of London...

... is one of the world's most famous palaces but despite a grim[1] reputation as a place of torture and death, there are many other stories to be told. Discover this powerful and enduring[2] symbol of the Norman Conquest, which has been enjoyed as a royal palace, served as an armoury and even housed a zoo.

Familiarise yourself with the palace's intriguing cast of characters who have all left their mark on its history, including the jewel thief Colonel Blood, tortured Gunpowder plotter[3] Guy Fawkes and three queens of England beheaded on Tower Green.

1. *sinistre* **2.** *(ici) éternel* **3.** *conspirateur*

LES ÉTAPES À SUIVRE

1 Prenez une feuille format A4 divisée en trois parties et notez au brouillon les éléments que vous mettrez sur le recto et sur le verso.

2 Mobilisez vos connaissances en relisant les documents étudiés dans cette unité, par exemple p. 217 pour le vocabulaire ou p. 218 pour les structures. Relevez-y tous les outils linguistiques utiles pour la rédaction de votre brochure (lexique, structures, citations).

3 Complétez éventuellement vos connaissances sur Internet. Sources possibles :
www.nottinghillcarnival.biz
www.nottinghillcarnival.org.uk

4 Réutilisez les procédés repérés dans le prospectus sur la Tour de Londres pour inciter les touristes à se rendre au carnaval de Notting Hill.

5 Vous devez inclure les points suivants :
- *Dates*
- *Days: on Saturday, on Sunday*
- *Time*
- *Route map and how to get to and from the Carnival*
- *Safety tips, survival guide*
- *Origin of the carnival*
- *Creation in... (p. 216)*
- *What did these immigrants come to Britain for? (pp. 211, 213, 214)*
- *Difficulties for the first immigrants (p. 214)*
- *Music (p. 216): Steel pan • Calypso • Soca • Mas • Sound systems*
- *Costumes (p. 216)*
- *You may include one of these Carnival mottos: "Every spectator is a participant" • "Unity in Diversity" (p. 216)*
- *You may add a few references to the food the spectators will try.*
- *You may include photos to illustrate your production.*

6 Relisez-vous minutieusement.
⚠ **ATTENTION** à la ponctuation et aux majuscules.

RAPPELS
– En anglais, les **adjectifs de nationalité** et tous les mots dérivés de **noms de pays** prennent une majuscule, contrairement au français.
– Il faut mettre une majuscule aux **jours de la semaine** et aux **mois**.

⚠ Vérifiez la place des mots.

RAPPEL
Les expressions qui indiquent un moment (*the day before, the next / following day*) se placent soit en tête de phrase soit en fin de phrase.

⚠ Trois mots à éviter : *good, beautiful, big*. Employez des adjectifs plus précis.
– *~~good~~: great, exciting, pleasant, enjoyable, memorable...*
– *~~beautiful~~: colourful, striking, gorgeous, wonderful, fantastic...*
– *~~big~~: tall, high, huge, large, enormous, gigantic...*

RÉDIGER UN TEXTE

A Avant de vous lancer

Avant de vous lancer dans la rédaction, vous devez :
– réfléchir au type de sujet qu'on vous demande d'écrire (dialogue, sujet d'opinion, narration, récit, lettre, mail...)
– vous interroger sur les mots clés du sujet
– mobiliser le lexique, les structures et le maximum d'idées qui s'y rapportent

1 Lisez les deux sujets suivants :

a. Samuel writes an e-mail to his best friend to tell him about the concert he went to.

b. Would you like to spend your holidays on a desert island? Why? Why not?

2 Pour chaque sujet, identifiez le type de rédaction attendu.

3 Observez le sujet a, où les mots clés ont été soulignés.

Dans le sujet **b**, repérez à votre tour les mots clés.

4 Sur papier libre, notez les idées, le lexique et les structures qui se rapportent aux mots clés du sujet a.

Voici un exemple pour le sujet **b**.

For	*rest, be exciting, get away from it all, be on my own, have a lot of free time, forget the real world...*
Structures	*Purpose (but): in order to + V...*
	Cause: because
	Likes: I enjoy / love / am keen on + V-ing...
	Opinion: I think, believe, to my mind...
Against	*miss my friends, feel very lonely / scared, be boring, have nothing to do, get mad, cry all the time...*
Structures	*Dislikes: hate + V-ing, can't stand + V-ing, be fed up with +V-ing, be sick of +V-ing...*
	If: If I was / were..., I would...

B À votre tour !

1 Voici le début de la rédaction du sujet a.

a

From: Samuel
To: Tom
Object: Amazing concert!

Hi Tom!
Guess what happened to me last night! I went to a concert. I arrived early and I saw...

2 Rédigez les sujets a et b en entier sur papier libre (80 mots).

C Apprenez à étoffer un récit

1 Lisez l'extrait suivant.

On a December night I was coming home from school, when suddenly two big, strong, hooded men with dark clothes kidnapped me. I screamed like mad, punched them, called for help again and again, but there was nobody around. They took me to a house in the woods where they locked me in. They tied me to a chair, then left me alone for what seemed like hours. I was desperate and panic-stricken. All of a sudden, I realized my cellphone was in my pocket! I managed to get one hand free and grab it to send an SOS to my parents. A few hours later, I heard police sirens: people were finally coming to my rescue. I was free at last!

2 Identifiez la situation.

a. Les circonstances : le lieu, le moment de la journée et les personnages présents.
b. Relevez les adjectifs décrivant les sentiments du narrateur.
c. Résumez rapidement en français ce qui se passe dans cet extrait.

3 Repérez ces éléments.

a. Faites la liste des formes verbales utilisées dans le récit ; nommez le temps grammatical utilisé et indiquez sa valeur.
b. Relevez les termes utilisés pour décrire les deux hommes.
c. Relevez les mots de liaison et les marqueurs de temps.

4 Observez comment on peut étoffer un récit.

Voici le squelette de l'histoire. Comment est-on passé d'une phrase simple à une phrase complexe ?

Squelette de l'histoire	Récit étoffé
I was coming home from school; two men kidnapped me.	**On a December night** I was coming home from school, **when suddenly** two **big, strong, hooded** men **with dark clothes** kidnapped me.
They took me to a house.	They took me to a house **in the woods where they locked me in. They tied me to a chair, then left me alone for what seemed like hours.**
I grabbed my mobile phone. I sent an SOS to my parents.	I **managed to get one hand free and** grabbed my mobile phone **to send** an SOS to my parents.
People were coming to my rescue.	**A few hours later, I heard police sirens**: people were **finally** coming to my rescue. **I was free at last!**

5 Construisez un récit.

– Déterminez les circonstances (temps, lieux).
– Imaginez vos personnages (description physique, personnalité, sentiments, émotions).
– Imaginez les moments forts de votre récit (mots de liaison, marqueurs de temps) et faites un plan (respectez un ordre chronologique).
– Mobilisez le lexique et les structures adaptées au contexte.

6 À votre tour !

Voici le squelette d'un récit. Réécrivez-le en étoffant chaque phrase afin d'obtenir 120 mots.

In the middle of the night, I heard a noise. I decided to get up. I saw a shadow, but nothing else. I felt a blow on my head. The next morning, I woke up; nothing had changed in the house.

RÉDIGER UNE LETTRE

Une lettre est un type d'écrit particulier, dans la mesure où elle doit respecter un certain nombre de règles concernant sa présentation.

11 Earlbank Avenue
Scotstoun
Glasgow G14 9EA → 1

8th April, 2008 → 2

Dear all, → 3

Yes, we're on the move again. We've left our flat near the river and moved into a proper house.
Come and visit us soon, Glasgow has a lot to offer!
Are you all well? I hope so.
See our new address.

Love, → 4
Teresa
XXX → 5

1 Repérez la structure de cette lettre.

Associez chacun des numéros à la définition correspondante ci-dessous.

a. La date.
b. L'adresse complète, qui figure en haut et à droite.
c. X représente un baiser, c'est une marque d'affection.
d. Formule d'introduction pour une lettre personnelle.
e. Formule de conclusion d'une lettre personnelle : cette formule n'exprime pas de sentiment amoureux, mais de l'affection.

2 Repérez le destinataire de cette lettre.

S'agit-il d'un employeur, d'un professeur, de grands-parents, d'amis ?
Quels éléments de la lettre vous ont aidé(e) à trouver la réponse ?

3 Utilisez la bonne formule.

Sur papier libre, classez les formules suivantes en deux colonnes et indiquez à chaque fois si la situation est formelle ou informelle.

Dear Mr Rogers, • *Sincerely yours,* • *My darling Betty,* • *Dear Sir / Madam,*

4 Écrivez un mot d'excuse.

a. Examinez ce mot.

> Dear Mrs Barnes,
> I am writing this note because I am so sorry I couldn't attend your class yesterday. I do apologize for missing your lesson, but I had to go to hospital for a visit. I intend to make up for lost time as soon as possible. Could you please send me the homework to do?
> Thank you very much in advance,
> Sue

b. Repérez ces éléments :
la formule d'introduction – les formules d'excuse – l'excuse donnée – la formule de conclusion

c. À votre tour !

You write to a friend because you couldn't attend his / her birthday party. (30-40 words)	You are on holiday. Write a postcard to an English-speaking friend. (50 words)	You are going to spend a week at your penfriend's house. You must thank the family for welcoming you, and give basic information about your tastes and habits. (150 words)

RÉDIGER UN DIALOGUE

1 Lisez ce dialogue.

The phone rang on the table in front of Rob and he answered it immediately. Maybe it was Ashley. He was expecting a phone call from her.
"Hi, honey," said Rob cheerfully. "Still got far to come?"
"I'm on my way," replied Ashley.
"Where exactly?" he asked impatiently.
There was a pause. "Er... I've only just got past Pembroke."
"Why did you leave so late? You knew you'd be late, didn't you?"
"And why are you making a big fuss about it?" she snapped. "Are you mad at me?"

2 Identifiez la situation.

a. Qui sont les personnages présents ?
b. Est-ce une situation formelle ou informelle ?
c. Résumez rapidement en français ce qui se passe dans cet extrait.

3 Repérez les éléments suivants dans le texte.

a. Quelle est la ponctuation utilisée ? Que se passe-t-il à chaque changement de locuteur ?
b. Relevez les verbes introducteurs utilisés dans ce dialogue.
c. Quels adverbes ont été utilisés pour définir le ton de chaque personnage ?
d. Donnez des exemples de langue orale (formes contractées des verbes, *gap filler*, *tag* interrogatif).

4 Apprenez à utiliser les adverbes qui conviennent.

Associez les bulles au ton correspondant.

- I couldn't care less!
- Can I help you?
- Don't ever do it again!
- I just adore him
- You let me down again!

, he said sadly.	, she said kindly.	, she said passionately.	, she said rudely.	, he said furiously.

5 Variez les verbes.

Choisissez dans cette liste : *asked* • *replied* • *told* • *answered* • *explained* • *shouted* • *declared.*
Marge is waiting for Phil. He finally arrives three hours later.
"Where have you been?", she ... [1] him. "I've been waiting for you for three hours!", she ... [2] .
"You'll never believe me!", he ... [3] . "I got arrested by the police", he ... [4] .
"You what?", she ... [5] . "What happened?", she was getting hysterical.
"I was on my way home and a policeman jumped on me and arrested me", he simply ... [6] her.
"But why?", she ... [7] .

6 À votre tour !

Imagine the dialogue between Garfield and Jon (80 words).

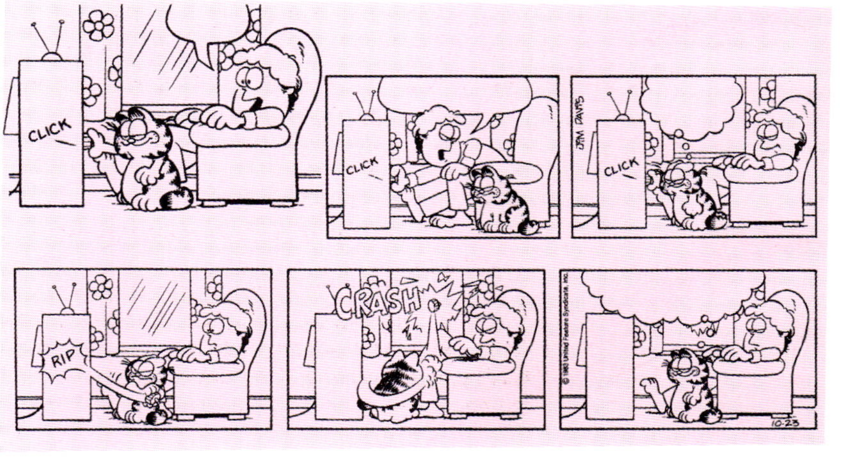

ÉVALUATION

J'ÉVALUE MES PROGRÈS

À la suite de ces trois unités, évaluez vos progrès et faites le bilan de vos compétences.

1 Je me prépare

1. You have lost your notes and you need them for a test about South Africa. You write an e-mail to a friend. In your mail you need to:
– ask for his/her help
– explain you will photocopy the notes
– ask him/her when and where you can have them
– thank him/her
(40 words)

2. You went to a reggae concert last night.
The concert was horrible.
You post a note on your blog and you tell your friends why you are so angry.
(40 words)

3. On your blog you want to tell your friends what you have been doing recently. Choose one of the following topics:
a. Your resolutions: more sport. Which sports did you choose to practise?
b. A film you have just seen. Give your opinion on it.
(60 words)

4. Write a story beginning with:
"I was sleeping when the phone rang in the middle of the night."
Don't forget to include your feelings and reactions at that moment.
(80 words)

5. Write a story beginning with:
"The door closed and Pamela realized she was a prisoner."
Explain why she was captured and how she will escape.
(100 words)

6. Correct the grammar or spelling mistakes that are underlined.

An old woman <u>was walk</u> in the park pushing her cart <u>who</u> was full of <u>bag</u>. She <u>sit</u> on a bench next to me and we <u>start</u> talking. She <u>had</u> eighty, her <u>hairs were</u> <u>whites</u>, she <u>looked like</u> very tired. She <u>said</u> me the story of her life. At twenty she was <u>a</u> actress and married to a very rich man. Fifteen years later he <u>felt</u> in love with <u>an other</u> woman and she <u>get</u> divorced. She found a job, worked for <u>much</u> years. Then she lost her job and was homeless. She didn't want <u>that I give</u> her any money. She said she didn't need much.

2 Je m'auto-corrige

Consultez les corrigés sur le site compagnon et comparez vos productions à celles proposées.

SOMMATIVE

Writing

JE FAIS LE BILAN

Analysez vos résultats à l'aide de cette grille d'évaluation où sont définis les différents paliers de compétences en expression écrite.

Sujet 1 : Je peux…	**Paliers**
… écrire des textes courts et simples, des lettres personnelles simples pour remercier ou m'excuser.	**A2**
… rédiger des messages pour demander des informations, communiquer des faits ou exposer des problèmes.	**B1**

Sujets 2 et 3 : Je peux…	**Paliers**
… faire une description brève et élémentaire de moi-même, de ma famille, de mes activités, d'événements.	**A2**
… écrire un texte simple et cohérent sur des sujets familiers ou de la vie quotidienne.	**B1**
… écrire un point de vue personnel (sentiments ou réactions) ou une opinion.	**B1**
… rédiger un compte rendu portant sur un film, un livre, etc.	en route vers **B2**

Sujet 4 : Je peux…	**Palier**
… écrire un texte simple et cohérent sur des sujets familiers ou de la vie quotidienne.	**B1**

Sujet 5 : Je peux…	**Palier**
… décrire un événement, raconter une histoire.	**B1**

ÉVALUATION

Votre professeur va maintenant vous distribuer une fiche d'évaluation.
Une fois l'évaluation terminée, il / elle pourra ainsi déterminer à quel palier vous vous situez par rapport à la grille d'évaluation du Cadre Européen Commun de Référence pour les Langues.

This is my land

Henry Page and his family set off with their wagon train across the wide prairies of the Middle West. He learned to ride a horse, to drive a team of horses, and to mend[1] the wagons when they broke down. He never saw an Indian until he reached Black River Bend. He wondered what all the fuss was about, the Indians there were thin and unhappy people, living on scraps[2] of food and working for the white settlers, doing the worst jobs and spending what little money they got on cheap whisky. Most of the time they were drunk, they never looked anything like Henry had been expecting. They were poor, ignorant savages. Henry felt sorry for them.

At Black River Bend Henry heard about the land which was being given to settlers. The best pieces had already gone but if you would take a risk and settle your family in the wilds[3] you could have as much land as you wanted. All you had to do was to take a horse and a bundle of marker posts[4] and set off at dawn. You put down a marker post every hour and you could have as much land as you could mark off in twenty-four hours.

Henry rode out way beyond the furthest settlement and picked out a beautiful valley for himself. There was a clear river running through it, masses of trees on the slopes of hills all around and good grassland on both sides of the river. He set out at sunrise one morning and rode like the wind for the rest of that day. He did not stop to eat and only drank in the saddle as he raced along. By dawn the next day he had managed to mark off the whole valley. He rode back to Black River Bend and claimed[5] the valley as his own, naming it Valley Page. His claim was marked off on the map of the State and Henry Page was now a landowner.

From Charles Murray he got an axe and a saw, a sack of nails, and a hammer. He set to work to clear a space by the river and built himself a small log cabin. Mary fished the river and turned the cabin into a home. They were still very poor but they were very happy.

1. *réparer* **2.** *des restes* **3.** *territoires inhabités* **4.** marker posts: *piquets* **5.** *revendiqua*

Jeremiah Johnson, Sydney Pollack, 1972

Henry worked like a demon. He worked every hour there was in the day and went to his homemade bed tired and aching all over. Slowly he made his farm, with axe and saw and hammer he built his fences[6] and cleared the ground. As much as possible he made with his own hands, other things he had to pay for at Murray's store in Black River Bend and to get money he cut timber[7] and floated it down the river into the little town.

He and his family kept themselves to themselves[8]. When winter came he went hunting in his valley and came back with deer and wild birds to eat. The little log cabin was warm and snug. Henry and his family were happy.

The years passed. Page Six arrived, a girl who was given the name of Ruth. The little cabin was no longer big enough and Henry set to work to build a really nice house, with a garden and stables[9] and a barn[10]. He began to farm the land and the soil was good. He cleared more ground and got horses to draw the plow. He sowed corn and maize and raised good crops[11]. He was beginning to make money at last. His crops sold for a good price and he was able to buy cattle[12].

6. *clôtures* **7.** *du bois* **8.** kept themselves to themselves: *restaient isolés* **9.** *écuries* **10.** *grange* **11.** *récoltes* **12.** *bovins*

More ground was needed and so more trees came down, more fences went up and more plowing was done. After ten years Henry Page could look out on his farm and feel pleased with himself.

And then one day he went riding down to the far end of his valley. Mary had told him that the fish hadn't been coming down the river lately, that something must be blocking their run. He rode along the river's edge and came at last to the waterfall where the river ran into the valley.

There, just below the tumbling waters where the river was narrow, sat an Indian family. They had nets[13] slung across the river from bank to bank and a heap of shining silvery fish lay on the grass.

Henry went up to them. They stood up as he reached them and Henry saw that the man had an old shotgun in his hand. His wife and three children hid themselves behind a skin tent. The man waited until Henry was facing him.

"This is my land," said Henry. "And those are my fish."

The Indian's eyes glittered. He looked at Henry for a long time before he spoke. He raised a hand and swept it all around him[14] at the wooded slopes of the valley.

"This – my people's land. Not your land. All this belong my people."

Henry frowned. How could you tell an Indian savage about the white man's laws?

"Listen! You take your family and clear out of it, see? You not take any more fish, understand? You go..."

Henry had a Winchester rifle[15] in his saddle-holster.

13. *filets de pêche* **14.** swept it all around him: *balaya d'un geste large* **15.** *fusil*

He looked at the Indian and felt the man's hatred[16] blazing in his eyes. Henry walked away and made his way back to his house feeling rather sad. He wasn't a hard man, he didn't want to drive the Indian family away... and yet he'd spoken to them like all the other Whites. He told Mary what had happened.

"We are all alone out here," she said. "There's no helping us if we're attacked. And there's the children—"

Henry went into Black River Bend and bought two more Winchesters and a large amount of ammunition. He told the storekeeper about the Indian family on his land.

"Give me ten dollars," said the storekeeper. "You won't be bothered[17] by them varmints[18] any more." Then, seeing that Henry was still worried, he went on "There's a trapper I know... He'll move'em on, nice and peaceful like."

Henry paid the man, glad to have someone else to do the job for him. Next morning he heard the sound of shots from the far end of the valley. He saddled his horse and rode out there. He met the trapper, Luke, coming back.

Luke grinned[19] at him. "Guess you won't be having any more trouble from them," he said. And laughed.

Henry rode past the man. He reached the waterfall and the first thing he saw was a blazing[20] tent. There was blood on the ground and the fishing net was ripped into pieces. The Indian woman stood some way off, the three children huddled around[21] her. She faced him as he walked up to her and Henry saw that she was standing in front of the man's body.

Henry felt ashamed. He held out both hands to show that he carried no weapon. He knelt beside the fallen Indian and saw that the man had a gaping wound[22] in his side. But he was not dead, though he had lost much blood.

Henry ripped[23] the sleeve from his own shirt and bound the wound as best he could. The woman watched him silently while he did his clumsy best to stop the bleeding. He was shaking like a leaf[24] as he helped the Indian to his feet and he walked him across to his horse. Gently he lifted the man into the saddle[25] and then walked off down the river's edge towards his house. Looking back he saw the woman and her children following him at a distance. The woman was carrying the old shotgun but she didn't know how to use it. Henry was thankful for that.

Mary rushed out to meet him as he came to the house. Henry snapped at her, told her to get a bed ready, to get herbs and bandages. He took the Indian off the horse and carried him in his arms into the house.

The Indian made a slow recovery[26]. Almost three weeks went by before he was on his feet again. Henry tried his best to be friendly but the man uttered not one word[27] in all that time. When at last the time came for him to go, Henry offered the man a new fishing net and ten dollars in money.

The Indian turned his back on Henry and walked into the sunshine without a word.

William Charles Henry Chalk, *Jim Silent*, 1971

16. *haine* **17.** *embêtés* **18.** *animaux nuisibles* **19.** *regarda avec un large sourire* **20.** *en feu* **21.** huddled around: *blottis contre* **22.** gaping wound: *blessure béante* **23.** *arracha* **24.** was shaking like a leaf: *tremblait comme une feuille* **25.** lifted the man into the saddle: *mit l'homme en selle* **26.** made a slow recovery: *se remit lentement* **27.** uttered not one word: *ne prononça pas un mot*

Ations[1]

If we meet and I say, “Hi,”
That’s a salutation.
If you ask me how I feel,
That’s consideration.
If we stop and talk a while,
That’s a conversation.
If we understand each other,
That’s communication.
If we argue[2], scream and fight,
That’s an altercation.
If later we apologize[3],
That’s reconciliation.
If we help each other home,
That’s cooperation.
And all these ations added up
Make civilization.

(And if I say this is a wonderful poem,
Is that exaggeration?)

Shel Silverstein, *A Light in the Attic*, 1981

1. /ˈeɪʃəns/ **2.** /ˈɑːgjuː/ *on se dispute* **3.** *on s’excuse*

Alfred Hitchcock, *Psycho*, 1960

The landlady

***O**n arriving in Bath, where he was going to start a new job, Billy Weaver, aged seventeen, took a room at a Bed and Breakfast run by an old landlady*[1]*. After he had written his name and address in the guest book, he noticed that there were only two names above his.*

He crossed the room slowly, and sat down on the edge of the sofa. She placed his teacup on the table in front of him.

" There we are," she said. "How nice and cozy[2] this is, isn't it?"

Billy started sipping his tea. She did the same. For half a minute or so, neither of them spoke. But Billy knew that she was looking at him. Her body was half-turned towards him, and he could feel her eyes resting on his face, watching him over the rim of her teacup. Now and again, he caught a whiff[3] of a peculiar smell that seemed to emanate directly from her person. It was not in the least unpleasant, and it reminded him – well, he wasn't quite sure what it reminded him of. Pickled walnuts? New leather? Or was it the corridors of a hospital?

"Mr. Mulholland was a great one for his tea" she said at length. Never in my life have I seen anyone drink as much tea as dear, sweet Mr. Mulholland."

"I suppose he left fairly recently," Billy said. He was still puzzling his head about the two names. He was positive now that he had seen them in the newspapers – in the headlines.

"Left?" she said, arching her brows[4]. "But my dear boy, he never left. He's still here. Mr. Temple is also here. They're on the fourth floor, both of them together."

Billy set down his cup slowly on the table and stared at his landlady. She smiled back at him, and then she put out one of her white hands and patted him comfortingly on the knee. "How old are you, my dear?" she asked.

1. *logeuse* **2.** *douillet, confortable* **3.** *bouffée* **4.** /braʊ/ (*ici*) *fronça les sourcils*

"Seventeen."

"Seventeen!" she cried. "Oh, it's the perfect age! Mr. Mulholland was also seventeen. But I think he was a trifle shorter than you are; in fact I'm sure he was, and his teeth weren't quite so white. You have the most beautiful teeth, Mr. Weaver, did you know that?"

"They're not as good as they look," Billy said. "They've got simply masses of fillings[5] in them at the back."

"Mr. Temple, of course, was a little older," she said, ignoring his remark. "He was actually twenty-eight. And yet I never would have guessed it if he hadn't told me, never in my whole life. There wasn't a blemish[6] on his body."

"A what?" Billy said.

"His skin was just like a baby's."

There was a pause. Billy picked up his teacup and took another sip of his tea; then he set it down again gently in its saucer. He waited for her to say something else, but she seemed to have lapsed into another of her silences. He sat there staring straight ahead of him into the far corner of the room, biting his lower lip. "That parrot," he said at last. "You know something? It had me completely fooled when I first saw it through the window. I could have sworn[7] it was alive."

"Alas, no longer."

"It's most terribly clever the way it's been done," he said. "It doesn't look in the least bit dead. Who did it?"

"I did."

" You did?"

"Of course," she said. "And have you met my little Basil as well?" She nodded towards the dachshund[8] curled up so comfortably in front of the fire. Billy looked at it. And suddenly, he realized that this animal had all the time been just as silent and motionless as the parrot. He put out a hand and touched it gently on the top of its back. The back was hard and cold, and when he pushed the hair to one side with his fingers, he could see the skin underneath, grayish black and dry and perfectly preserved.

"Good gracious me," he said. "How absolutely fascinating." He turned away from the dog and stared with deep admiration at the little woman beside him on the sofa. "It must be most awfully difficult to do a thing like that."

"Not in the least," she said. "I stuff[9] all my little pets myself when they pass away[10]. Will you have another cup of tea?"

"No, thank you," Billy said. The tea tasted faintly of bitter almonds[11], and he didn't much care for it.

"You did sign the book, didn't you?"

"Oh, yes."

"That's good. Because later on, if I happen to forget what you were called, then I can always come down here and look it up. I still do that almost every day with Mr. Mulholland and Mr. . . . Mr. . . ."

"Temple," Billy said, "Gregory Temple. Excuse my asking, but haven't there been any other guests here except them in the last two or three years?"

Holding her teacup high in one hand, inclining her head slightly to the left, she looked up at him out of the corners of her eyes and gave him another gentle little smile.

"No, my dear," she said. "Only you."

Roald Dahl, *The Landlady*, 1959

5. *plombages* **6.** *marque/défaut* **7.** *jurer* **8.** *teckel* **9.** *empaille* **10.** *meurent* **11.** /ˈɑːmənd / *amandes amères*

Father

Father: the magistrate, into whose courtroom I would sometimes slip during a trial[1], to crouch in a back seat, trying to relate to the stranger up there on the high bench[2], in his ample black gown, remote and stern, dispensing justice. However strange he seemed, I was proud, immensely proud. This is my father, I wanted everyone to know, this man who can listen to all these people and then decide, just like that, what is right, what is wrong. *He* knows. Then, one Saturday while he was playing golf, a man came to the back door to ask for him, a black man in such rags and tatters[3] one could see parts of his bare body right through them, his baggy trousers tied to his thin waist[4] with string, the front fastened with an inadequate safety pin; but what shocked me was that his whole face was covered in dried blood. He was unsteady[5] on his legs, but whether he was drunk or whether it was from pain I couldn't tell, I was too young, and certainly too terrified. Mother was inside, practising arpeggios, the door closed, which meant *Keep out;* Anna was in the bath preparing for an evening out. So I had to deal with him. He wouldn't go away. When I told him Father was out, he said he'd wait, he *had* to see him. Why? Because his baas[6], he said, had beaten him – "Look at me!" and he began to cry, it was the first time I'd seen a man cry – and he wanted justice. Those were his words. "I want justice."

1. *procès* **2.** *(ici) fauteuil du magistrat* **3.** in rags and tatters: *en haillons* **4.** *taille* **5.** was unsteady: *ne tenait pas* **6.** master

I offered him water from one of the tin mugs Mother kept under the sink for the servants, or for blacks like this one who came to the back door. He gulped it down thirstily. "Why don't you go to the police?" I asked, all stupid innocence. He just shook his head and sat down on the back step. From time to time he moaned in pain[7]. I stood there all the time, watching in horror and misery. Until Father came home. I ran to the garage to tell him about the man. He tried to shake me off[8]. "This is not the time, Kristien. I have to shower first." And he walked right past the man into the house. It must have been almost an hour before Father emerged from their bedroom again; he was pouring his whisky when I entered and reminded him. He was ready to dismiss[9] me, I could see; but I stood my ground. "If you don't come out to see him," I said, "I'm going to bring him in here." "Don't use that tone of voice with me," he warned. "The man is in pain," I said, "he's been beaten, he has come to you for help."

7. moaned in pain: *geignait de douleur* **8.** shake me off: *se débarrasser de moi* **9.** *renvoyer*

Making no attempt to hide his displeasure he came past me, the glass still in his hand. "Yes? What do you want?" he brusquely asked at the back door. The man staggered to his feet[10]. The front of his trousers was all wet. He began to tell his story. Even before he'd finished, Father curtly interrupted him: "Go to the police. This is their business, not mine. If it comes to court I can deal with it, but not here." "But Baas," said the man, "I already gone to the police. They just beat me some more and chase me away." "Then I'm sorry," said Father, "but I can't interfere. It would be highly improper. Now go away. Look how you've messed up[11] the place." And he went inside. I fled. I couldn't look the man in the face again. I stopped at the door to the lounge. "I don't understand you!" I shouted, tears streaming down my face. *"I don't understand you!"* And then I ran to our bathroom – it was still steamed up with Anna's fragrant ablutions – and vomited in the toilet. I still don't understand.

Andre Brink, *Imaginings of Sand*, 1996

10. staggered to his feet: *se leva en chancelant* **11.** messed up: *sali*

■ More about...

Visit the following website to collect information about Andre Brink.

www.answers.com/topic/andr-brink

a. When and where was Andre Brink born?

b. What is his mother tongue *(langue maternelle)*?

c. Where was he educated?

d. What was his relationship with black people in Paris? Why was it different from home? What impact did it have on Andre Brink?

e. What cause did he start to defend after 1968?

f. What are his most famous novels?

g. Which one has been made into a film?

Wuthering Heights[1]

Out on the wiley[2], windy moors[3]
We'd roll and fall in green
You had a temper like my jealousy
Too hot, too greedy[4]

How could you leave me
When I needed to possess you?
I hated you, I loved you too

Bad dreams in the night
You told me I was going to lose the fight
Leave behind my wuthering, wuthering
Wuthering Heights

Heathcliff, it's me, Cathy, I've come home
I'm so cold, let me in your window
Heathcliff, it's me, Cathy, I've come home
I'm so cold, let me in your window

Ooh, it gets dark, it gets lonely
On the other side from you
I pine[5] a lot, I find the lot
Falls through without you

I'm coming back, love
Cruel Heathcliff, my one dream
My only master

Too long I roamed[6] in the night
I'm coming back to his side to put it right
I'm coming home to wuthering, wuthering
Wuthering Heights
Heathcliff, it's me, Cathy, I've come home
I'm so cold, let me in your window
Heathcliff, it's me, Cathy, I've come home
I'm so cold, let me in your window

1. *Les Hauts de Hurlevent* (voir p. 224-225) **2.** wiley = wily: *trompeuse*
3. /mʊəʳz/ *lande* **4.** *avide* **5.** *me languis* **6.** *(ici) j'ai erré*

Ooh, let me have it
Let me grab[7] your soul away
Ooh, let me have it
Let me grab your soul away
You know it's me, Cathy
Heathcliff, it's me, Cathy, I've come home
I'm so cold, let me in your window

Heathcliff, it's me, Cathy, I've come home
I'm so cold, let me in your window
Heathcliff, it's me, Cathy, I've come home
I'm so cold

Heathcliff, it's me, Cathy, I've come home
I'm so cold, yeah

It's me, Cathy, I've come home
I'm so cold, yeah

Kate Bush, *The Kick Inside*, 1978

7. *saisir*

The living dead

Mr Lockwood is trying to sleep after a tiring day but a constant noise from outside keeps awaking him.

"I must stop it nevertheless!" I muttered, knocking my knuckles[1] through the glass, and stretching an arm out to seize the importunate branch: instead of which, my fingers closed on the fingers of a little, ice-cold hand!

The intense horror of nightmare came over me; I tried to draw back my arm but the hand clung to it, and a most melancholy voice sobbed[2],

"Let me in – let me in!"

"Who are you?" I asked, struggling, meanwhile to disengage myself.

"Catherine Linton," it replied shiveringly [...] "I'm come home, I'd lost my way on the moor[3]!"

As it spoke, I discerned, obscurely, a child's face looking through the window – terror made me cruel; and finding it useless to attempt shaking the creature off, I pulled its wrist[4] on to the broken window-pane, and rubbed it to and fro[5] till the blood ran down and soaked the bed-clothes: still it wailed, "Let me in!" and maintained its tenacious grip, almost maddening me with fear.

"How can I!" I said at length. "Let *me* go, if you want me to let you in!"

The fingers relaxed, I snatched mine through the hole, hurriedly piled the books up in a pyramid against it, and stopped my ears to exclude the lamentable prayer.

1. *jointures des doigts* **2.** *sanglota* **3.** /mʊəʳ/ *lande* **4.** *poignet* **5.** rubbed to and fro: *frotta d'avant en arrière*

I seemed to keep them closed above a quarter of an hour, yet, the instant I listened again, there was the doleful cry moaning on!

"Begone!" I shouted, "I'll never let you in, not if you beg for twenty years."

"It's twenty years," mourned[6] the voice, "twenty years, I've been a waif[7] for twenty years!"

Thereat began a feeble scratching outside, and the pile of books moved as if thrust forward.

I tried to jump up, but could not stir a limb[8]; and so yelled aloud, in a frenzy of fright.

To my confusion, I discovered the yell was not ideal[9]. Hasty footsteps approached my chamber door: somebody pushed it open, with a vigorous hand, and a light glimmered through the squares of the top of the bed. [...]

Heathcliff stood near the entrance, in his shirt and trousers, with a candle dripping over his fingers and his face as white as the wall behind him. [...]

"It is only your guest, sir," I called out [...]. "I had the misfortune to scream in my sleep, owing to a frightful nightmare. I'm sorry I disturbed you."

"Oh, God confound you, Mr Lockwood! I wish you were at the –" commenced my host, setting the candle on a chair, because he found it impossible to hold it steady.

"And who showed you up into this room?" he continued, crushing his nails into his palms, and grinding his teeth. [...] "I've a good mind to turn them out of the house this moment!"

"It was your servant, Zillah," I replied. [...] "I should not care if you did, Mr Heathcliff; [...] Well, it is – swarming[10] with ghosts and goblins!"

"What do you mean?" asked Heathcliff. [...]

"If the little fiend[11] had got at the window, she probably would have strangled me!" I returned. [...] "That Catherine Linton told me she had been walking the earth these twenty years: a just punishment for her mortal transgressions, I've no doubts." [...]

Heathcliff got on to the bed, and wrenched open the lattice[12], bursting, as he pulled at it, into an uncontrollable passion of tears.

"Come in! Come in!" he sobbed. "Cathy, do come. Oh do – *once* more! Oh! My heart's darling! Hear me *this* time – Catherine at last!"

The spectre showed a spectre's ordinary caprice; it gave no sign of being; but the snow and wind whirled wildly through, even reaching my station, and blowing the light out.

Emily Brontë, *Wuthering Heights*, 1847

6. *se lamenta* **7.** *enfant abandonnée* **8.** *membre* **9.** the right thing to do **10.** *grouillant* **11.** *démon*
12. wrenched open the lattice: *arracha le treillage*

A portrait of Emily Brontë by her brother Patrick, around 1833

More about...

Visit the following websites to collect information about Emily Brontë.

a. When was Emily Brontë born?
b. Where did she spend most of her life? Give the name of the place, the type of area and landscape.
www.poetry.com
www.beautifulbritain.co.uk/htm/outandabout/haworthhtm

c. How many brothers and sisters did she have? What was her sisters' occupation?
d. Where was Emily educated?
e. What were her hobbies as a child?
www.poetry.com

f. What is she famous for?
g. When did she die? What did she die of?
www.answers.com/topic/emily-bront

ART PROJECT

NEW YORK CITY IN ART

YOUR TASK AT THE END OF THIS PROJECT

You are writing a guidebook on New York City and you want to create a section entitled “New York City in Art”. You will include information collected in this project to draw a timeline on the American artists whose works are presented in the following pages.

Seasons in New York

Maurice Prendergast, *Central Park*, 1901

1 Observe these two paintings and react

a. What strikes you (colours, season, place, people, activities, clothes, atmosphere, ...)?
b. Does *Central Park* remind you of paintings by: Leonardo da Vinci – Constable – Monet – Renoir – Picasso – Warhol?
(Use a dictionary if necessary).
c. Justify your answer (theme, technique, period).

MORE ABOUT

To help you answer these questions go to:
http://www.artchive.com/artchive/P/prendergast.html
http://20thcenturyart.suite101.com/article.cfm/robert_henri

Robert Henri, *Snow in New York*, 1902

Help!

Central Park	Snow in New York	Technique
horse carriage: *calèche* crowded smartly-dressed go for a walk /wɔːk/ stroll: *flâner* bench: *banc*	coach: *diligence* streetlamp snowstorm: *tempête de neige* bleak: *lugubre* plod through: *marcher péniblement à travers*	everyday life scene urban landscape brushstroke: *coup de pinceau* blurred /blɜːd/ : *flou, estompé* sketchy outline: *contours esquissés* give / convey an impression of

2 A calendar

PREPARE YOUR TASK

The museum you work in will organise an exhibition entitled "Views of New York City at the Turn of the 20th Century". Which of these two paintings will you print on the ticket? Defend your choice.

A city of steel

Charles C. Ebbets, *Lunch Atop a Skyscraper*, 29 September 1932

1 Observe and speak

a. React to this document (date, country, city, place, people's attitudes, activities).

b. What do you know about the period when the photo was taken?

c. In your opinion, what were the photographer's intentions?

MORE ABOUT

Go on these websites to learn more about New York architecture and skyscrapers.

What inventions made the building of skyscrapers possible?

http://inventors.about.com/library/inventors/blskyscapers.htm

http://www.pbs.org/wgbh/buildingbig/skyscraper/index.html

http://www.madehow.com/Volume-6/Skyscraper.html

Help!

Reactions	Working conditions	Photographer's intentions
lunch box steel beam /stiːl biːm/: *poutre en acier* emptiness = the void: *le vide* blue-collar worker : *ouvrier* relaxed feel dizzy /fiːl ˈdɪzɪ/, giddy /ˈgɪdɪ/ = afraid of heights /haɪts/: *avoir le vertige* dangle /dæŋgl/ rest: *se reposer*	construction site: *chantier* safety harness: *harnais de sécurité* low wages /ləʊ ˈweɪdʒɪz/: *salaires bas* strenuous /ˈstrenjʊəs/ = hard, difficult skilled: (*ici*) *habile, qualifié* risk one's life hire /ˈhaɪəʳ/: *engager*	power high-angle shot blurred /blɜːd/: *flou* towering /ˈtaʊərɪŋ/: *imposant, démesuré* soar /sɔːʳ/: *s'élancer (vers le ciel)* glorify give / convey an impression of

Joseph Stella,
The Voice of the City of New York Interpreted: The Bridge,
1920–1922

2 An audio guide

a. Listen to the audio guide and learn about the artistic movement Joseph Stella belonged to.

b. Read the following transcriptions, then write the words corresponding to them, and translate them with the help of a dictionary if necessary. Listen to them and repeat them.
/ˈdaɪnəmɪzəm/ /ˈkænvəsɪz/ /ˈfræktʃəd/ /kəˈlaɪdəskəʊp/ /steɪnd ˈglɑːs/

3 Oral account

Prepare a one-minute oral account of the document that includes the following points: painter's place and date of birth – main elements or characteristics of the painting – technique used – name of the artistic movement – artist's final goal – painter's date of death

The p**ai**nting dates back to...
This p**e**riod corresp**o**nds to...
The c**a**nvas incl**u**des...
Joseph St**e**lla gl**o**rified...
He beli**e**ved...
He was conv**i**nced...

4 Write an article

PREPARE YOUR TASK

You are in charge of the architecture section of a guidebook on New York City. Here are two titles:
– A city of steel
– The tallest, the highest.
Write a paragraph illustrating one of them.

Neighbourhoods

Red Grooms, *Little Italy*, 1989

Help!

Scenes of New York

cab: *taxi*
pram: *landau*
passer-by
crowd /kraʊd/
zebra-crossing
traffic-jam / congestion
fire escape
pavement / sidewalk
stroll: *flâner*
overlook a street

Impressions

hustle and bustle: *frénésie*
frantic
crammed
oversized
noisy / deafening

1 A quick look

a. Observe *Little Italy* for 30 seconds. Then close your book and try to remember three characters and three objects.

b. What is the weather like?

c. Where are the characters and objects?
(See p. 281-282 '*Commenter un document visuel*').

2 React

a. What are the dominant colours?

b. What impression does this painting give?
Choose from this list: vitality – solitude – crowd – movement – emptiness – joy – sadness – dynamism – diversity – uniformity – chaos

c. Justify your choice(s) by listing people's activities.

d. Is it a stereotyped view of New York? What district is represented here? What do you know about it?

3 Technique

Is this work of art realistic – naive – abstract – futuristic? Explain your choice with elements from the painting.

Richard Estes, *The Canadian Club, New York*, 1974

4 Observe and react

a. Which of these reactions would you choose? (several possible answers)

- How true to life!
- How crowded!
- It's so much like a photograph!
- It's so realistic!
- What a deserted street!
- It must be an old photograph!
- It can't be a painting!
- It's a lifeless world!

b. Richard Estes is a photorealist. Can you guess what this term means? Use elements from the painting to justify your answer.

c. A journalist has interviewed an art critic about Richard Estes. Here's an extract. Get ready to read it aloud.

Journalist: How does Estes find the subject matter for his paintings?
Art critic: He just wanders around and looks at things. He takes a lot of pictures if something strikes him and he thinks it's interesting. And he didn't really want to do things just out of his mind, to make up things.

PREPARE YOUR TASK

5 Record an audio guide

Select one of these two paintings. Record an audio guide (one to two minutes). Use notes only. Describe the painting briefly, talk about the artist and his technique. You may include the reactions and feelings of the public when this painting was shown for the first time.

Help!

concrete /ˈkɒnkriːt/: *béton*
billboard/hoarding: *panneau publicitaire*
dehumanized
close /kləʊs/ to reality

The city that never sleeps

Georgia O'Keeffe, *City Night*, 1970s

1 Fill in the blanks

a. Fill in the blanks with words taken from the list below.

canyons – concrete – convey – corporations – deserted – economic – geometric – gloomy – height – human – imposing – inhuman – low-angle shot – power – tiny

This painting shows two skyscrapers at night. It relies on … design. This painting looks dark, … and fascinating at the same time. The … was chosen to … an impression of … and …, to reinforce the vertical lines of the composition. The viewer feels … compared to the huge and … skyscrapers that are reaching for the sky. The only ray of light comes from the moon. The world of … represented here looks cold and … . No … presence can be noticed. The skyscrapers may represent the … power of big … . People live and work in a metallic and … world. It conveys the impression that streets are … and that people are overpowered.

b. What keywords from this paragraph can you remember?

Edward Hopper, *Nighthawks*, 1942

MP3

PREPARE YOUR TASK

2 An interview

We interviewed Potter Guifford, an art expert on Hopper. Listen to his comments on *Nighthawks* and learn more.

PREPARE YOUR TASK

3 Watch a film clip

a. Go on the following website and use the links.

b. Note down as much information as you can on Hopper: historical period, movement, type of subjects painted, dominant theme.

MORE ABOUT

http://www.nga.gov/exhibitions/hopperinfo.shtm
Related resources – Watch a film clip.

PREPARE YOUR TASK

4 Write a biography

Use the information collected to write a short biography of Edward Hopper and illustrate it with the painting you preferred. Justify your choice.

YOUR TASK AT THE END OF THIS PROJECT

A few tips for the final task

- ✔ Collect as much information as you can on the artists and the movements they belong to.
- ✔ Draw the timeline, write the dates in colour.
- ✔ Write short paragraphs on the main artists.
- ✔ Illustrate with paintings you like.

Renforcement lexical

LES PRINCIPAUX PRÉFIXES ET SUFFIXES

Formation des noms (abstraits et collectifs)			
		Sens	Exemples
Préfixe	*mis- / mal-*	péjoratif, contraire	*misbehaviour*
	non-	contraire	*non-violent*
	super-	au-dessus	*superhero*
Suffixe	*-er / -or / -ar / -ess / -ist*	agent, profession, instrument	*scientist, laser-pointer*
	-ation	fonction, condition	*occupation*
	-dom /dəm/	rang, condition, domaine	*kingdom, boredom*
	-hood /hʊd/	condition, état, âge	*childhood*
	-ism	doctrine, pratique	*racism, optimism*
	-ness /nəs/	état, caractéristique	*loneliness*
	-ship	état, condition	*friendship*
Formation des adjectifs			
		Sens	Exemples
Préfixe	*dis- / im- / in- / ill- / ir- /*	contraire	*disloyal, unscrupulous, illegal*
	un- / over-	excès	*overworked*
Suffixe	*-able / -ible* /əbᵊl/	capable de	*reliable*
	-al / -y / -ish / -ic	se rapportant à, comme	*realistic, skinny*
	-ful /fəl/	plein de	*powerful*
	-en	matière	*golden*
	-ed / -ing / -ly	pourvu de, ayant la qualité de	*oppressed, caring, lovely*
	-less /ləs/	sans, dépourvu de	*defenceless*
	-some /səm/	qui provoque	*lonesome*
	-ch / -sh / -ss / -ese / -an	nationalité	*Indian, Japanese*
Formation des verbes			
		Sens	Exemples
Préfixe	*dis- / un-*	contraire	*displace, unlock*
	re-	répétition	*reorganize*
Suffixe	*-en*	transformation	*blacken*
Formation des adverbes			
		Sens	Exemples
Suffixe	*-ly*	manière	*shyly*

1 SONG OF MYSELF

■ Sur papier libre, trouvez un maximum de mots dans les quatre rubriques. Aidez-vous d'un dictionnaire, si nécessaire.

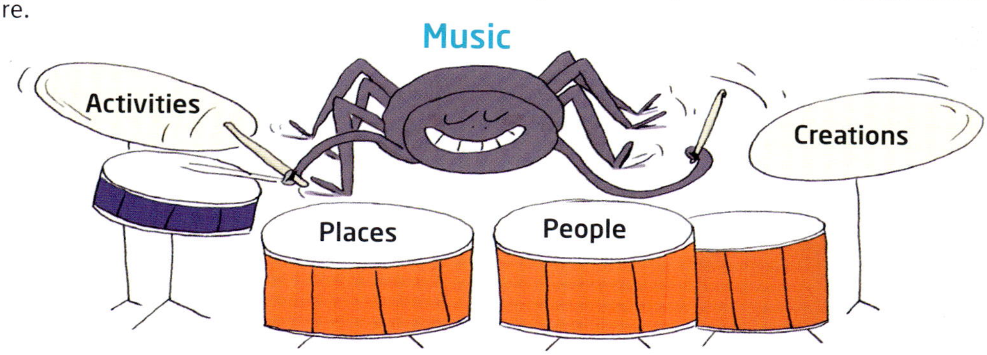

2 HALL OF FAME

■ Chassez l'intrus dans ces listes de mots de sens voisins.

1. attractive, heavy, lovely, pretty, cute
2. upset, ugly, horrid, hideous, dull
3. huge, large, enormous, big, deep
4. joyful, dreadful, pleased, merry, happy
5. evil, cruel, noisy, wicked, nasty
6. kind, sweet, savoury, friendly, nice
7. tiny, small, slim, short, little
8. smart, clever, intelligent, brainy, confident

3 MAKE A WISH

■ Donnez le contraire de chacun des adjectifs suivants. Classez-les dans un tableau à deux colonnes : positif et négatif.

optimistic hopeful exciting generous idealistic strong broad-minded

4 HEROES

■ Étoffez votre vocabulaire. Au lieu d'utiliser des mots simples (A2) utilisez un vocabulaire plus précis (B1). Trouvez le plus de mots possible grâce au lexique donné dans l'unité.

Physical description

A2	B1
strong →	m______r, a______c
nice →	h______e, g__d-l_____g, a________e

Personality

A2	B1
brave →	d____g, a_________s, f______s,
active →	e_______c, e__________g

Life

A2	B1
dangerous →	r___y, e______l
sad →	m_______e, d______l
lucky →	s_________l, f_______e

Involvement

A2	B1
generous →	d_____d, c____g, s______s
concerned →	c_______d, d________d, d_______d

5 CITY OF GLASS

■ Sur papier libre, recopiez les séries suivantes en éliminant l'intrus. Déterminez le champ sémantique auquel ces séries de mots appartiennent. Aidez-vous d'un dictionnaire, si nécessaire.

a. opportunity – determined – achieve – park – future – emigrate – integrate into – fulfil – foreigner – hopeful

b. maze – soulless – flashy billboards – hustle and bustle – hectic – dehumanized – get lost – gloomy – passport – anonymous – depressing – dizzy

c. monument – culture – visit – museums – tourism – harbour – audio-guide – ticket – wheelchair access – queuing – heritage – entertainment

6 WILD WILD WEST

■ Voici une liste de mots de liaison utiles pour raconter l'histoire de l'Ouest américain. Classez-les selon leurs valeurs, puis traduisez-les en français.

after that, so, eventually, but, suddenly, later on, on the contrary, to start with, that's why, then, for example, also, first of all, such as, at last, therefore, whereas, because, thanks to, consequently, besides

give a chronology	express cause	introduce examples	express opposition
conclude	begin	express consequence	add new elements

7 ROBOT DREAMS

■ Sur papier libre, reformulez les phrases en complétant les espaces blancs avec un mot de la même famille que le mot en italiques.

a. Elvex felt miserable when he realized robots *worked too much*.
→ Elvex felt miserable when he realized robots were … .

b. Human beings can be really weak when confronted with a robot *with no soul*.
→ Human beings can be really weak when confronted with a … robot.

c. Robots can be very useful when your house is *in a mess*.
→ Robots can be very useful when your house is all … .

d. Dr Calvin must have *feared* Elvex's reactions when she realized he had acted as a human being.
→ Dr Calvin must have felt … of Elvex's reactions when she realized he had acted as a human being.

8 TRUE BRITS

■ Complétez les blancs avec la préposition prise dans cette liste: ***about, at, by, of, to, with***.
Les prépositions peuvent être utilisées plusieurs fois. Utilisez un dictionnaire si nécessaire.

1. When visiting London last Christmas, we were amazed … the decorations in the streets.
2. French visitors are often worried … the traffic coming from the right and not the left and they are surprised … the kindness of the people. But they are also confused … their accent.
3. My friend was shocked … the prices in the shop windows.
4. The whole group was interested … the exhibition at the Tate Gallery and satisfied … the restaurant we had booked for them. Everybody was excited … the show at the Globe later on.
5. When we went to the Tower of London, we were scared … pickpockets, and very tired … queuing for so long before getting in.

9 DESTINATION LIVERPOOL

■ Ces mots sont dans le désordre. Ré-écrivez-les correctement et classez-les dans ce tableau. Pour vous aider, la première et la dernière lettres ont été mises en gras.

1. nleir 2. tccoaob 3. ronccet 4. ssngeerpa 5. usrpoterp 6. rfreeee 7. adiceune 8. lennsaveetm

Merseyside Maritime Museum	INTERNATIONAL SLAVERY MUSEUM	Liverpool Football Club	The Beatles Story

10 LIFE IS ART

■ À partir des mots donnés dans les colonnes de gauche, trouvez les termes qui ont la même racine et entourez la voyelle accentuée. Utilisez un dictionnaire si besoin.

Verbe	Nom
criticize	
standardize	
consume	
recognize	
possess	

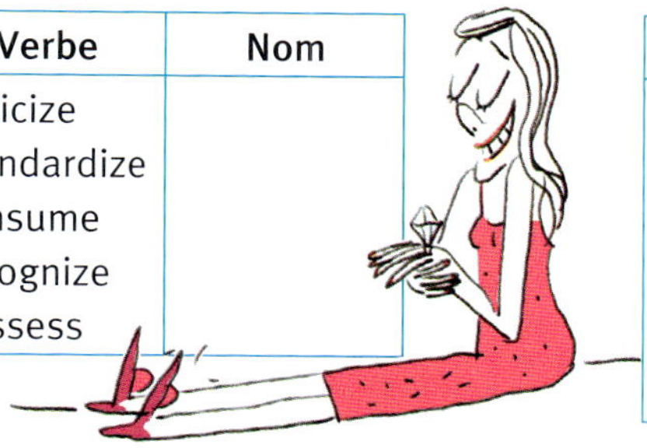

Nom	Adjectif
geometry	
luxury	
need	
wealth	
reality	
success	

Adjectif	Verbe
resigned	
revolting	

11 A WORLD OF GEEKS

■ Sur papier libre, indiquez les antonymes (≠) ou synonymes (=) des mots suivants.

a. addicted to = … b. harmless ≠ … c. isolated = …
d. sociable ≠ … e. noisy = … f. preposterous = …

12 MOTHER EARTH

■ Formez des noms composés en associant un mot de la liste A à un mot de la liste B.

Liste A

oil – rubbish – nuclear – water – mass

Liste B

murder – dump – spill – supply – waste – shortage

13 ALL THE WORLD'S A STAGE

■ Trouvez l'adjectif formé à partir de ces noms ou de ces verbes et, à l'aide d'un dictionnaire, marquez l'accent tonique du mot formé.

1. obey 2. submit 3. authority 4. inquire 5. care
6. caution 7. hesitate 8. contempt 9. scorn 10. aristocrat

14 A MIND TO MURDER

■ Sur papier libre, classez les mots ci-dessous dans le champ lexical qui leur correspond : *Crime – Investigation – Defence*. Aidez-vous d'un dictionnaire si nécessaire.

court /kɔːʳt/– weapon – witness – shadow – sleuth /sluːθ/– aggressor – description – mug shot – alibi /ˈæləbaɪ/– fingerprints – DNA – blood – testimony – blackmailer – track – stab – lawyer /ˈlɔːjəʳ/

15 OVER THE RAINBOW

■ Ajoutez aux mots entre parenthèses les préfixes et/ou suffixes appropriés choisis dans la liste ci-dessous. Écrivez le nouveau mot formé entièrement sur papier libre. Attention aux changements nécessaires.

Préfixes: *in-, imp-, un-*

Suffixes: *-hood, -ic, -ion, -ly, -ment, -ship*

Steve Biko was one of South Africa's most famous political activists. While he was at medical school, Biko started denouncing the (justice) of the apartheid regime, poverty and (employ). He couldn't stand social and (economy) (discriminate) because it was (fair). He realized that Blacks living in (town), that is to say very poor (neighbour), were treated as second-class citizens. He believed he lived in a (dictator) because Afrikaners were ready to crush any (rebel) or (demonstrate) (brutal). One day he was caught, (prison), was tortured in (detain) and died during his (interrogate). His death was a (violate) of Human Rights.

16 JAMAICAN COLOURS OF LONDON

■ Sur papier libre, recopiez les mots sur une colonne puis suivez les indications.

1. Donnez les contraires des mots suivants : ***enthusiastic – happy – unusual – lifeless – employment***
2. Donnez un équivalent pour chacun des mots suivants : ***enormous – awful – intriguing – isolated – surprising – welcome – big – beautiful – good***

Précis grammatical

Sommaire

1 L'auxiliaire *BE*

	Formes affirmatives	Formes négatives	Formes interrogatives
Présent	I **am** / **'m** happy. You **are** / **'re** happy. He / She / It **is** / **'s** happy. We / You / They **are** / **'re** happy.	I **am not** / **'m not** happy. You **are not** / **aren't** /ɑːnt/ happy. He / She / It **is not** / **isn't** happy. We / You / They **are not** / **aren't** happy.	**Am** I happy? **Are** you happy? **Is** he / she / it happy? **Are** we / you / they happy?
Prétérit	I **was** /wɒz/ /wəz/ happy. You **were** /wɜːʳ/ /wəʳ/ happy. He / She / It **was** happy. We / You / They **were** happy.	I **was not** /**wasn't** /ˈwɒznt/ happy. You **were not** / **weren't** /ˈwɜːʳnt/ happy. He / She / It **was not** / **wasn't** happy. We / You / They **were not** / **weren't** happy.	**Was** I happy? **Were** you happy? **Was** he / she / it happy? **Were** we / you / they happy?

Participe passé : *been* ; forme en *-ing* : *being.*

Dans certains cas, l'anglais emploie une construction en *be* alors que le français emploie une construction en « avoir ».

*He**'s** hungry. / He**'s** thirsty.* Il **a** faim. / Il **a** soif.

*I**'m** cold. / I**'m** hot.* J'**ai** froid. / J'**ai** chaud.

*You**'re** lucky.* Tu **as** de la chance.

"*How old **is** she?*" "*She**'s** 16.*" « Quel âge **a**-t-elle ? » « Elle **a** 16 ans. »

2 *There is / there are*

■ L'élément conjugué est *BE*.

*There **is** / There**'s** a problem.* Il y a un problème.

*There **was** a problem.* Il y avait / Il y a eu / Il y eut un problème.

*There **will be** a problem.* Il y aura un problème.

*There **must be** a problem.* Il doit y avoir un problème.

■ Il y a obligatoirement un accord au **singulier** ou au **pluriel** avec le sujet « réel » (qui est placé après *BE*).

There is <u>a problem</u>. / There are <u>two problems</u>. Il y a un problème. / Il y a deux problèmes.

There weren't <u>many passengers</u>. Il n'y avait pas beaucoup de voyageurs.

En français, on a toujours le singulier (« Il y a », « Il y avait »).

■ À la forme interrogative, l'inversion se fait avec l'élément ***there***.

There is a problem. → ***Is there** a problem?* Est-ce qu'il y a un problème ?

N'utilisez pas la construction *there is / there are* comme equivalent anglais de « il y a » qui signifie « depuis ».

Il y a deux mois qu'il est ici. *He's been here for two months.*

Il y a trois ans qu'elle est partie. *She left three years ago.* (voir § 9, p. 260)

3 Have

1 *Have* peut exprimer la possession au sens large du terme (avoir un ordinateur / un rhume / des enfants). On peut alors employer *have* seul, ou suivi de *got* (*have got*).

He ***has*** *a lot of friends. / He****'s got*** *(=* ***has got****) a lot of friends.* Il a beaucoup d'amis.

Have got est employé dans la langue courante ou familière. Les deux formes ne fonctionnent pas de la même façon à la forme interrogative et à la forme négative :

- *Have* employé seul fonctionne comme un **verbe ordinaire** : il se construit alors avec les auxiliaires ***do / does / did*** au présent et au prétérit simples négatif et interrogatif.

She ***doesn't*** *have a computer.* Elle n'a pas d'ordinateur.

Did *Alice* ***have*** *children?* Est-ce qu'Alice avait des enfants ?

- Dans l'expression ***have got***, l'élément *have* fonctionne comme un **auxiliaire**.

She ***hasn't got*** *a computer.* Elle n'a pas d'ordinateur.

Has *she* ***got*** *a DVD player?* Est-ce qu'elle a un lecteur de DVD ?

En anglais US, on dira habituellement : *She* ***doesn't have*** *a computer. /* ***Does*** *she* ***have*** *a DVD player?*

2 Le verbe *have* peut être utilisé dans le sens de « prendre », ou dans un sens voisin (manger, boire, etc.).

Have a nice weekend! Bon week-end !

They're having lunch. Ils sont en train de déjeuner.

We'll have a good time. On va bien s'amuser.

Have est ici un verbe **d'action** et il ne peut pas être remplacé par *have got*. La négation et l'interrogation se forment obligatoirement avec *do / does / did*.

They ***didn't have*** *a nice weekend.* Ils n'ont pas passé un bon week-end.

What time ***do you have*** *dinner?* Vous dînez à quelle heure ?

3 *Have* est également utilisé pour former le ***present perfect*** et le ***past perfect***.

I have / I had finished. J'ai / J'avais fini. (voir § 6 p. 258 et § 12 p. 261)

4 Le présent simple

1 Conjugaison

Forme affirmative	Forme interrogative	Forme négative
I **work**. You **work**. He / She / It **works**. We / You / They **work**.	**Do** I **work**? **Do** you **work**? **Does** /dʌz/ he / she / it **work**? **Do** we / you / they **work**?	I **do not** / **don't** /dəʊnt/ **work**. You **do not** / **don't work**. He / She / It **does not** / **doesn't work**. We / You / They **do not** / **don't work**.

2 Terminaison *-s* à la 3e personne du singulier : modifications orthographiques

- Quand la base verbale se termine par *-s, -x, -z, -ch, -sh* ou *-o*, on ajoute ***-es***.

pass → *pass**es***
fix → *fix**es***
watch → *watch**es***
wash → *wash**es***
go → *go**es***

- Quand la base verbale se termine par un ***-y*** précédé d'une consonne, ce *-y* devient ***-i*** et on ajoute ***-es***.

try → *tr**ies**, marry* → *marr**ies*** (mais dans *play* le *-y* est précédé d'une voyelle, donc *play* → *plays*)

3 Terminaison *-s* à la 3e personne du singulier : prononciation

- La terminaison écrite ***-es*** se prononce /ɪz/ lorsqu'elle **suit une consonne** *(passes, fixes, judges)*.

- Dans tous les autres cas, la terminaison écrite ***-s*** ou ***-es*** se prononce soit /z/ *(plays, knows, goes, lies)*, soit /s/ *(looks, sits)*.

Deux cas particuliers : ***does*** se prononce /dʌz/ et ***says*** se prononce /sez/.

4 Emplois du présent simple

Le présent simple est utilisé pour parler d'un fait ou d'une série de faits, considérés au moment présent et **vus dans leur totalité**.

■ Je parle d'une **caractéristique du sujet.**

Laura plays the piano (= Laura is a pianist). Laura joue du piano.

Ted likes hip hop. Ted aime le hip hop.

■ Je parle d'un **comportement habituel.**

Ted plays football every Saturday. Ted joue au foot tous les samedis.

■ Je parle d'une **action** qui est située au moment présent, et qui est **considérée dans sa totalité.**

I click on this icon, and the menu opens. Je clique sur cette icône, et le menu s'ouvre.

And now Ricardo gets the ball, he shoots, and he scores! Maintenant Ricardo prend la balle, il shoote, et il marque !

5 Le présent en *BE* + *-ING*

Le présent en *BE* + *-ING* s'oppose au présent simple. Le présent simple voit l'événement **dans son ensemble.** Le présent en *BE* + *-ING* réalise un « coup de projecteur » **sur un moment de l'événement** (ou sur plusieurs moments). Ce « coup de projecteur » peut prendre plusieurs formes.

■ Il se situe **au moment où on parle.**

*Look, he**'s trying** to open the door.* Regarde, il essaie (= est en train d'essayer) d'ouvrir la porte.

■ Il porte sur un événement **futur** (expression d'une **intention**).

*Tomorrow evening **I'm watching** the match on TV.* Demain soir je regarde le match à la télé.

Certains verbes sont difficilement compatibles avec *BE* + *-ING* : ce sont des verbes comme *know* (savoir, connaître) ou *look* (employé dans le sens de « sembler ») ; ces verbes expriment un sentiment ou un état mental vus nécessairement « en bloc » :
I know him. Je le connais.
It looks easy. Ça a l'air facile.

6 Le *present perfect* simple

1 Forme

Auxiliaire *HAVE* conjugué au présent + **participe passé** du verbe :

I have finished my work. J'ai fini mon travail.

Pour les verbes réguliers, le participe passé se forme comme le prétérit : on ajoute la terminaison *-ed* à la base verbale. Pour les verbes irréguliers, voir p. 275.

Forme affirmative	Forme interrogative	Forme négative
I **have finished.** You **have finished.** He / She / It **has finished.** We / You / They **have finished.**	**Have** I **finished**? **Have** you **finished**? **Has** he / she / it **finished**? **Have** we / you / they **finished**?	I **have not / haven't finished.** You **have not / haven't finished.** He / She / It **has not / hasn't finished.** We / You / They **have not / haven't finished.**

2 Valeur de résultat

■ On s'intéresse au **résultat présent d'un événement passé.**

*I've **fixed** the TV.* J'ai réparé la télé.

Ce qui importe ici pour l'énonciateur, c'est le résultat : « la télé fonctionne ». En revanche, on utilise le **prétérit** quand on s'intéresse en premier lieu à l'événement passé, ou à ses circonstances :

"When did you fix it?" "(I fixed it) this morning."
« Quand est-ce que tu l'as réparée ? » « Ce matin. »

Pour le même événement passé, on peut donc choisir, **en fonction du point de vue qu'on adopte,** soit le *present perfect* soit le prétérit.

■ Avec le *present perfect*, on emploie souvent des adverbes ou compléments de temps comme *already, ever / never, not... yet, over the past few weeks / months,* qui font implicitement référence au moment présent : *He **has** already **finished** his work* (Il a déjà fini son travail), *I **have sent** six text messages so far* (J'ai envoyé six SMS jusqu'à maintenant).

En revanche, certains adverbes, ainsi que les indications de date, d'heure, etc., sont **incompatibles avec le *present perfect,*** et exigent l'emploi du prétérit :
I sent six SMS messages yesterday / on February 7th / two weeks ago.

3 Passé récent

Associé à l'adverbe ***just***, le *present perfect* exprime un passé récent.

I've just seen her. Je viens de la voir.

En anglais US, on emploie le prétérit pour exprimer un passé récent : *I **just saw** her.*

4 Valeur de durée

On emploie le *present perfect* pour une action ou un état qui a commencé dans le passé et qui **dure encore au moment présent**.

I have known him for six months. Je le connais depuis six mois. / Il y a six mois que je le connais.

I have known him since last year. Je le connais depuis l'an dernier.

Notez les deux **équivalents du français « depuis »** :

– ***for*** + present perfect : indication d'une **durée** (*for six months, for ten years,* etc.).

– ***since*** + *present perfect* : indication du **point de départ** de l'événement (*since June 5th, since 2 o'clock,* etc.).

For peut aussi indiquer la durée d'un événement qui est **entièrement coupé du présent**, et donc est exprimé avec un **prétérit**. Comparez :

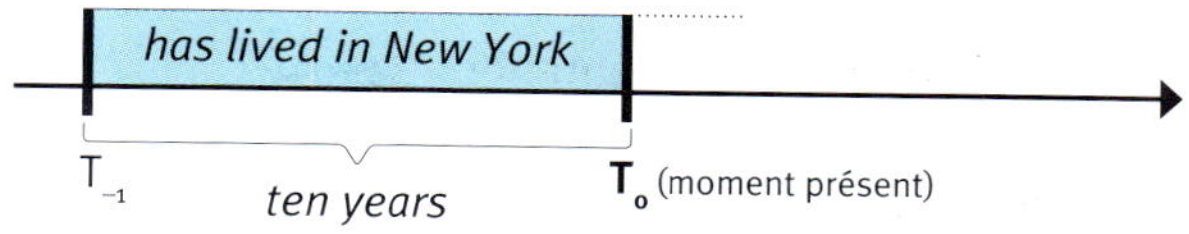

*He **has lived** in New York **for ten years**.* Il habite New York **depuis** dix ans. (Il y habite encore.)

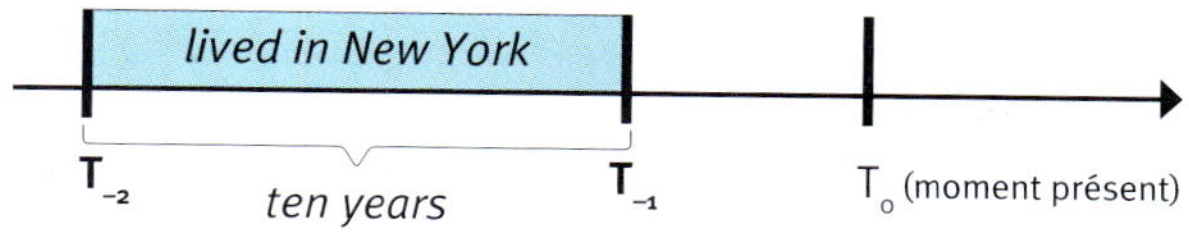

*He **lived** in New York **for ten years**.* Il a habité New York **pendant** dix ans. (Il n'y habite plus.)

L'emploi du prétérit est normal dans le second cas : l'événement est séparé du présent.

7 Le *present perfect* en BE + -ING

1 Valeur de résultat

	Forme	Valeur
Present perfect **simple**	*Jenny **has washed** the dog. He doesn't smell any more.* Jenny a lavé le chien. Il ne sent plus mauvais.	Exprime simplement un résultat : le chien est propre.
Present perfect **en *BE + -ING***	A: *There's water everywhere! What's happened?* B: *Ted **has been washing** the dog.* A: Il y a de l'eau partout. Qu'est-ce qui s'est passé ? B: Ted a lavé le chien.	On a constaté un résultat (« Il y a de l'eau partout »), et la forme verbale en *BE + -ING* exprime un « coup de projecteur » sur **l'action qui a provoqué le résultat** (sur l'action « Ted a lavé le chien »).

Notez qu'en français on a la même forme verbale dans les deux cas (« a lavé le chien »).

2 Valeur de durée

Avec les verbes *know* ou *look, understand,* etc. difficilement compatibles avec *BE + -ING* (voir § 6 p. 258), on utilise obligatoirement le ***present perfect*** simple.

I've known him for ten years. Je le connais depuis dix ans.

Avec les autres verbes, on utilise généralement le ***present perfect*** en *BE + -ING*.

She's been playing computer games for an hour. Elle joue à des jeux sur ordinateur depuis une heure.

8 Le prétérit simple : formes

1 Conjugaison

■ **Forme affirmative.** À toutes les personnes, on ajoute la terminaison ***-ed***.

I worked from 9 to 5. Je travaillais de 9 heures à 17 heures.

Attention au cas particulier des **verbes irréguliers** (voir p. 275).

■ **Formes interrogative et négative.** À toutes les personnes, on utilise l'auxiliaire ***did*** et la base verbale.

Did her brother work in a bank? Est-ce que son frère travaillait dans une banque ?

They did not / didn't work very much. Ils / Elles ne travaillaient pas beaucoup.

2 Terminaison *-ed* du prétérit : modifications orthographiques

■ *try* → ***tried***, *marry* → ***married*** : *y* qui suit une consonne devient *i*.

■ *stop* → ***stopped*** : une consonne finale qui suit une voyelle est redoublée dans les verbes d'une seule syllabe *(stop)*, ou si la syllabe finale est accentuée : *prefer* → *preferred* (mais *offer* → *offered*).

3 Terminaison *-ed* du prétérit : prononciation

■ On prononce /ɪd/ après *t* ou *d* : *started, needed.*

■ Dans les autres cas, on prononce soit /d/ *(played, loved)*, soit /t/ *(looked, stopped, missed)*.

9 Le prétérit simple : emplois

1 Le prétérit de récit

■ Le prétérit est utilisé dans le récit d'événements passés, vus comme **nettement séparés du présent.**

Marilyn Monroe was a great actress. She played in about 30 movies. Marilyn Monroe était une grande actrice. Elle a joué dans environ 30 films.

■ L'événement passé est **repéré dans le temps** par un adverbe (*yesterday*, etc.), par une date, par l'indication d'une période ou d'une heure *(last year)* ou par le contexte.

Il peut également être repéré dans le temps par une construction formée avec ***ago***.

He arrived in London two years ago / one week ago. Il est arrivé à Londres il y a deux ans / il y a une semaine.

2 Le prétérit imaginaire

■ Le verbe au prétérit peut renvoyer à un événement « contraire à la réalité ».

If I knew her phone number I could call her. Si je connaissais son numéro de téléphone, je pourrais l'appeler. (sous-entendu : je ne le connais pas)

Pour *BE*, il existe une forme pour exprimer ce prétérit imaginaire : *were* utilisé à toutes les personnes. Exemple : *If I were rich...* (Si j'étais riche...). Dans la langue courante, on dit *If I was rich...*

■ On trouve aussi ce prétérit après :

- le verbe ***wish*** (souhaiter, regretter que... ne... pas).

I wish I knew her phone number! Je regrette de ne pas connaître son numéro de téléphone.

- ***If only...!***

If only I knew her telephone number! Si seulement je connaissais son numéro de téléphone !

- ***It's time...***

It's time the children went to bed. Il est temps que les enfants aillent se coucher.

10 L'hypothèse exprimée par *if...*

Hypothèse **possible** (sur un fait présent ou futur)	*If it **is** sunny, we **will** go to the seaside.*	S'il fait beau, nous irons au bord de la mer. (Je ne sais pas s'il fait / fera beau.)
Hypothèse **irréelle** portant sur un fait **présent**	*If it **was** sunny, we **would** go to the seaside.*	S'il faisait beau, nous irions au bord de la mer. (Je sais qu'il ne fait pas beau.)
Hypothèse **irréelle** portant sur un fait **passé**	*If it **had been** sunny, we **would have gone** to the seaside.*	S'il avait fait beau (hier), nous serions allés au bord de la mer.

11 Le prétérit en *BE* + *-ING*

■ **Forme** : l'auxiliaire est ici ***was* / *were***.

"What were you doing yesterday at 8 p.m.?" "I was watching TV." « Qu'est-ce que tu faisais hier à 8 heures du soir ? » « Je regardais la télé. »

■ Le **repère dans le temps** est ici un moment du passé. Dans l'exemple ci-dessus, le moment-repère est *yesterday at 8 p.m.* ; le prétérit en *BE + -ING* désigne une action qui est en cours de déroulement à ce moment-repère.

Le moment-repère peut être constitué par un autre événement.

When I entered the room, he was watching TV. Quand je suis entré dans la pièce, il regardait la télé.

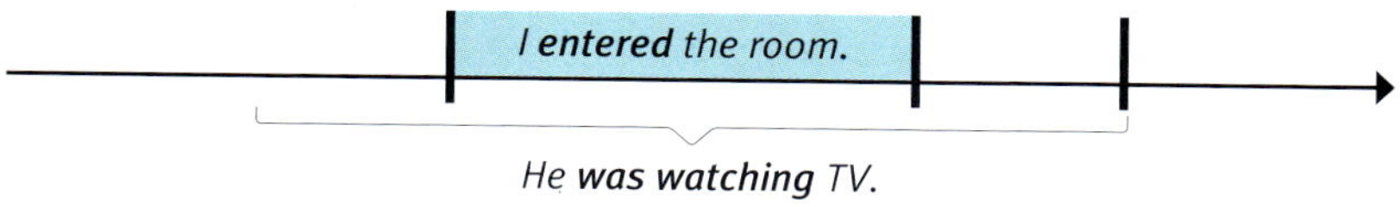

12 Le *past perfect* (ou *pluperfect*)

■ **Forme**

Auxiliaire *HAD* (forme contractée : ***'d***) pour toutes les personnes + participe passé. Exemple : *I / You / He / She / It / We / You / They* ***had finished***.

■ **Valeur de résultat**

*I **had fixed** the TV. So they were able to watch it.* J'avais réparé la télé. Donc ils ont pu la regarder.

Différence avec le *present perfect* : il s'agit d'un résultat **par rapport à un moment du passé**, et non par rapport au moment présent.

■ **Valeur de durée**

*I **had known** him for six months / since 2003.* Je le connaissais depuis six mois / depuis 2003.

L'événement dure jusqu'à un moment du passé. En français, le temps utilisé est ici **l'imparfait**.

■ **Valeur imaginaire**

L'élément « prétérit » contenu dans l'auxiliaire *had* peut aussi avoir une valeur « imaginaire ».

*If I **had finished** I would tell you.* Si j'avais fini je te le dirais.

13 Les modaux : généralités

Présent	can /kæn/ /kən/	may /meɪ/	must /mʌst/ /məst/	shall /ʃæl/ /ʃəl/	will /wɪl/, 'll /l/
Prétérit	could /kʊd/ /kəd/	might /maɪt/		should /ʃʊd/ /ʃəd/	would /wʊd/ /wəd/, 'd

Cannot s'écrit en un seul mot ; *can't* se prononce /kɑːnt/ en anglais GB et /kænt/ en anglais US.

■ **Formes modales simples et composées** (exemples avec *may*)

Modal + base verbale	*He may / might work.*
Modal + *BE* + *V-ING*	*He may / might **be** work**ing**.*
Modal + *have* + participe passé	*He may / might **have** work**ed**.*
Modal + *have been* + *V-ING*	*He may / might **have been** work**ing**.*

■ **Caractéristiques de forme des modaux**

- Ce sont des auxiliaires : ils forment directement (sans *do / does / did*) leur interrogation et leur négation.
- Ils ne prennent pas de *-s* à la troisième personne du singulier.
- Ils ne sont jamais précédés ni suivis de *to*. Ils n'ont pas d'infinitif, ni de forme en *-ing*, ni de participe passé.
- Dans un groupe verbal, il ne peut y avoir qu'un seul modal, qui est nécessairement placé en tête.

14 Les modaux : capacité, permission, obligation

1 « Je peux » = « Je suis capable de » : *I can*

He can help us. Il peut nous aider.

Can I help you? Je peux vous aider ?

Sorry, I cannot / can't help you. Désolé, je ne peux pas vous aider.

■ En français, l'équivalent est quelquefois « savoir ».

Can you swim? Est-ce que vous savez nager ?

■ On utilise ***be able to*** pour une capacité portant :

- sur un **fait futur**. *Next year he'**ll be able to** help us.* L'an prochain il pourra nous aider.
- sur un **fait passé réalisé**. *As I had the key I **was able to** go in.* Comme j'avais la clé j'ai pu entrer.

2 « Je peux » = « J'ai la permission de » : *I can*

You can use my scooter if you like. Tu peux te servir de mon scooter si tu veux.

Can I have some more coffee? Je peux avoir un peu plus de café ?

■ Pour demander une permission de façon très polie, et un peu « formelle », on peut utiliser *May I...?*

May I have some more coffee?

Can I / Could I have some more coffee? Je peux / Je pourrais avoir un peu plus de café ?

3 « Je dois » = « Il faut que je » : *I must*

■ *Must* exprime la volonté ou l'opinion personnelle de l'énonciateur.

You must help me. Il faut que tu m'aides.

Dans un style plus neutre, ou moins recherché, on utilise *have to,* qui n'est pas un modal : *You have to help me.*

- **Obligation future :** *I'll have to get up early tomorrow morning.* Demain matin il va falloir que je me lève de bonne heure.
- **Obligation passée :** *I had to hurry.* Il a fallu que je me dépêche.

À la forme négative, *must* et *have to* ont deux sens très différents.

You mustn't /ˈmʌsnt/ *go!* Il ne faut pas que tu partes ! (= obligation de ne pas / interdiction de)

You don't have to go! Tu n'es pas obligé de partir ! (= non obligation de)

4 « Je devrais » = « Il faudrait que je » (conseil, etc.) : *I should*

She should be more careful. Elle devrait être plus prudente.

You shouldn't tell him. Tu ne devrais pas le lui dire.

Pour exprimer un reproche concernant un fait passé, on utilise souvent *should not have* + participe passé.

You shouldn't have told him. Tu n'aurais pas dû le lui dire.

15 Les modaux : expression d'un degré de probabilité

1 « Je peux » = « Il se peut que je... » : *I may*

He may be ill. Il peut être malade. / Il se peut qu'il soit malade.

They may win the match. Il se peut qu'ils gagnent le match.

2 « Je pourrais » = « Il se pourrait que je... » : *I might*

I might be wrong. Il se pourrait que je me trompe.

They might win the match. Il se pourrait qu'ils gagnent le match.

En anglais comme en français, il faut faire attention aux sens différents des formes négatives.

*He **may not be** at home.* Il **peut ne pas** être chez lui.

*He **cannot** / He **can't be** at home.* Il **ne peut pas** être chez lui.

3 « Je dois » = « Il est probable que je... » : *I must*

I must be ill. Je dois être malade.

He must have been ill. Il devait / Il a dû être malade.

Attention aux équivalents anglais de « j'ai dû... » : s'agit-il d'une obligation ou d'une probabilité ?

À cause de la pluie ils **ont dû** arrêter le match. (obligation) *Because of the rain they had to stop the match.*

Ils ne sont pas encore là. Ils **ont dû** manquer le train. (probabilité) *They haven't arrived yet. They must have missed the train.*

16 Exprimer le futur

■ Le français utilise souvent le **présent** pour parler de l'avenir : « Demain, il est à Paris. » L'anglais fait de même, mais attention, il faut choisir entre le présent simple et le présent en *BE + -ING*.

• On emploie le **présent simple** pour un événement qui fait partie d'un **programme** (planning, horaire de trains...).

Tomorrow night there is a good film on TV. Demain soir, il y a un bon film à la télé.

• On emploie **le présent en *BE + -ING*** pour exprimer une intention.

Tomorrow evening I'm watching the match on TV. Demain soir je regarde le match à la télé.

■ L'équivalent anglais du futur simple est en général le modal ***will***.

Je m'en souviendrai. *I'll remember it.*

■ L'équivalent anglais de « aller + infinitif » est souvent ***be going to***.

Il va pleuvoir. *It's going to rain.*

■ Mais on emploie ***will*** pour exprimer une **décision prise au moment où l'on parle.**

D'accord, je vais leur demander. *OK, I'll ask them.*

17 Équivalents anglais de « quand... »

a) *I don't know **when we'll see** them again.* Je ne sais pas quand nous les reverrons.

b) *I'll tell them **when I see** them.* Je le leur dirai quand je les verrai.

■ Dans l'énoncé a) la proposition introduite par *when* est une **subordonnée interrogative** (cf. *When will we see them?* Quand est-ce qu'on les reverra ?). On peut utiliser ***will*** pour exprimer un futur.

■ Dans l'énoncé b) la proposition introduite par *when* (*as soon as* ou *until*) est une **subordonnée de temps** (qui pourrait être remplacée par *tomorrow* ou *next time*). Dans les subordonnées de temps, on ne peut pas employer *will* pour exprimer un futur : on utilise le **présent simple**.

18 Exprimer l'habitude

■ L'habitude s'exprime souvent au moyen du **présent** ou du **prétérit** simples, avec un **adverbe** ou un **complément de temps**.

She goes jogging every day. / She often went jogging. Elle fait du jogging tous les jours. / Elle faisait souvent du jogging.

■ Pour exprimer le sens de **« être habitué à »**, on peut utiliser ***be used to V-ING*** (à ne pas confondre avec *used to* + base verbale).

He was used to being treated like a child. Il avait l'habitude d'être traité comme un enfant.

■ Pour exprimer le sens de **« s'habituer à »**, on peut utiliser ***get used to V-ING***.

He soon got used to getting up at 5 every morning. Il s'est vite habitué à se lever à 5 heures tous les matins.

■ Pour exprimer un **comportement habituel**, on peut utiliser ***will*** (présent) ou ***would*** (passé).

He'll listen to that music for hours. Il écoute cette musique pendant des heures.

She'd go jogging every evening. Elle faisait du jogging tous les soirs.

19 L'impératif

2e personne du singulier ou du pluriel	Base verbale (*don't* + BV pour la négation)	*Be careful!* Fais / Faites attention ! *Don't ask him!* Ne lui demande / demandez pas.
1re personne du pluriel	*Let's* + base verbale (*let's not* à la forme négative)	*Let's ask him!* Demandons-lui ! *Let's not be pessimistic!* Ne soyons pas pessimistes !

20 Noms dénombrables et noms indénombrables

■ **Nom dénombrable** (*a cat / two cats, an orange / many oranges*, etc.) : il est possible de **compter des éléments**, et donc de mettre le nom au pluriel.

■ **Nom indénombrable** (*milk, courage*, etc.) : le nom représente **une « masse » qui ne se subdivise pas en éléments séparés les uns des autres** ; donc, on ne peut pas utiliser l'article *a / an*, ni mettre le nom au pluriel.

En français, il y a également des noms indénombrables, mais beaucoup moins qu'en anglais. Voici une liste de noms indénombrables anglais courants qui peuvent poser problème aux francophones :

accommodation	logement	*information*	renseignement(s)
advice	conseils	*knowledge*	connaissances
baggage	bagages	*news*	nouvelles
business	affaires	*progress*	progrès
evidence	preuve(s)	*toast*	toast, pain grillé
furniture	meubles	*traffic*	circulation
garbage	ordures	*weather*	temps (météo)
hair	cheveux	*work*	travail (action de travailler)

■ Ne mettez pas les noms indénombrables au pluriel, et faites l'accord du verbe au singulier.

Ses conseils sont sensés. *His / Her advice* ***is*** *sensible.*

Les nouvelles étaient bonnes. *The news* ***was*** *good.*

■ N'employez pas l'article indéfini *a / an* devant les indénombrables.

C'est un grand progrès. *That's great progress.*

Si on veut absolument « dénombrer », on peut dans certains cas utiliser ***a piece of***.

C'est un renseignement intéressant. *It's an interesting piece of information.*

21 Le pluriel des noms dénombrables

■ Pour les noms réguliers, on ajoute la terminaison **-*s*** (*one dog* → *two dogs*). Les modifications orthographiques sont les mêmes qu'avec la terminaison *-s* des verbes à la 3e personne du singulier du présent (voir § 4 p. 228).

bus → *bus**es***

beach → *beach**es***

party → *part**ies***, etc.

Les règles de prononciation sont les mêmes que pour la terminaison *-s* des verbes : *dogs* /dɒgz/, *cats* /kæts/, *buses* /ˈbʌsɪz/, etc.

■ Principaux pluriels irréguliers

child /tʃaɪld/ (enfant)	→ *children* /ˈtʃɪldrən/
man /mæn/ (homme)	→ *men* /men/
woman /ˈwʊmən/ (femme)	→ *women* /ˈwɪmɪn/
foot /fʊt/ (pied)	→ *feet* /fiːt/
tooth /tuːθ/ (dent)	→ *teeth* /tiːθ/
mouse /maʊs/ (souris)	→ *mice* /maɪs/

■ Certains noms qui se terminent par **-*f*** ou **-*fe*** ont un pluriel en **-*ves*** :

half → *halves*

wife → *wives* (mais *roof* → *roofs*)

Parmi les plus courants : *life*, *shelf* (étagère), *knife*, *leaf* (feuille), *wolf* (loup).

■ Avec ***people*** employé dans le sens de « personnes » et ***police***, l'accord au pluriel est obligatoire.

There ***were*** *ten* ***people*** *present.* Il y avait dix personnes présentes.

The police are *ready to intervene.* La police est prête à intervenir.

22 L'article « zéro » (∅)

L'article ∅, ou absence d'article, existe également en français : « Il est sorti de **prison** » n'a pas le même sens que « Il est sorti de **la prison**. » En anglais, cependant, il est beaucoup plus fréquent qu'en français.

■ On utilise l'article ∅ quand on veut parler de quelque chose « **en général** », avec les noms **indénombrables au singulier** et les **dénombrables au pluriel**.

He doesn't like chocolate / oranges. Il n'aime pas le chocolat / les oranges.

En français, on utilise dans ce cas l'article « le / la / les ».

■ On utilise l'article ∅ pour désigner une chose du point de vue de son **utilisation**, de sa **fonction sociale**, etc.

She's going to school. Elle va à l'école.

He'll soon get out of prison. Il va bientôt sortir de prison.

■ On utilise l'article ∅ devant les noms de pays, continents ou régions : *Germany* (l'Allemagne), *Africa* (l'Afrique), *Alaska* (l'Alaska). Exception pour les noms de pays au pluriel : *the USA* (les États-Unis), *the Netherlands* (les Pays-Bas).

■ On utilise aussi l'article ∅ devant les noms de titre suivis d'un nom propre (*President Obama, Queen Elizabeth,* etc.).

23 L'article *a/an*

1 Formes

■ On utilise l'article ***a*** /ə/ devant un son « consonne » : *a cat*. Attention à certains mots qui, **dans leur forme écrite**, commencent par une voyelle, mais **dans leur prononciation** commencent par une consonne.

a uniform (voyelle transcrite /juː/)

a European city (même chose)

a one-man show (voyelle transcrite /wʌ/)

Attention aussi au *h* initial, qui est une consonne **prononcée** *(a happy day)*, sauf dans *honest, hono(u)r, hour* et *heir* (« héritier ») : *an honest man, an hour.*

■ On utilise l'article ***an*** /ən/ devant un son « voyelle » *(an orange)*.

2 Emploi particulier en anglais

Pour indiquer le métier de quelqu'un, on utilise *a / an* + **nom de métier**.

She's an engineer. Elle est ingénieur.

24 L'article *the*

1 Prononciation

L'article *the* se prononce :

- /ðə/ devant un son « consonne »

the cat /kæt/

the uniform /ˈjuːnɪfɔːm/

the one-man /wʌn mæn/ *show*

- /ði/ devant un son « voyelle »

the orange /ˈɒrɪndʒ/

the hour /aʊəʳ/

2 Emploi

Attention à cette différence avec les articles « le / la / les » du français : on emploie ∅ pour parler de **quelque chose « en général »**, devant les **indénombrables au singulier** et devant les **dénombrables au pluriel.**

Jazz was born sometime around 1895 in New Orleans.

Le jazz est né aux alentours de 1895 à la Nouvelle-Orléans.

*He loves **comic strips**.* Il adore **les bandes dessinées.**

25 Les quantifieurs : *some, any, no, many, much*, etc.

1 « Une certaine quantité de... » : *some* ou *any*

	Indénombrable (singulier)	Dénombrable au pluriel
Affirmations : *some* /səm/	*There's some milk in the fridge.* Il y a du lait dans le frigo.	*There are some potatoes in the fridge.* Il y a des pommes de terre au frigo.
Questions pour offrir / demander qqch : *some*	*Would you like some / some more coffee?* Tu veux du / un peu plus de café ?	*Would you like some / some more sandwiches?* Tu veux des / d'autres sandwichs ?
Autres interrogations : *any* /ˈeni/	*Is there any milk left?* Est-ce qu'il reste du lait ?	*Are there any potatoes?* Est-ce qu'il y a des pommes de terre ?

Les articles français « du / de la / des » ont pour équivalent *some / any* quand ils signifient « un certain nombre / une certaine quantité de... ». Toutefois, s'ils servent à indiquer la **nature** de quelque chose, sans idée de quantité, comme dans : « Tu veux du thé ou du café ? », ils ont pour équivalent l'article zéro : *Would you like tea or coffee?*

Any est souvent utilisé dans des énoncés affirmatifs avec le sens de « n'importe quel(s) / n'importe quelle(s) » : *Just take a card – any card.* Prends simplement une carte. N'importe quelle carte.

2 Quantité nulle (= « pas de... », « aucun... », etc.) : *not any* ou *no*

	Indénombrable (singulier)	Dénombrable au pluriel
Construction négative + *any*	*There isn't any milk.* Il n'y a pas de lait.	*There aren't any yoghurts.* Il n'y a pas de yaourts.
Construction affirmative + *no*	*There is no milk.* Il n'y a pas de lait.	*There are no yoghurts.* Il n'y a aucun yaourt.

Le pronom qui correspond à *no* est ***none*** /nʌn/ : *I wanted some milk / some yoghurts but there was / there were none.* (... il n'y en avait pas / il n'y en avait aucun.) Ne pas confondre avec *no one* (= personne, voir § 26 p. 267).

3 Grande et petite quantité : *a lot of / many / much, few / little*

	Indénombrable (singulier)	Dénombrable au pluriel
beaucoup de	*There's **a lot of / lots of** milk.* Il y a beaucoup de lait. *Is there **much** milk?* *There isn't **much** milk.*	*There are **a lot of / lots of** oranges.* Il y a beaucoup d'oranges. *Are there **many** oranges?* *There aren't **many** oranges.*
peu de, pas de, beaucoup de	*There's **little** milk.* Il y a peu de lait.	*There are **few** oranges.* Il y a peu d'oranges.
un peu de, quelques	*There's **a little** milk left.* Il reste un peu de lait.	*There are **a few** oranges left.* Il reste quelques oranges.

4 Tous et chacun : *all, every, each*, etc.

all = tout(e), tous, toutes	*all the bread / all the sandwiches*
the whole = la totalité (de)	*He drank the whole bottle.* Il a bu toute la bouteille.
every = chaque	*Every solution **has** its problem.* Chaque solution a son problème. (= Toutes les solutions ont leur problème.) Notez l'emploi du **singulier** à la suite de *every*.
each = chaque, chacun(e)	*Each situation is particular.* Chaque situation est particulière.
both = les deux (sous-entendu : pas seulement un / une)	*I've met both brothers.* J'ai rencontré les deux frères. (= pas seulement l'un des deux)

26 Les composés de *some / any / no / every*

someone / somebody quelqu'un	*anyone / anybody* quelqu'un	*no one / nobody* personne	*everyone* tout le monde *everybody* tout le monde (+ singulier)
something quelque chose	*anything* quelque chose	*nothing* rien	*everything* tout (+ singulier)
somewhere quelque part	*anywhere* quelque part	*nowhere* nulle part	*everywhere* partout

En anglais (à la différence du français), on emploie **une seule négation par proposition** :
Il ne parle jamais à personne. → *He never speaks to anybody.*

27 Les démonstratifs *this / these* et *that / those*

■ ***This*** /ðɪs/ (+ nom au **singulier**) et ***these*** /ði:z/ (+ nom au **pluriel**) s'emploient pour désigner ce qui est proche de l'énonciateur dans l'espace ou le temps, ou ressenti comme proche.

This city is marvellous. Cette ville (= la ville où nous sommes) est merveilleuse.

I love these songs. J'adore ces chansons (= les chansons que nous écoutons).

■ ***That*** /ðæt/ (+ nom au **singulier**) et ***those*** /ðəʊz/ (+ nom au **pluriel**) s'emploient pour désigner ce qui est éloigné de l'énonciateur (ou ressenti comme éloigné), ou a déjà été mentionné.

I hate that song. J'ai horreur de cette chanson.

I hate those songs. J'ai horreur de ces chansons.

28 Les adjectifs

■ Les adjectifs anglais sont **invariables**.

These chairs are very comfortable. Ces chaises sont très confortables.

■ Les adjectifs **épithètes** (= rattachés directement au nom) se placent **avant le nom.**

He bought six very comfortable chairs. Il a acheté six chaises très confortables.

■ En anglais, on emploie les adjectifs comme noms pour désigner **l'ensemble d'une catégorie**.

The poor are more numerous than the rich. Les pauvres sont plus nombreux que les riches.

Notez que l'adjectif est précédé de ***the***, qu'il reste invariable, et que le groupe *the* + adjectif a un **sens pluriel**.

Dans les autres cas, l'adjectif est obligatoirement **associé à un nom ou au pronom *one*** :
Il y a deux Français. *There are two French people.*
Je préfère le bleu. *I prefer the blue one.*

■ Certains adjectifs sont formés à partir de **verbes**, auxquels on ajoute :

– soit la terminaison *-ing* (*amuse* → *amusing*, amusant)

– soit la marque du participe passé *-ed* (*amuse* → *amused*, amusé).

Attention : la terminaison *-ing* équivaut à la terminaison française « -ant ».

interesting intéressant — *tiring* fatigant
interested intéressé — *tired* fatigué

29 La comparaison des adjectifs

■ **Adjectifs courts** : une syllabe, ou deux syllabes avec terminaison *-y* ou *-er*.

■ **Adjectifs longs** : autres adjectifs

	Adjectifs courts	Adjectifs longs
Comparatif de supériorité (= plus... que...)	*Ella is **taller than** /ðæn/ Lucy.* Ella est plus grande que Lucy.	*Nora is **more gifted** than Lyn.* Nora est plus douée que Lyn.
Comparatif d'infériorité (= moins... que...)	*The book is **not as interesting as** the film.* Le livre est moins intéressant que le film. *It's **less** interesting.* C'est moins intéressant.	
« de plus en plus... »	*It's **easier and easier**.* C'est de plus en plus facile.	*It's **more and more interesting**.* C'est de plus en plus intéressant.
« de moins en moins... »	*It's **less and less easy / interesting**.* C'est de moins en moins facile / intéressant.	
Comparatif d'égalité (= aussi... que...)	*Jane is **as** /əz/ **tall / as gifted as** Lisa.* Jane est aussi grande / aussi douée que Lisa.	
Superlatif de supériorité (= le plus...)	*Ann is **the tallest** girl in the class.* Ann est la fille la plus grande de la classe.	*Liz is **the most gifted** girl in the class.* Liz est la fille la plus douée de la classe.

■ Le complément du superlatif est introduit par ***in***, sauf s'il désigne un ensemble d'éléments *(the tallest girl **of** all)* ou une période de temps *(the longest day **of** the year)*.

■ Modifications orthographiques avec les terminaisons *-er* / *-est* :
– *happy* → *happier, happiest* : un *y* qui suit une consonne devient *i*.
– *big* → *bigger, biggest* : une consonne finale qui suit une voyelle est doublée.

■ **Comparatifs et superlatifs de supériorité irréguliers**

good bon ***well*** bien	***better*** meilleur / mieux	***the best*** le / la / les meilleur(e)(s) / mieux
bad mauvais	***worse*** /wɜːʳs/ pire	***the worst*** /wɜːʳst/ le / la / les pire(s)
far loin	***farther*** ou ***further*** plus loin	***the farthest*** ou ***the furthest*** le / la / les plus éloigné(e)(s)

30 Nom + 's (ou « génitif »)

La terminaison ***'s*** ajoutée à un nom exprime la **possession au sens large du terme** (incluant les liens de parenté, etc.).

1 Forme

John's brother lives in Paris. Le frère de John vit à Paris.

His parents' house is in the country. La maison de ses parents est à la campagne.

Il n'y a jamais d'article devant le second nom. Il n'y a pas non plus d'article devant le premier nom s'il s'agit d'un **nom propre** : opposez *John's car* à *the doctor's car* (la voiture du docteur).

2 Emplois

■ La terminaison ***'s*** est utilisée notamment avec les noms désignant :
– des personnes ;
– des animaux familiers (*the cat's legs*, les pattes du chat) ;
– des villes, des institutions, etc. *(London's buses, the UNO's decision)* ;
– des repères temporels *(yesterday's paper)*.

■ Quand le second nom désigne un magasin, un lieu de travail ou une habitation, ce nom est généralement omis.

I have to go to the dentist's / Claire's. Je dois aller chez le dentiste / chez Claire.

31 Les noms composés

■ Ce sont des noms constitués de plusieurs mots, écrits séparément ou en un seul mot.

a phone number un numéro de téléphone

a teacup une tasse à thé

a ten-dollar bill un billet de dix dollars

baby milk powder lait en poudre pour bébés

■ Le dernier nom est le **nom principal** (*a racehorse* = un cheval de course, *a horse race* = une course de chevaux).

■ Les noms qui le précèdent jouent le rôle d'adjectifs, et ils sont invariables : notez la forme singulier de *horse* dans *horse race*, de *dollar* dans *ten-dollar bill*, etc.

■ C'est en général le premier nom qui est accentué.

*a **race**horse*

*a **horse** race*

*a **phone** number*

*a **tea**cup*

32 La famille des pronoms personnels

Pronoms sujets	Pronoms compléments	Déterminants possessifs	Pronoms possessifs	Pronoms réfléchis (voir §33)
I	*me*	*my* (mon / ma / mes)	*mine* (le mien / la mienne / les miens / les miennes)	*myself* (accentuation sur *self*)
you	*you*	*your* /jɔːʳ/	*yours* /jɔːʳz/	*yourself*
he	*him*	*his*	*his*	*himself*
she	*her*	*her*	*hers*	*herself*
it	*it*	*its*	*its own*	*itself*
we	*us*	*our* /aʊəʳ/	*ours* /aʊəʳz/	*ourselves*
you	*you*	*your*	*yours*	*yourselves*
they	*them*	*their*	*theirs*	*themselves*

Les possessifs (*my, your,* etc. ; *mine, yours,* etc.) s'accordent uniquement avec le « possesseur ».

***He** introduced me to **his** sister / **his** brother.* Il m'a présenté à sa sœur / son frère.

***She** introduced me to **her** sister / **her** brother.* Elle m'a présenté à sa sœur / son frère.

33 Équivalents anglais des verbes pronominaux français

■ Le français utilise la même forme pour le sens **réfléchi** (Ils se sont vus dans la vidéo = chacun a vu lui-même) et pour le sens **réciproque** (Ils se sont vus [= rencontrés] hier).

■ En anglais :

– pour le sens **réfléchi**, on utilise un **pronom réfléchi** (*myself, yourself*, etc., voir § 32).

They saw themselves in the video.

– pour le sens **réciproque**, on utilise l'un des deux **pronoms réciproques *each other* / *one another*** (le choix étant libre).

They saw each other / one another yesterday.

■ Les verbes comme *get up*, *shave*, *dress*, *wash*, *meet* et *quarrel* se construisent sans pronom réfléchi ou réciproque (en effet, le sens réfléchi ou réciproque est évident).

He got up at seven, shaved, and dressed carefully. Il s'est levé à 7 heures, s'est rasé, et s'est habillé avec soin.

They often meet and quarrel. Ils se rencontrent et se disputent souvent.

34 Les constructions interrogatives

Ces constructions exigent l'emploi d'un **auxiliaire,** qui est *do / does / did* pour le présent et le prétérit simples.

Did she like the film? Elle a aimé le film ?

Elles peuvent être introduites par un mot interrogatif ou une expression interrogative, dont voici les principaux.

- ***Who** did they contact?* Ils ont contacté qui ?
- ***Whose** DVD is this?* Il est à qui ce DVD ?
- ***How many** people attended the meeting?* Combien de personnes ont assisté à la réunion ?
- ***How much** money did he want?* Il voulait combien ?
- ***How long** did he stay?* Il est resté combien de temps ?
- ***How tall** is he?* Il mesure combien ?
- ***How far** did he go?* Il est allé jusqu'où ? / Il est allé loin ?
- ***How often** do you change the batteries?* Tu changes les piles tous les combien ?
- ***How** is Sandra?* Elle va comment Sandra ? (interrogation sur la santé)
- ***What** is Sandra **like**?* Elle est comment, Sandra ? (interrogation sur l'allure, le caractère, etc.)

Opposez ***Who** did they see*? (Qui ont-ils vu ?) et ***Who** saw them*? (Qui les a vus ?) : quand le mot interrogatif ou l'expression interrogative est sujet du verbe, on emploie une construction affirmative (cf. *John saw them*), sans *do / does / did* au présent ou au prétérit simples.

35 Les constructions exclamatives

■ Selon que l'exclamation porte sur un nom ou sur un adjectif, ces constructions peuvent être introduites par ***what / such*** ou par ***how / so***.

What a (strange) story! Quelle histoire (bizarre) !

How strange (it is)! Comme c'est bizarre !

It's such a strange story! C'est une histoire tellement bizarre !

It's so strange! C'est tellement bizarre !

■ Si le nom qui suit *what* ou *such* est un indénombrable, il ne peut pas être précédé de l'article *a / an*, et il faut employer l'article zéro.

What strange weather! Quel temps bizarre !

It's such strange weather! C'est un temps tellement bizarre !

36 Les prépositions

Attention aux différences de construction entre le français et l'anglais.

J'attends Tim. *I'm waiting <u>for</u> Tim.* (pas de préposition en français, préposition en anglais)

Il a emprunté l'argent <u>à</u> son frère. *He borrowed the money <u>from</u> his brother.* (préposition « à » en français après « emprunter », *from* en anglais après *borrow*)

37 La place des adverbes

■ Les **adverbes de fréquence** usuels (essentiellement *sometimes, rarely, often, always, never* et *ever*) se placent **devant le verbe** et, quand il y a un auxiliaire (*be, have, can*, etc.), **après l'auxiliaire**.

She sometimes eats cornflakes. Elle mange quelquefois des cornflakes.

He is often in front of his computer. Il est souvent devant son ordinateur.

I've never eaten Jamaican food. Je n'ai jamais mangé de nourriture jamaïcaine.

■ **L'adverbe ne doit pas séparer le verbe de son complément d'objet.**

Il connaît <u>bien</u> le Portugal. *He knows Portugal **well**.*

38 Le passif

1 Forme

Construction active	Construction passive (*BE* + participe passé)
German engineers ***built*** *the bridge*. Des ingénieurs allemands ont construit le pont.	*The bridge* ***was built*** *by German engineers*. Le pont a été construit par des ingénieurs allemands.

■ Si le complément du verbe se construit avec une **préposition**, cette dernière se place **après le verbe**.

Le billet avait déjà été payé. *The ticket had already been paid* ***for***.

■ Avec certains **verbes à deux compléments** comme *give, ask, show, tell, offer* et *send*, deux constructions passives sont possibles.

They showed me the photos. → ***I was shown*** *the photos*. On m'a montré les photos.

Cette construction est plus courante que la construction avec *to* : *The photos* ***were shown*** *to me*.

2 Emplois

On utilise le passif, en particulier, quand on ne peut pas ou qu'on ne veut pas dire qui accomplit l'action. Dans ce cas, le français utilise généralement **« on »**.

On lui a volé ses clés. *His /Her keys were stolen.*

On m'a dit qu'il avait eu un accident. *I was told he'd had an accident.*

39 Équivalents du français « faire faire »

■ Assez souvent, l'équivalent anglais du français « faire + verbe » est un **verbe simple**.

Fais-moi voir ce que tu as acheté. ***Show*** *me what you've bought*.

Il **a fait bouillir** l'eau. *He* ***boiled*** *the water*.

■ Dans les autres cas, « faire » peut avoir pour équivalent *make, have* ou *get*, dans des constructions différentes.

• ***Make*** **+ nom / pronom + base verbale** exprime une idée de cause ou de forte contrainte.

They made them get off the plane. Ils les ont fait descendre de l'avion.

She made that poor child cry. Elle a fait pleurer ce pauvre enfant. (Notez l'ordre des mots en anglais.)

• ***Have*** **+ nom / pronom + base verbale** exprime une contrainte plus neutre.

I'll have him take your baggage upstairs. Je vais lui faire monter vos bagages.

• ***Have / get*** **+ nom / pronom + participe passé** : on s'intéresse au résultat plus qu'à la personne qui accomplit l'action.

I'll have / I'll get my hair cut. Je vais me faire couper les cheveux.

40 Équivalents du français « laisser faire »

L'équivalent anglais du français « laisser + verbe » est la construction : ***let*** (= autoriser) **+ nom / pronom + base verbale** (attention à l'ordre des mots en anglais).

He let the children go. / He let them go. Il a laissé partir les enfants. / Il les a laissés partir.

Ne confondez pas les verbes *leave* et *let*. « Laisser = abandonner / ne pas prendre, etc. » a généralement pour équivalent *leave*.

He left a message on a post-it note. Il a laissé un message sur un post-it.

41 La proposition infinitive

■ Après les verbes qui expriment une volonté ou un souhait, et en particulier après *want*, *prefer* et *would like*, on utilise non pas une proposition en *that* (~~*I want that...*~~), mais une proposition formée avec un infinitif.

*He **wants** everybody to keep silent.* Il veut que tout le monde reste silencieux.

*I **prefer** them to stay here.* Je préfère qu'ils restent ici.

***Would** you **like** me to help you?* Est-ce que tu voudrais que je t'aide ?

■ Si on utilise un **pronom** dans cette construction, il est à la **forme complément** (*him, them*, etc.).

42 La forme *V-ING*

■ *V-ING* peut avoir notamment une fonction d'**adjectif** *(It's an amusing story)* ou de **nom** (*He loves skateboarding*. Il aime beaucoup le skateboard). Cet emploi de *V-ING* avec une valeur de nom est appelé **gérondif**.

■ L'emploi de *V-ING* est obligatoire :

– après une **préposition** *(about, after, at, before, of, without...)*.

***Before opening** the window, she turned the heating off.* Avant d'ouvrir la fenêtre, elle a coupé le chauffage.

*He took the DVD **without asking** permission.* Il a pris le DVD sans demander la permission.

– après les verbes qui expriment une **appréciation** ou un **jugement**.

*He **can't stand seeing** such poverty.* Il ne peut pas supporter de voir une telle pauvreté.

*I **don't feel like going** out tonight.* Je n'ai pas envie de sortir ce soir.

– après la plupart des verbes qui indiquent la **continuation** ou la **fin** d'une action, notamment *carry on / keep (on) / go on* (continuer à) et *stop / quit* (arrêter de).

*He **gave up** / **quit smoking** last year.* Il a arrêté de fumer l'an dernier.

43 Équivalents anglais de « pendant »

1 « Pendant » = « sur une durée de » = *for*

Il a travaillé pendant deux heures. *He worked **for** two hours.*

Question correspondante : ***How long** did he work?* (Pendant combien de temps a-t-il travaillé ?)

2 « Pendant » = « au cours de » = *during*

Il a travaillé pendant les vacances. *He worked **during** the holidays.*

Question correspondante : ***When** did he work?* (Quand a-t-il travaillé ?)

44 Les subordonnées de but

■ ***So (that)*** peut exprimer le but.

He lowered his voice so (that) I couldn't hear. Il a baissé la voix pour que je n'entende pas.

I gave him some money so that he can buy DVDs. Je lui ai donné de l'argent pour qu'il s'achète des DVD.

■ Le but peut également être exprimé par ***to***, ou (style recherché) par ***in order to / so as to***.

He got up early to /in order to /so as to catch the 7.15 train. Il s'est levé de bonne heure pour avoir / afin d'avoir le train de 7 h 15.

45 Les propositions relatives

■ Les propositions relatives sont introduites par des pronoms relatifs, qui sont :

– les **pronoms relatifs** en *wh-* (***who*** /hu:/, ***which, whose*** /hu:z/) ;

– ***that*** (prononcé /ðət/) ;

– **le relatif « zéro »** (∅), c'est-à-dire un vide. Exemple : *The girl I met is Irish*. La fille que j'ai rencontrée est irlandaise.

■ Le choix est déterminé par :

– le type d'**antécédent** (c'est-à-dire de nom que le pronom relatif remplace) ;

– la **fonction** du pronom relatif (sujet du verbe, complément du verbe, ou complément d'un nom).

Il y a souvent plusieurs choix possibles. Dans la pratique les relatifs sont utilisés comme indiqué dans le tableau ci-dessous.

■ **Règles à appliquer absolument :**

– ***who*** uniquement pour les personnes et ***which*** uniquement pour les choses ;

– **∅ n'est jamais utilisé en fonction sujet.** Il ne peut pas remplacer *who / which / that* dans des phrases comme *The girl who called yesterday is my sister*. (La fille qui a appelé hier est ma sœur.) ou comme *The book which / that is on the top shelf is a dictionary*. (Le livre qui est sur l'étagère du haut est un dictionnaire.)

	Antécédent humain	Antécédent non humain
Sujet	*The girl* ***who called yesterday...*** La fille qui a appelé hier...	*The book* ***which / that is on the top shelf...*** Le livre qui est sur l'étagère du haut...
Complément direct	*The girl ∅* ***I met...*** La fille que j'ai rencontrée...	*The book ∅* ***you bought...*** Le livre que tu as acheté...
Complément indirect	*The girl ∅* ***I told you about...*** La fille dont je t'ai parlé...	*The book ∅* ***I told you about...*** Le livre dont je t'ai parlé...
Complément de nom	*The girl* ***whose father...*** La fille dont le père...	*The book* ***whose title...*** Le livre dont le titre...

Si le verbe se construit avec une **préposition** (ci-dessus, préposition *about*) : avec le **relatif ∅**, la préposition est obligatoirement **placée après le verbe** (et éventuellement après son complément direct). Voir aussi le **passif** (§ 38 p. 271).

46 Comment rapporter des paroles ou des pensées

Discours direct	Discours indirect
He said, "I want to go."	*He said that he wanted to go.*
He said, "I have finished the work."	*He said that he had finished the work.*
He said, "I will help them."	*He said that he would help them.*
He said, "They may be late." (Ils peuvent être en retard.)	*He said that they might be late.* (Il a dit qu'ils pouvaient être en retard.)

1 Caractéristiques du discours indirect

■ Au discours indirect, on n'utilise pas les guillemets.

■ Il peut être introduit par la **conjonction *that*** (prononcée /ðət/) ou la **conjonction « zéro »**.

■ Certains **pronoms** doivent être modifiés (dans l'exemple, *I* devient *he*).

■ Il faut respecter les règles dites de **concordance des temps** ; ces règles s'appliquent dans les récits au passé, quand le verbe qui introduit le discours indirect est au **prétérit** *(He said / He thought that...)* :

– le **présent** du discours direct devient un **prétérit** (voir tous les exemples du tableau) ;

– le **prétérit** du discours direct devient généralement un ***past perfect***.

He said, "I saw her on May 1st." Il a dit : « Je l'ai vue le 1er mai. »

→ *He said that he had seen her on May 1st.*

■ Les **adverbes de lieu et de temps** peuvent être modifiés.

He said, "I will stay here until tomorrow". Il a dit : « Je vais rester ici jusqu'à demain. »

→ *He said that he would stay there until the day after.*

Autres changements de ce type :

– *yesterday* → *the day before*

– *last week / month / year* → *the week / month / year before*

– *ago* → *before*

2 Le cas particulier des questions

■ Les questions rapportées au style indirect sont à la **forme affirmative** : il n'y a pas d'inversion sujet-auxiliaire, ni d'auxiliaire *do / does / did*, ni de point d'interrogation.

She asked me, "Where does Susan live?"

→ *She asked me where Susan lived.*

■ Pour rapporter au style indirect une *Yes / No* question, on utilise ***if*** (***whether*** dans un style recherché).

He asked me, "Do you want some more coffee?"

→ *He asked me if I wanted some more coffee.*

VERBES IRRÉGULIERS COURANTS

	Base verbale	Prétérit	Participe passé	Traduction
B	be	was / were	been	*être*
	bear /ɜə/	bore /ɔ:/	borne /ɔ:/	*porter*
	beat /i:/	beat /i:/	beaten /i:/ /ə/	*battre*
	become /ɪ/ /ʌ/	became /ɪ/ /eɪ/	become /ɪ/ /ʌ/	*devenir*
	begin /ɪ/ /ɪ/	began /ɪ/ /æ/	begun /ɪ/ /ʌ/	*commencer*
	bend /e/	bent /e/	bent /e/	*courber*
	bet /e/	bet /e/	bet /e/	*parier*
	bite /aɪ/	bit /ɪ/	bitten /i:/ /ə/	*mordre*
	bleed /i:/	bled /e/	bled /e/	*saigner*
	blow /əʊ/	blew /u:/	blown /əʊ/	*souffler*
	break /eɪ/	broke /əʊ/	broken /əʊ/ /ə/	*casser*
	breed /i:/	bred /e/	bred /e/	*élever*
	bring /ɪ/	brought /ɔ:/	brought /ɔ:/	*apporter*
	build /ɪ/	built /ɪ/	built /ɪ/	*bâtir*
	burn /ɜ:/	burnt /ɜ:/, burned /ɜ:/	burnt /ɜ:/, burned /ɜ:/	*brûler*
	burst /ɜ:/	burst /ɜ:/	burst /ɜ:/	*éclater*
	buy /aɪ/	bought /ɔ:/	bought /ɔ:/	*acheter*
C	cast /ɑ:/	cast /ɑ:/	cast /ɑ:/	*lancer*
	catch /æ/	caught /ɔ:/	caught /ɔ:/	*attraper*
	choose /u:/	chose /əʊ/	chosen /əʊ/ /ə/	*choisir*
	come /ʌ/	came /eɪ/	come /ʌ/	*venir*
	cost /ɒ/	cost /ɒ/	cost /ɒ/	*coûter*
	cut /ʌ/	cut /ʌ/	cut /ʌ/	*couper*
D	deal /i:/	dealt /e/	dealt /e/	*distribuer*
	do /u:/	did /ɪ/	done /ɒ/	*faire*
	draw /ɔ:/	drew /u:/	drawn /ɔ:/	*tirer*
	dream /i:/	dreamt /e/, dreamed /i:/	dreamt /e/, dreamed /i:/	*rêver*
	drink /ɪ/	drank /æ/	drunk /ʌ/	*boire*
	drive /aɪ/	drove /əʊ/	driven /ɪ/ /ə/	*conduire*
E	eat /i:/	ate /e/	eaten /i:/ /ə/	*manger*
F	fall /ɔ:/	fell /e/	fallen /ɔ:/ /ə/	*tomber*
	feed /i:/	fed /e/	fed /e/	*nourrir*
	feel /i:/	felt /e/	felt /e/	*(res)sentir*
	fight /aɪ/	fought /ɔ:/	fought /ɔ:/	*combattre*
	find /aɪ/	found /aʊ/	found /aʊ/	*trouver*
	fly /aɪ/	flew /u:/	flown /əʊ/	*voler (dans les airs)*
	forbid /ə/ /ɪ/	forbad(e) /ə/ /eɪ/	forbidden /ə/ /ɪ/ /ə/	*interdire*
	forget /ə/ /e/	forgot /ə/ /ɒ/	forgotten /ə/ /ɒ/ /ə/	*oublier*
	forgive /ə/ /ɪ/	forgave /ə/ /eɪ/	forgiven /ə/ /ɪ/ /ə/	*pardonner*
	freeze /i:/	froze /əʊ/	frozen /əʊ/ /ə/	*geler*
G	get /e/	got /ɒ/	got /ɒ/, gotten /ɒ/ /ə/ (US)	*obtenir*
	give /ɪ/	gave /eɪ/	given /ɪ/ /ə/	*donner*
	go /əʊ/	went /e/	gone /ɒ/	*aller*
	grow /əʊ/	grew /u:/	grown /əʊ/	*pousser (= croître)*
H	have /æ/	had /æ/	had /æ/	*avoir*
	hang /æ/	hung /ʌ/	hung /ʌ/	*pendre, suspendre*
	hear /ɪə/	heard /ɜ:/	heard /ɜ:/	*entendre*
	hide /aɪ/	hid /ɪ/	hidden /ɪ/ /ə/	*cacher*
	hit /ɪ/	hit /ɪ/	hit /ɪ/	*frapper*
	hold /əʊ/	held /e/	held /e/	*tenir*
	hurt /ɜ:/	hurt /ɜ:/	hurt /ɜ:/	*blesser*
K	keep /i:/	kept /e/	kept /e/	*garder*
	know /əʊ/	knew /u:/	known /əʊ/	*connaître*
L	lay /eɪ/	laid /eɪ/	laid /eɪ/	*poser à plat*
	lead /i:/	led /e/	led /e/	*mener*
	leap /i:/	leapt /e/	leapt /e/	*sauter*
	learn /ɜ:/	learnt, learned /ɜ:/	learnt, learned /ɜ:/	*apprendre*

	Base verbale	Prétérit	Participe passé	Traduction
	leave /iː/	left /e/	left /e/	*quitter*
	lend /e/	lent /e/	lent /e/	*prêter*
	let /e/	let /e/	let /e/	*laisser*
	lie /aɪ/	lay /eɪ/	lain /eɪ/	*être couché*
	light /aɪ/	lit /ɪ/	lit /ɪ/	*éclairer*
	lose /uː/	lost /ɒ/	lost /ɒ/	*perdre*
M	make /eɪ/	made /eɪ/	made /eɪ/	*faire*
	mean /iː/	meant /e/	meant /e/	*signifier*
	meet /iː/	met /e/	met /e/	*rencontrer*
P	pay /eɪ/	paid /eɪ/	paid /eɪ/	*payer*
	put /ʊ/	put /ʊ/	put /ʊ/	*mettre*
R	read /iː/	read /e/	read /e/	*lire*
	ride /aɪ/	rode /əʊ/	ridden /ɪ/ /ə/	*aller à cheval*
	ring /ɪ/	rang /æ/	rung /ʌ/	*sonner*
	rise /aɪ/	rose /əʊ/	risen /ɪ/ /ə/	*s'élever*
	run /ʌ/	ran /æ/	run /ʌ/	*courir*
S	say /eɪ/	said /e/	said /e/	*dire*
	see /iː/	saw /ɔː/	seen /iː/	*voir*
	sell /e/	sold /əʊ/	sold /əʊ/	*vendre*
	send /e/	sent /e/	sent /e/	*envoyer*
	set /e/	set /e/	set /e/	*placer*
	shake /eɪ/	shook /ʊ/	shaken /eɪ/ /ə/	*secouer*
	shoot /uː/	shot /ɒ/	shot /ɒ/	*faire feu, tirer*
	show /əʊ/	showed /əʊ/	shown /əʊ/	*montrer*
	shut /ʌ/	shut /ʌ/	shut /ʌ/	*fermer*
	sing /ɪ/	sang /æ/	sung /ʌ/	*chanter*
	sink /ɪ/	sank /æ/	sunk /ʌ/	*couler, sombrer*
	sit /ɪ/	sat /æ/	sat /æ/	*être assis*
	sleep /iː/	slept /e/	slept /e/	*dormir*
	smell /e/	smelt /e/	smelt /e/	*sentir*
	speak /iː/	spoke /əʊ/	spoken /əʊ/ /ə/	*parler*
	spell /e/	spelt /e/	spelt /e/	*épeler*
	spend /e/	spent /e/	spent /e/	*dépenser*
	spill /ɪ/	spilt /ɪ/	spilt /ɪ/	*répandre (par mégarde)*
	split /ɪ/	split /ɪ/	split /ɪ/	*fendre*
	spoil /ɔɪ/	spoilt /ɔɪ/	spoilt /ɔɪ/	*gâter*
	spread /e/	spread /e/	spread /e/	*répandre, étaler*
	spring /ɪ/	sprang /æ/	sprung /ʌ/	*bondir*
	stand /æ/	stood /ʊ/	stood /ʊ/	*être debout*
	steal /iː/	stole /əʊ/	stolen /əʊ/ /ə/	*voler (qqch)*
	stick /ɪ/	stuck /ʌ/	stuck /ʌ/	*coller*
	strike /aɪ/	struck /ʌ/	struck /ʌ/	*frapper*
	swear /ɜə/	swore /ɔː/	sworn /ɔː/	*jurer*
	sweep /iː/	swept /e/	swept /e/	*balayer*
	swim /ɪ/	swam /æ/	swum /ʌ/	*nager*
	swing /ɪ/	swung /ʌ/	swung /ʌ/	*(se) balancer*
T	take /eɪ/	took /ʊ/	taken /eɪ/ /ə/	*prendre*
	teach /iː/	taught /ɔː/	taught /ɔː/	*enseigner*
	tear /ɜə/	tore /ɔː/	torn /ɔː/	*déchirer*
	tell /e/	told /əʊ/	told /əʊ/	*dire*
	think /ɪ/	thought /ɔː/	thought /ɔː/	*penser*
	throw /əʊ/	threw /uː/	thrown /əʊ/	*lancer*
U	understand /ʌ/ /ə/ /æ/	understood /ʌ/ /ə/ /ʊ/	understood /ʌ/ /ə/ /ʊ/	*comprendre*
W	wake /eɪ/	woke /əʊ/	woken /əʊ/ /ə/	*réveiller*
	wear /ɜə/	wore /ɔː/	worn /ɔː/	*porter (un vêtement)*
	win /ɪ/	won /ʌ/	won /ʌ/	*gagner*
	write /aɪ/	wrote /əʊ/	written /ɪ/ /ə/	*écrire*

A LES SONS DE L'ANGLAIS (VOYELLES ET CONSONNES)

1 Voyelles (anglais britannique)

	Mot type
/iː/	sea
/ɪ/	fish
/i/*	happy
/e/	bed
/æ/	cat
/ɑː/	car
/ɒ/	pot

	Mot type
/ɔː/	door
/ʊ/	book
/uː/	shoe
/ɜː/	girl
/ʌ/	bus
/ə/	banana
/eɪ/	plane

	Mot type
/aɪ/	five
/aʊ/	mouse
/ɔɪ/	boy
/əʊ/	boat
/ɪə/	hear
/eə/	chair
/ʊə/	poor

* Prononcé /ɪ/ ou /iː/ selon la variété d'anglais. Généralement en voyelle finale non accentuée, écrite *y*, *ie*, etc.

Anglais américain : deux différences importantes

■ En anglais US, le son /ɒ/ n'existe pas. À la place, on a généralement /ɑː/ (*top* /tɑːp/). Dans certains mots, comme *dog*, on peut avoir /ɑː/ ou /ɔː/ (*dog* /dɑːg / ou /dɔːg/).

■ Dans *thought* (GB /θɔːt/), la voyelle est généralement prononcée /ɔː/ en anglais US : *thought* /θɑːt/. Dans *door*, c'est-à-dire devant un *r*, la voyelle est à peu près identique, mais le *r* est prononcé : *door* /dɔːr/.

2 Consonnes

a. Signes phonétiques qui n'existent pas dans l'alphabet latin

	Mot type
/ð/	this
/θ/	thanks
/ʒ/	pleasure*
/ʃ/	sure**
/ŋ/	song

* son « j » du français « jour »
** son « ch » du français « chou »

• Notez également le signe /j/ (mot type : *yes*).

■ Les consonnes suivantes peuvent poser des problèmes aux francophones, parce qu'il s'agit de sons qui n'existent pas en français, ou sont différents :

• /ð/ (*this*), /θ/ (*thanks*), /r/ (*rain*) et /ŋ/ (*song*) ;
• /p/, /t/ et /k/ placés au début d'une syllabe accentuée (par exemple dans *pencil*, *ten* et *key*) ;
• /l/ placé en fin de mot et devant une consonne (par exemple dans *well* et *milk*).
• Notez également qu'en début de syllabe, *h* (*happy*) est toujours prononcé, sauf dans *hour*, *hono(u)r*, *heir* (« héritier ») et *honest*.

b. Une différence importante entre l'anglais GB et l'anglais US : prononciation de *r*

En anglais US, le *r* est toujours prononcé. En anglais GB, le *r* final (dans *hear, chair, poor*, etc.) n'est prononcé que pour une « liaison » avec le mot suivant, si celui-ci commence par une voyelle (*that poor ‿ animal*).

B LE RYTHME ET L'INTONATION

1 Le rythme

Le rythme de l'anglais est très différent de celui du français.

- En **français**, toutes les syllabes ont approximativement la même longueur dans le temps (on dit que le français est une langue à **rythme syllabique**).
- En **anglais**, le **rythme** est **accentuel** : il se caractérise par l'alternance de syllabes accentuées et de syllabes inaccentuées, et les syllabes inaccentuées sont en quelque sorte « compressées » entre les syllabes accentuées – d'où l'existence, à l'oral, de **formes réduites** qui donnent parfois l'impression d'être « avalées ».

Ainsi, dans la phrase *She'll **never ask** them to **help** her*, seuls sont accentués les mots *never*, *ask* et *help*.

Quant aux autres mots (tous des mots grammaticaux), ils ne sont pas prononcés sous leur forme pleine, mais sous leur forme réduite.

Formes pleines	Formes réduites
she /ʃiː/	she /ʃi/
will /wɪl/	'll /l/
them /ðem/	them /ðəm/
to /tuː/	to /tə/

2 L'accent de mot

- Les mots de plusieurs syllabes ont toujours une syllabe qui est plus accentuée que les autres, et qu'on appelle l'accent principal : ***gar**den*, *ho**tel***, etc.
- Certains mots (en général des mots de plus de deux syllabes) peuvent également avoir un accent secondaire, c'est-à-dire un accent un peu moins fort que l'accent principal.
- Dans les transcriptions en signes phonétiques, on utilise les signes ˈ et ˌ placés avant la syllabe accentuée, pour noter ces deux types d'accent :

hospitality /ˌhɒspɪˈtæləti/, *garden* /ˈɡɑːdən/, *hotel* /həʊˈtel/.

Accents de mot
Accent principal / ˈ / → /həʊˈtəl/
Accent secondaire / ˌ / → /ˌhɒspɪˈtæləti/

3 L'intonation

L'intonation est la « musique » de l'énoncé parlé. Elle comporte deux éléments essentiels :

a. les variations de hauteur (ton montant, ton descendant, etc.) ;

b. le rythme, constitué par l'accentuation de certains mots, ou plus précisément de certaines syllabes. Tous les accents n'ont pas le même relief. Il y a toujours, dans une phrase ou une proposition, au moins un mot qui a plus de relief que les autres. Ce relief est marqué par une variation de hauteur. Comparez, dans la phrase *My **brother** has **bought** a **scooter*** (Mon frère a acheté un scooter), ces accentuations différentes :

*My **BROTHER** has **bought** a **scooter*** : mon frère (pas mon père, etc.) a acheté un scooter.
*My **brother** has **BOUGHT** a **scooter*** : mon frère a acheté (pas loué, etc.) un scooter.
*My **brother** has **bought** a **SCOOTER*** : mon frère a acheté un scooter (pas une voiture, etc.).

> Comme nous l'avons vu, les mots grammaticaux sont habituellement inaccentués. Cependant, on peut leur donner un relief particulier pour exprimer une opposition.
> *"Your brother intends to buy a scooter."* — Ton frère a l'intention d'acheter un scooter.
> *"He HAS bought a scooter."* — Il a (déjà) acheté un scooter.

1 LE MONDE DU CINÉMA

a. Dans le paragraphe suivant, remplacez chaque chiffre par un des mots de la liste.
actor • adapted • blockbuster • directed • location • novel • stars • played • studios • stuntman

The new MGM ... 1 has already sold twenty million tickets. It is ... 2 by Steven Spielberg and ... 3 from a ... 4 by the science fiction writer Isaac Asimov. The movie ... 5 Will Smith, the former ... 6 of the TV series *Fresh Prince of Bel-Air*. Mr Smith took a lot of risks: He ... 7 some dangerous scenes without any ... 8 . The outside scenes were shot on ... 9 but most of the movie was shot in the MGM ... 10 in Hollywood.

b. Fermez votre livre. De quels mots vous souvenez-vous ?

2 ÊTES-VOUS UN VRAI FAN DE CINÉ ?

Associez chaque film de la colonne de gauche au genre qui lui correspond dans la colonne de droite. Attention, un même film peut correspondre à plusieurs genres.

Films	Genres
Titanic	thriller / detective film
Bowling for Columbine	adventure film
West Side Story	musical /mjuːzɪkəl/
Saw	disaster film
Brave Heart	documentary
Pirates of the Caribbean	comedy
Shrek	horror film
Saving Private Ryan	drama
The Matrix	war film
Pretty Woman	science /ˈsaɪəns/ fiction film
Bend It Like Beckham	historical film
Wild Wild West	romantic comedy
The Silence of the Lambs	western
	(animated) cartoon

3 LE VOCABULAIRE DU 7e ART

Les mots suivants se rapportent tous au cinéma.

a. Trouvez le sens de chaque mot. Utilisez un dictionnaire si nécessaire.
special effects • credits • set • film score • subtitles /ˈsʌbˌtaɪtls/ *• voice-over • soundtrack • sound effects • lighting • camera movements*

b. Classez ces mots dans la colonne leur correspondant : image ou son ?

Image	Son

4 PLANS ET ANGLES

Les plans les plus fréquents sont :

Long shot *(plan d'ensemble)*	The camera shows a distant object or a landscape.
Full shot *(plan moyen)*	The camera shows characters standing.
Medium shot *(plan américain)*	The characters are seen from head to knees.
Close-up *(gros plan)*	The camera focuses on the characters' heads and shoulders.
Extreme close-up *(très gros plan)*	The viewer can see details on a face or an object to express (= convey) an emotion.

Deux angles sont essentiellement utilisés :

High-angle shot *(en plongée)*	This shot makes the character look smaller, weaker. The viewer dominates the scene.
Low-angle shot *(en contre-plongée)*	The character is seen from below. The viewer feels dominated.

5 À VOTRE TOUR !

a. Observe the different stills (= pictures from a film) and decide what shots or angles they correspond to.

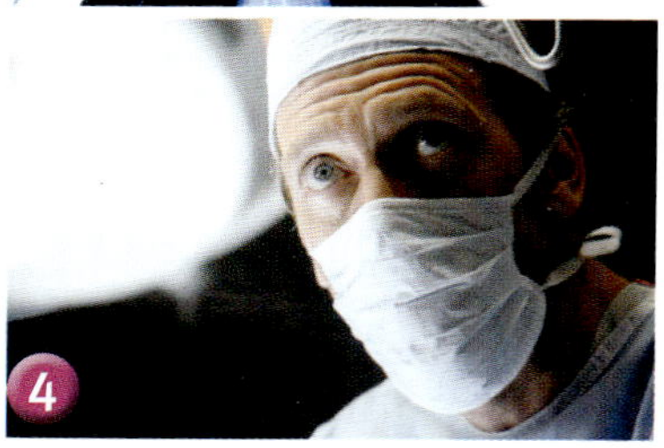

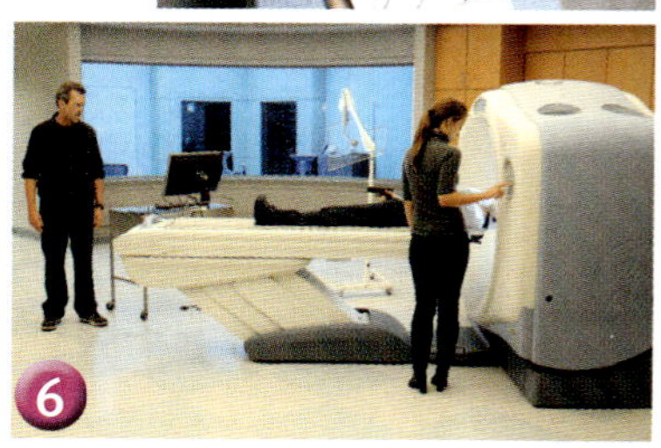

b. What impact do these different shots and angles have on you?

Help!

viewer detail surroundings = setting: *cadre / décor*	powerless ≠ powerful weak inferior threatened / endangered determined	dominate ≠ feel dominated convey an impression of / a feeling of focus the attention on introduce the viewer to sth: *présenter qqch au spectateur* let the viewer share: *faire partager au spectateur*

COMMENTER UN DOCUMENT VISUEL

On vous demandera souvent de commenter un document visuel.
Pour l'analyse de ce type de document, observez les étapes suivantes :
1. repérez les éléments clés
2. interprétez et analysez ces éléments
3. donnez votre opinion personnelle

1 REPÉREZ LES ÉLÉMENTS CLÉS

A Indiquez la nature du document.

– dessin	*drawing*
– tableau	*painting*
– dessin humoristique	*cartoon*
– bande dessinée + bulle	*strip cartoon / comic strip + balloon*
– photo(graphie)	*photo(graph) ≠ photography* = l'art de la photo
– pub(licité) + légende	*advert(isement)* /əd'vɜːtɪsmənt/, *advert, ad + caption*
– image tirée d'un film	*still*
– graphique	*chart*
– carte	*map*
– affiche	*poster*

B Présentez le document.

Source	*This ... is taken from...*
Date	*It was published in...*
Auteur	*It was drawn by / painted by / made by... an artist / a painter / a photographer / a cartoonist / an advertiser.*
Exemple de présentation	*This is a painting by David Hockney.* *It was painted in 1967 and is called Big Splash.*

C Présentez le sujet du document.

Pour ce faire, sélectionnez les éléments essentiels :
- *The scene takes place in / at...*
- *It shows / represents, illustrates, focuses on, advertises...*
- *We are shown... / We can see...*
- *It's composed of / made up of...*

D Localisez les objets et / ou les personnages.

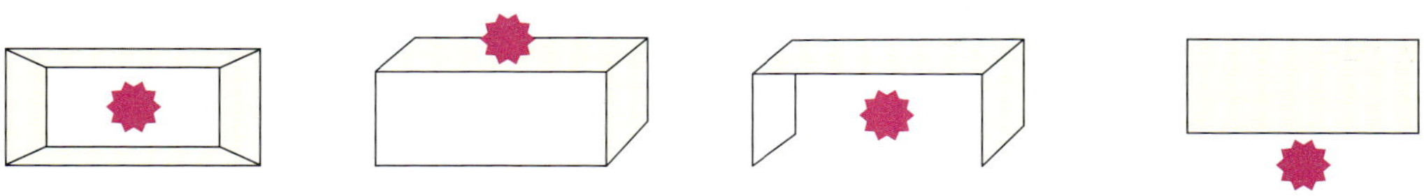

in *on* *under* *below*

above *over* *on (the) top of* *in front of*

RAPPEL Pour réaliser un « coup de projecteur » **sur un moment de l'événement** (ou sur plusieurs moments) on utilise le présent en BE + -ING.
Indiana Jones is running away from his attackers.

2 INTERPRÉTEZ ET ANALYSEZ

Tâchez d'interpréter le message du document et les intentions de l'auteur.
Pour ce faire, vous devez vous poser les bonnes questions par rapport à la nature du document. Une publicité, par exemple, est toujours destinée à vendre un produit. Vous devez donc vous demander quel est le public visé ou si elle est efficace.

– *It symbolises / stands for / embodies* (incarne)…
– *The author highlights / illustrates / shows…*
– *He / She means / wants to suggest…*
– *His / Her purpose / goal / aim is to make fun of / criticize…*
– *He / She wants to denounce / draw our attention to / make us realize that…*
– *This advertisement seems really efficient because…*
– *Teenagers / Adults… are the target audience.*

3 DONNEZ VOTRE OPINION

Réagissez personnellement au document.

– *As far as I'm concerned… / In my opinion… / To my mind…*
– *It reminds me of…*
– *It looks like…*
– *I find it amusing / moving / original / convincing…*

COMPRENDRE LES CONSIGNES

Avant de répondre à une question, vérifiez que vous avez bien compris ce qui vous est demandé.

1 REPÉREZ

- In this **text** / **paragraph** / **passage** / **extract**...: *Dans ce texte / ce paragraphe / ce passage / cet extrait...*
- **List** the characters present in the scene: *Faites la liste des personnages présents dans la scène.*
- Who are the **main characters**? *Qui sont les personnages principaux ?*
- Who **is mentioned** in this scene? *Qui est mentionné / cité dans cette scène ?*
- **When** does the scene take place? *Quand la scène se passe-t-elle ?*
- **Where** does the scene take place? / **Where** is the scene set?: *Où se passe l'action ?*
- **Locate**: *Situez.*
- **Location**: *lieu.*
- **Choose**: *Choisissez.*
- Find a **clue**: *Trouvez un indice.*
- **Check**: *Vérifiez.*
- **Find** the **keyword** / the name of... / one adjective / one verb...: *Trouvez le mot clé / le nom de... / un adjectif / un verbe...*
- **Pick out** the words...: *Relevez / Repérez les mots...*
- **List** the words which **are connected with** / **are related to** / **refer to**...: *Relevez les mots qui se rapportent à / qui font référence à...*
- What do the **following figures** refer to? *À quoi les chiffres suivants font-ils référence ?*
- Who or what do the **underlined** pronouns **refer to**? *À qui ou à quoi les pronoms soulignés font-ils référence ?*
- **Fill in** the **grid** / **table** / **columns below**: *Remplissez la grille / le tableau / les colonnes ci-dessous.*
- Find the **equivalent of** / the word **corresponding to** the following definition: *Trouvez l'équivalent de / le mot correspondant à la définition suivante.*
- Find the **opposite** of...: *Trouvez le contraire de...*

2 JUSTIFIEZ VOS RÉPONSES

- **Quote** / **Give a quote** / **quotation**: *Citez. / Donnez une citation.*
- **Justify** using keywords from...: *Justifiez vos réponses à l'aide de mots clés tirés de...*
- Quote one **sentence**: *Citez une phrase.*
- Quote one **phrase**: *Citez un groupe de mots.*
- **Explain** your view: *Expliquez votre point de vue.*

3 ASSOCIEZ

- **Match** the following words with their definitions: *Associez les mots suivants à leur définition.*
- Which of the following words **apply to**...?: *Parmi les mots suivants, lesquels s'appliquent à... ?*

4 RÉSUMEZ

- **Complete** this paragraph: *Complétez ce paragraphe.*
- **Fill in** the **blanks** in the following **summary**: *Complétez le résumé suivant par les mots qui manquent.*
- **Sum up** the story: *Résumez l'histoire.*
- **Sum up** this text **in your own words**: *Résumez ce texte en utilisant vos propres mots.*
- Sum up **what you have learnt so far**: *Résumez ce que vous appris jusqu'à présent.*
- Sum up the **reasons** why...: *Résumez les raisons pour lesquelles...*

5 REMETTEZ DANS L'ORDRE

- **Put** the following words in the right column: *Classez les mots suivants dans la colonne correspondante.*
- **Re-order** / **Re-organize** the following **events** in **chronological order**: *Classez les événements suivants par ordre chronologique.*

6 À VOUS D'AGIR !

- **Act out** the dialogue / the scene in front of an audience: *Jouez le dialogue / la scène face à un public.*
- **Confront** your results with your neighbour: *Comparez vos résultats avec ceux de votre voisin(e).*
- **Report** your findings to the class: *Rendez compte de ce que vous avez trouvé à la classe.*
- **Listen** and **answer**: *Écoutez et répondez.*
- Read **carefully**: *Lisez attentivement.*
- **Read aloud**: *Lisez à haute voix.*
- **Turn to** your Workbook for help: *Consultez votre cahier d'exercices pour plus d'informations.*
- Write down on a **separate piece of paper**: *Écrivez sur papier libre.*
- Make a one or two-minute **oral presentation** / **account** / **report of...**: *Faites une présentation orale de... pendant une ou deux minutes.*
- What can you **guess** about the themes of the song?: *Devinez quel sont les thèmes de la chanson.*

Crédits textes

p. 19 : © Mary Glasgow Magazines, Scholastic Inc. D.R. - **p. 26-27 :** From The Growing Pains of Adrian Mole by Sue Townsend. Reprinted by permission of The Random House group Ltd. - **p. 32 :** John Lennon © 1971 Lenono Music - **p. 34 :** From THE HOUSE ON MANGO STREET. Copyright © 1984 by Sandra Cisneros. Published by Vintage Books, a division of Random House, inc., and an hardcover by Alfred A. Knopf in 1994. Reprinted by permission of Susan Bergholz Literary Services, New York, NY and Lamy, NM. All rights reserved. - **p. 35 :** "Dreams", from THE COLLECTED OF LANGSTON HUGHUES by Langston Hughes, edited by Arnold with David Roessel, Associate Editor - **p. 36 :** From Newsweek, 21/01/2008 © 2008 Newsweek, Inc. All rights reserved. Used by permission and protected by the Copyright Laws of the United States. The printing, copying, redistribution, or retransmission of the material without express written permission is prohibited. www.newsweek.com - **p. 40 :** © Shel Silverstein - **p. 44 :** From JOURNEY THROUGH HEARTSONGS by Mattie J.T. Stepanek. Copyright © 2001 Mattie J.T. Stepanek. Reprinted by permission of Hyperion. All rights reserved. - **p. 45 :** © TIME For Kids. Reprinted by permission. - **p. 46 :** The MY HERO Project http://myhero.com - **p. 47 :** © Telegraph Media Group Limited 2009 - **p. 48 :** Ismael Beah, A Long Way Gone, 2007 © Farrar, Straus and Giroux. DR - **p. 63 :** © Russel Freedman, Immigrant Kids, Puffin Books, 1995. D.R. - p. 73 : Copyright Nomad Press 2007. Used by permission Nomad Press LLC - **p. 74 :** © Sally S. Isaacs, America in the Time of Lewis and Clark, 1998. Heinemann D.R. - **p. 76 :** © Chester Anders Fee, Chief Joseph: The Biography of a Great Indian, Wilson-Erickson, 1936. D.R. - **p. 82 :** Copyright Nomad Press 2007. Used by permission Nomad Press LLC - **p. 85 :** Reprinted with permission from Reader's Digest. Copyright © 2008 by the Reader's Digest Association, Inc. - p. 88 et 90 : Isaac Asimov, Robot Dreams, 1986, Byron Preiss Visual Publications. D.R. - **p. 95 :** "Research seeks to replace service dogs with robots" from the October 28, 2008 edition of EE Times. - **p. 96 :** "Harry Potter & the Prisoner of Azkaban" © J.K. Rowling - **p. 98 :** From A Coal Miner's Bride, The Diary of Anetka Kaminska by Susan Campbell Bartoletti © Scholastic Inc. DR. - **p. 106 :** www.fodors.com D.R. - **p. 108 :** From A Year in the Merde by Stephen Clarke, published by Bantam Press. Reprinted by permission of The Random House Group Ltd. - **p. 115 :** www.liverpool08.com - **p. 116 :** Reproduced with permission from Britain/5th Edition © 2003 Lonely Planet publications Pty Ltd. - **p. 117 :** pitchproseproductions © pitchprose.org © ELLJAY - **p. 118 et 123 :** www.liverpoolmuseums.org.uk D.R. - **p. 128 :** © « MOUNTAINS O' THINGS » Paroles et musique : Tracy Chapman © EMI April Music Inc – Purple Rabbit Music. Avec l'aimable autorisation d'EMI Songs France - **p. 146 :** From The New York Times, 24/02/2005 © 2005 The New York Times All rights reserved. Used by permission and protected by the Copyright Laws of the United States. The printing, copying, redistribution, or retransmission of the Material without express written permission is prohibited. www.nytimes.com - **p. 146 :** From The New York Times, 03/05/2006 © 2006 The New York Times All rights reserved. Used by permission and protected by the Copyright Laws of the United States. The printing, copying, redistribution, or retransmission of the Material without express written permission is prohibited." www.nytimes.com - **p. 148 :** © Matthew Campbell, 23/07/2006. Reprinted with permission of Sunday Times. - **p. 158 :** © Nathalie Merchant/Christian Burial Music. D.R. - **p. 186 :** © David Cobb, Puzzles for English Practice, Pearson Education Limited © Longman group Ltd. 1978 - **p. 190 :** www.mysterynet.com. D.R. - **p. 192 :** Reprinted/used with the permission of Simon & Schuster, Inc. from TWO LITTLE GIRLS IN BLUE by Mary Higgins Clark. Copyright © 2006 by Mary Higgins Clark. Reprinted with the permission of Simon & Schuster, Inc. from I'LL BE SEEING YOU by Mary Higgins Clark. Copyright © 2006 by Mary Higgins Clark. Reprinted with the permission of Simon & Schuster, Inc. from A STRANGER IS WATCHING by Mary Higgins Clark. Copyright © 1977 by Mary Higgins Clark. Reprinted with the permission of Simon & Schuster, Inc. from I HEARD THAT SONG BEFORE by Mary Higgins Clark. Copyright © 2007 by Mary Higgins Clark. - **p. 198-199 :** National Geographic Society - **p. 200 et 205 :** JOURNEY TO JO'BURG © 1986 BY BEVERLY NAIDOO. Used by permission of HarperCollins Publishers. - **p. 201 :** From MANDELA: FROM THE LIFE OF THE SOUTH AFRICAN STATESMAN by Floyd Cooper, © 1996 by Floyd Cooper. Used by permission of Philomel books, A Division of Penguin Young Readers Group, A Member of Penguin Group (USA) Inc., 345 Hudson Street, New York, NY 10014. All rights reserved. - **p. 202-203 :** "We are together" by Sally Williams © The Daily Telegraph, 1st March 2008. - **p. 204 :** BBC Motion Gallery - **p. 212 :** © National Geographic Atlas of the World, Eighth Edition, 2004. D.R. - **p. 213 :** © Windrush Child copyright @ 1985 by John Agard reproduced by kind permission of John Agard c/o Caroline Sheldon Literary Agency Limited - **p. 214 :** © Andrea Levy, 2000. Reprinted with permission of David Grossman Literary Agency Ltd. - **p. 228-231 :** Heinemann Education D.R. - **p. 232 :** © Shel Silverstein - **p. 233-234 :** Extract from The Landlady, KISS, KISS, Roald Dahl, Penguin © David Higham Associates Ltd. - **p. 235-237 :** From Imaginings of Sand by Andre Brink, published by Secker & Warburg. Reprinted by permission of The Random House Group Ltd. - **p. 238-239 :** WUTHERING HEIGHTS WORDS AND MUSIC BY KATE BUSH © 1977, REPRODUCED BY PERMISSION OF EMI MUSIC PUBLISHING LTD, LONDON W8 5SW

Crédits photos

8-1 ph © Emilio Suetone / hemis.fr
8-2 ph © Prod DB © Columbia - Marvel Entertainment / DR
8-3 ph © Jutta Klee / Corbis
8-4 ph © Photo12.com / Alamy
9-5 ph © Brian Lawrence / Imagestate / GHFP / Eyedea / ADAGP, Paris 2010
9-6 ph © Photo12.com / Alamy
9-7 ph © Volker Moehrke / Zefa / Corbis
10-8 ph © Photo12.com / Alamy
10-9 ph © Fausto Giaccone / Anzenberger / Ask Images
10-10 ph © Roy Lichtenstein / VG Bild-Kunst / Akg-Images / ADAGP, Paris 2010
11-11 ph © Roger Bamber / Alamy / Photo12.com
11-12 ph © Friedrich Saurer / Alamy / Photo12.com
11-13 Coll. Christophe L
12-14 ph © Photo12.com / Alamy
12-15 ph © Frans Lemmens / Zefa / Corbis
12-16 ph © Bettina Strenske / Alamy / Photo12.com
13-h ph © Prod DB © Warner Bros / DR
13-m ph © Charles C. Ebbets / Corbis
15 ph © Luke Tchalenko
16 ph © Aaron Kehoe / UPI / Eyedea
18 © DR
19 ph © Kuttig - People / Alamy / Photo12.com
20-hg ph © Emilio Suetone / hemis.fr
20-hd ph © Eyedea Illustration
21 ph © Diana Bier Speakers Corner UK / Alamy / Photo12.com
22 © www.CartoonStock.com
23 ph © Getty-Images / AFP
24-g ph © Prod DB © Bruckheimer - Touchstone - Walt Disney / DR
24-d ph © Prod DB © Fox Searchlight Pictures / DR
25-hg, hd ph © Eyedea
25-hmg © Jan Opdebeeck
25-hmd © Petar Pismestrovic / artizans.com
25-mg © Bernd Erti / artizans.com
25-md © Borot / Dalle
25-mmg © Petar Pismestrovic / artizans.com
25-mmd © Patrick Dea / artizans.com
26 ph © Ace Stock Limited / Alamy / Photo12.com
29 ph © Prod DB © Columbia - Marvel Entertainment / DR
30 © CALVIN AND HOBBES © 1990 Watterson. Dist. By UNIVERSAL PRESS SYNDICATE. Reprinted with permission. All rights reserved.
32 ph © Getty-Images / Stock Illustration
34 ph © 2008, Digital Image, The Museum of Modern Art, New York / Scala, Florence.
35-h ph © Bernard Starck
35-b ph © Jutta Klee / Corbis
36 ph © Denis Darzacq / Agence VU
39 © CALVIN AND HOBBES © 2007 Watterson. Dist. By UNIVERSAL PRESS SYNDICATE. Reprinted with permission. All rights reserved.
41 ph © The Estate of Keith Haring
42 © Appel Press, Londres
44 ph © Photo12.com / Alamy
45 ph © Peter Kramer / AP / Sipa Press
46 ph © Fossey / Sipa Press
47 ph © Wayne Drought / AP / Sipa Press
47 © Jacq Loeïza
48 © Harper Collins, Londres
51 ph © Photo12.com / Alamy
53 ph © Rex Features / Sipa Press
56 © Historic Denver
58 Coll. Christophe L
60-hg ph © Camille Moirenc / hemis.fr
60-hm ph © Jose Giribas / ROPI-REA
60-hd ph © Franck Charel / Hoa-Qui / Eyedea
60-mg ph © Kord.com / Eyedea
60-md ph © Brian Lawrence / Imagestate / GHFP / Eyedea / ADAGP, Paris 2010
61 ph © Prod DB © Universal Pictures / DR
62 ph © The Granger Collection NYC / Rue des Archives
63 ph © Bettmann / Corbis
65-h © Withney Museum
65-mg ph © Philippe Renault / hemis.fr
65-md ph © Raymond Depardon / Magnum Photos
66 © « Là où vont nos Pères » © 2007 Shaun Tan - Dargaud
69 ph © Prod DB © Centropolis Entertainment / DR
70 © Statue of Liberty, National Monument, New York
72 © Pascale Camps Vaquer
73 © «Stagecoach» © 1966 Twentieth Century Fox. All rights reserved. © 1966, The Norman Rockwell Family Entities Photograph Courtesy of the Denver Art Museum
74 ph © North Wind Pictures / Leemage
75 ph © David Nunuk / Firstlight / Eyedea
76 ph © North Wind Pictures / Leemage
77 ph © Christie's Images / Corbis
78-hg, md ph © The Bridgeman Art Library
78-hd ph © North Wind Pictures / Leemage
78-bg ph © AISA / Leemage
81 ph © Prod DB © Tig - Majestic / DR
82 ph © Photo12.com / Alamy
84 ph © Volker Moehrke / Zefa / Corbis
86 © www.CartoonStock.com
87 Coll. Grob / Kharbine-Tapabor
88 ph © Liu / Color China Photo / Sipa Press
90 ph © Firefly Productions / Corbis
93 Coll. Christophe L
94 ph © Jennie Hills / AFP Photo
95-h ph © Stéphane Audras / REA
95-b ph © Yuriko Nakao / Reuters
98 ph © Alex Bailey / WORKING TITLE / THE KOBAL COLLECTION
100 Coll. Christophe L
102 © WPL 1993
103 ph © The Bridgeman Art Library
104-1,2, 3, 4, 5 ph © Photo12.com / Alamy
104-6, 7, 8, mg ph © Eising / StockFood / StudioX
105 ph © Hulton-Deutsch Collection / Corbis
106 ph © Photo12.com / Alamy
107 ph © Photo12.com / Alamy
108 ph © Photo12.com / Alamy
109 © Peter Legon LGP, 2003
111-h ph © Mary Evans / Rue des Archives
111-b ph © Hartmut Krinitz / hemis.fr
112 ph © Photo12.com / Alamy
115 ph © Daniel Hopkinson / Arcaid / Corbis
116 ph © Ludovic Maisant / hemis.fr
117 ph © Akira Suemori / AP / Sipa Press
119 © National Maritime Museum, Greenwich, London
120 © Penguin Group (USA) Inc. Puffin 1998. Julius Lester « From slaves ship to Freedom road « illustrated by Rod Brown Books for Young Readers

123 © International Slavery Museum, Liverpool
124 Coll. Christophe L
125 ph © Fausto Giaccone / Anzenberger / Ask Images
126-hd ph © The Warhol Foundation for the visual arts / ADAGP, Paris 2010 / Corbis
126-b ph © 2008, Digital Image, The Museum of Modern Art, New York / Scala, Florence.
127 © The Bridgeman Art Library / ADAGP, Paris 2010
128 ph © Getty-Images
129 © Tate London 2008
130 © The Bridgeman Art Library / ADAGP, Paris 2010
131 ph © Henri Dauman Corbis The Warhol Foundation for the visual arts / ADAGP, Paris 2010
132 ph © VG Bild-Kunst / Akg-Images Estate of Roy Lichtenstein New York / ADAGP, Paris 2010
135 ph © VG Bild-Kunst / Akg-Images Estate of Roy Lichtenstein New York / ADAGP, Paris 2010
136 ph © The Bridgeman Art Library / ADAGP, Paris 2010
137 ph © Andy Rain / Epa / Corbis - Marilyn MonroeTM is a trademark of Marilyn Monroe LLC / The Warhol Foundation for the visual arts / ADAGP, Paris 2010
140 © from the How To Be British Collection © LGP, Brighton, UK www.lgpcards.com
142 Coll. Christophe L
145 © Owen Sherwood / Financial Times Magazine 12 Nov. 2005
146-h ph © Roger Bamber / Alamy / Photo12.com
146-b ph © Carol and Mike Werner / Alamy / Photo12.com
147 ph © Fabrice Lerouge / Photononstop
148 ph © Eurasia Press / Photononstop
149 ph © Peter Maltz / Images.com / Corbis
150-hg © 2000 Randy Glasbergen
150-hd © 1996 Randy Glasbergen
150-bg © 1998 Randy Glasbergen
150-bd © 2004 Mike Lane and Political / Cartoons.com
153 © CALVIN AND HOBBES © 2005 Watterson. Dist. By UNIVERSAL PRESS SYNDICATE. Reprinted with permission. All rights reserved.
155-hg ph © Double Touch / Photononstop
155-hd ph © Photo12.com / Alamy
155-mg ph © Laurent Hamels / Photononstop
155-md ph © Denis / REA
156-h © www.CartoonStock.com
156-b © Globecartoon
157 © Clay Bennett / The Christian Science Monitor
159 © DR
161-h ph © Lex Verspeek / HollandseHoogte-REA
161-m ph © Mike Nelson / Epa / Corbis
161-bg ph © Images.com / Corbis
161-bd ph © Frances Stéphane / hemis.fr
163 ph © Friedrich Saurer / Alamy / Photo12.com
164 Clay Bennett / The Christian Science Monitor
165 © Frederic Hanoteau
166-h © DR
166-b © www.marketforce.com.au / DR
167 © DR
168 ph © Michel Fainsilber / Photononstop
169 © Media Moguls / AFP
170 Coll. Christophe L
171 © www.CartoonStock.com
172 ph © Sotheby's / Akg-Images
174 ph © Prod DB © Working Title / DR
177 © CALVIN AND HOBBES © 1998 Watterson. Dist. By UNIVERSAL PRESS SYNDICATE. Reprinted with permission. All rights reserved.
178 ph © Nele Martensen / LAIF-REA
182 © Euro RSCG Helsinki / WWF Finland
184 Coll. Christophe L
187 ph © Mika / Zefa / Corbis
188 ph © M.G.M. / Album / Akg-Images
191 ph © Photo12.com / Alamy
192 ph © Gabe Palmer / Corbis
195 ph © Jeff Wall
198-hg ph © Gil Giuglio / hemis.fr
198-mg ph © Anna Zieminski / AFP
198-md ph © Frans Lemmens / Zefa / Corbis
200 ph © Graeme Williams / South-REA
201 ph © Lionel Healing / AFP
203-h ph © Roger De La Harpe / Gallo Images / Corbis
203-b ph © Scott Gries / Getty-Images For Keep A Child Alive
204 ph © Graham Mark / Gamma / Eyedea
209 © www.madamandeve.co.za
210 ph © Matthew Mawson / Alamy / Photo12.com
211 ph © Douglas Miller / Keystone / Getty-Images
212-h ph © Dorling Kindersley / Getty-Images
212-b ph © Jean-Pierre Amet / Corbis
213 ph © ImageState / Alamy / Photo12.com
214 ph © Haywood Magee / Getty-Images
216-h © Transport for London
216-b ph © Bettina Strenske / Alamy / Photo12.com
219 © Newsweek 2007
220 ph © Jack Sullivan / Alamy / Photo12.com
221 ph © Bettina Strenske / Alamy / Photo12.com
226 ph © © Alex Bailey / REALLY USEFUL FILMS / JOEL SCHUMACHER PRODS. / THE KOBAL COLLECTION
229 ph © Prod DB © Warner Bros / DR
230 ph © Layne Kennedy / Corbis
233 ph © PARAMOUNT / THE KOBAL COLLECTION
235 ph © Franklin McMahon / Corbis
236 ph © Abbas / Magnum Photos
237 ph © Louise Gubb / Corbis
239 ph © Nadia Isakova / Alamy / Photo12.com
240 Coll. Christophe L
241 ph © Rue des Archives / PVDE
242 Coll. Archives Hatier
243 ph © The Bridgeman Art Library
244 ph © Charles C. Ebbets / Corbis
245 ph © Art Resource, New-York / Scala, Florence © Joseph Stella D. R.
246 ph © Red Grooms / ADAGP, Paris 2010
247 ph © The Bridgeman Art Library © Richard Estes D. R.
248 ph © Photo Georgia O'Keeffe Museum, Santa Fe / Art Resource / Scala, Florence / ADAGP, Paris 2010
249 ph © Aisa / Leemage © Edward Hopper D. R.
280 ph © Rue des Archives / BCA
282 Coll. Christophe L

Droits réservés (DR) : malgré nos efforts, il nous a été impossible de joindre certains photographes ou leurs ayants-droit, ainsi que des éditeurs ou leurs ayants-droit de certains documents, pour solliciter l'autorisation de reproduction, mais nous avons naturellement réservé en notre comptabilité des droits usuels

Bourse
aux Livres fcpe
fcpedailly@gmail.com

Achevé d'imprimer par Rotolito Lombarda à Seggiano di Pioltello - Italie
Dépôt légal : 94428-4/07 - Juin 2012